STENDHAL'S LESS-LOVED HE[R]
FICTION, FREEDOM, AND THE

LEGENDA

LEGENDA, founded in 1995 by the European Humanities Research Centre of the University of Oxford, is now a joint imprint of the Modern Humanities Research Association and Routledge. Titles range from medieval texts to contemporary cinema and form a widely comparative view of the modern humanities, including works on Arabic, Catalan, English, French, German, Greek, Italian, Portuguese, Russian, Spanish, and Yiddish literature. An Editorial Board of distinguished academic specialists works in collaboration with leading scholarly bodies such as the Society for French Studies and the British Comparative Literature Association.

MHRA

The Modern Humanities Research Association (MHRA) encourages and promotes advanced study and research in the field of the modern humanities, especially modern European languages and literature, including English, and also cinema. It also aims to break down the barriers between scholars working in different disciplines and to maintain the unity of humanistic scholarship in the face of increasing specialization. The Association fulfils this purpose primarily through the publication of journals, bibliographies, monographs and other aids to research.

Routledge
Taylor & Francis Group

LONDON AND NEW YORK

Routledge is a global publisher of academic books, journals and online resources in the humanities and social sciences. Founded in 1836, it has published many of the greatest thinkers and scholars of the last hundred years, including adorno, einstein, Russell, Popper, Wittgenstein, Jung, Bohm, Hayek, Mcluhan, Marcuse and Sartre. Today Routledge is one of the world's leading academic publishers in the Humanities and Social Sciences. It publishes thousands of books and journals each year, serving scholars, instructors, and professional communities worldwide.

www.routledge.com

RESEARCH MONOGRAPHS IN FRENCH STUDIES

The *Research Monographs in French Studies* (RMFS) are selected, edited and supported by the Society for French Studies. The series seeks to publish the best new work in all areas of the literature, thought, theory, culture, film and language of the French-speaking world. Its distinctiveness lies in the tight focus and relative brevity of its publications (50,000–60,000 words).

As innovation is a priority of the series, volumes should predominantly consist of new material, although, subject to appropriate modification, previously published research may form up to one third of the whole. Proposals may include critical editions as well as critical studies. They should be sent with one or two sample chapters for consideration to the General Editor, Professor Diana Knight, at diana.knight@nottingham.ac.uk.

PUBLISHED IN THIS SERIES

www.legendabooks.com

Stendhal's Less-Loved Heroines

Fiction, Freedom, and the Female

MARIA C. SCOTT

Routledge
Taylor & Francis Group

LONDON AND NEW YORK

2013

First published 2013 by Modern Humanities Research Association and Routledge

2 Park Square, Milton Park, Abingdon, Oxfordshire OX14 4RN
52 Vanderbilt Avenue, New York, NY 10017

Routledge is an imprint of the Taylor & Francis Group, an informa business

First issued in paperback 2020

ISBN 978-1-907975-71-4 (hbk)
ISBN 978-0-367-60202-4 (pbk)

CONTENTS

FOR CIARA
AND OTHER MUCH-LOVED DAUGHTERS

ACKNOWLEDGEMENTS

If this book has taken a long time to complete, it is at least partly because I have enjoyed the journey so much. It has brought me into contact with a number of wonderful people who also happen to be outstanding Stendhal scholars. I am very grateful, in particular, to Yves Ansel, Xavier Bourdenet, Serge Linkès, and Catherine Mariette for their generosity and collegiality, and to Lucy Garnier and Francesco Manzini for being such selfless, enlightening, and sympathetic fellow travellers over the past few years; they have made me realize the great luck of the lone researcher who finds good company along the road. My debt to David Scott, my most long-standing academic friend and ally, is too fundamental to repay. I am also very thankful to Barbara Wright, who has shown much kindness to me over the years, especially on the day I landed in her office with a far-fetched theory about *Le Rouge et le Noir*. The Legenda team, and particularly Ann Jefferson, Diana Knight, Graham Nelson, Susan Wharton, and Jennifer Yee, have been extremely professional and supportive; the editorial committee, along with the anonymous reader of the manuscript, offered much wise and constructive advice. My thanks go too to Jean Anderson, for her help and advice at an early stage of the project, and to Susan Harrow, for the University of Bristol fellowship that ensured continuity of library access during a period of transition and displacement. This project would never have got off the ground without the generous assistance of the Irish Research Council for Humanities and Social Sciences, which funded an entire year of research leave in 2004–2005. I am indebted to my very hardworking colleagues at National University of Ireland, Galway, for facilitating that period of leave as well as a year of sabbatical research in 2008. Thank you to my husband, Simon Potter, for the time, in all senses, that he has given me. He and our children, Tommy and Ciara, have lived with this project for as long as they have known me. I think they will not miss it.

Some of the arguments made in the following chapters were previously published, in different form, in *French Studies*, 62 (2008), *The Irish Journal of French Studies*, 8 (2008), and *L'Année stendhalienne*, 11 (2012). Thank you to the editors of these journals for their encouragement and input.

All errors are, unfortunately, my own.

M.C.S., Bristol, March 2013

NOTE ON TRANSLATIONS

While translations are my own, I have consulted and occasionally borrowed from the following published sources: David Coward's 2002 translation of *Vanina Vanini*; T. W. Earp's 1952 translation of *Lamiel*; Richard Howard's 1988 translation of *Mina de Vanghel*; and Catherine Slater's 1991 translation of *Le Rouge et le Noir*.

INTRODUCTION

There is a very rich history of feminist critique in Stendhal studies. As early as the 1940s, Clara Malraux and Simone de Beauvoir published essays on the author that anticipated Anglo-American 'images of women' criticism, usually understood to originate with Kate Millett's *Sexual Politics*, published in 1970.[1] Many feminist critics of Stendhal have, like Malraux and Beauvoir, been attentive to his heroines. A second strand of feminist Stendhal criticism, often very closely related to and even overlapping with the first, is psychoanalytic in orientation, tending to focus on inscriptions of the maternal or feminine, as distinct from the female, in his writing; its most well-known exponent is Julia Kristeva.[2] A third identifiable strand of feminist Stendhal criticism, again often interwoven with and even inseparable from the previous two, analyses the implicit cultural and/or personal attitudes towards women that can be discerned from the author's writings.[3] While regular reference will be made in the course of this book to feminist criticism of Stendhal, the particular feminist approach adopted here will involve substantial engagement with, and contestation of, a somewhat more dominant tradition within Stendhal criticism: the androcentric one. This body of work crucially differs from feminist criticism in that it presents itself as gender-neutral rather than as biased towards one gender; occasionally it even lays claim to an objectivity free of any element of interpretation. Where it references feminist criticism at all, it tends to dismiss it as idiosyncratic and/or reductive. Because it presents itself as normative, androcentric criticism has historically dominated the way in which Stendhal has been taught and read; it seems likely that it continues to do so even today.

The influence of androcentric criticism reaches even into feminist criticism, as if to verify Judith Fetterley's theory about the 'immasculation of women by men'.[4] A particularly interesting and revealing instance of a female reader assuming a male heterosexual position is presented in Beauvoir's essay, 'Stendhal ou le romanesque du vrai' ['Stendhal, or the romance of the true'].[5] In this piece, which appears in *Le Deuxième Sexe* [*The Second Sex*], Beauvoir persuasively argues that Stendhal is an exception to the rule according to which male literary authors have historically represented women as a passive Other rather than as active subjects. Nevertheless, Beauvoir herself privileges those of Stendhal's heroines whom she describes as captives over his more obviously audacious, self-determining heroines. To borrow Jean Prévost's terminology, she seems to admire his angelic lovers more than she does his Amazons.[6] How might we make sense of this apparent contradiction?

Le Deuxième Sexe argues that women have traditionally occupied a paradoxical position in their relations with men, playing the role of Other despite experiencing themselves, at least partially, as subjects in their own rights. Beauvoir claims that women have traditionally been lured into a position of bad faith, that is, into the abdication of their responsibility to themselves as free human beings. She argues that, until her own time at least, the cost to a woman of acting in good faith, of authentically assuming her transcendent subjectivity, has always been prohibitively high as a result of the limiting social and corporeal situations of women. While women have been limited, moreover, by the role they play in male imaginations, Beauvoir's main thesis in her study of Stendhal is that his heroines depart from the usual myths of femininity by resembling flesh-and-blood women.[7] Instead of being mere avatars of the Other, narcissistic projections of a masculine consciousness, his heroines have independent destinies.

Stendhal does give an extraordinary degree of agency and centrality to his female characters, though not primarily to those whom Beauvoir treats as most illustrative of her argument; indeed, while she admires all of Stendhal's heroines for their unusual independence of character, she gives his less flagrantly autonomous females a privileged place in her essay. Beauvoir even obliquely argues that those of Stendhal's heroines who most resemble 'des prisonnières' [prisoners][8] are paradoxically freer and more authentic than those of his heroines who actively and self-consciously defy the restrictions of their situation. According to Beauvoir, Stendhal's heroines are shown, as a strange result of their oppression, to achieve a superior form of authenticity, or truth to themselves; they do not subscribe to that 'esprit de sérieux' [serious-mindedness] that characterizes most of the men and women around them; their freedom is interior rather than exterior.[9] By contrast, therefore, with Clara Malraux, who in 1944 had published a short article strongly in favour of energetic, self-motivating literary heroines (epitomized for her by Mathilde de La Mole), and critical of the more traditional hero-dependent heroine (typified for her by Madame de Rênal), Beauvoir qualifies her praise of Stendhal's more independent heroines.[10] She appears to find something that rings false in the latter; and it is Stendhal's interest in real (as distinct from fantasized) women that interests her above all else. While Beauvoir may, then, elsewhere in *Le Deuxième Sexe*, scorn that 'liberté docile' [docile freedom] which she claims men have habitually sought in women,[11] her essay on Stendhal appears to suggest that a mitigated form of freedom is preferable to a kind that is too far-fetched, too egregious. Stendhal's captive heroines seem genuine to Beauvoir precisely on account of their failure to assert their freedom, a failure for which she claims they cannot be held personally responsible. This reading is compatible with Beauvoir's nuancing, in *Le Deuxième Sexe*, of Jean-Paul's Sartre's stark alternative between good and bad faith. For Sartre, an individual's situation can offer no excuse for the failure to grasp his or her freedom; a slave is always at liberty, he claims, to break his chains.[12] Beauvoir, by contrast, holds that women's situations have until recently restricted their freedom to act in good faith; her favouring of Stendhal's less freely self-determining heroines can be explained at least partly by this position.

A passage from Beauvoir's essay on Stendhal suggests a less philosophical explanation of her privileging of Stendhal's prisoner-heroines over his more audacious creations:

> La seule liberté ne suffirait pas à les douer de tant d'attraits romanesques: une pure liberté, on la reconnaît dans l'estime mais non dans l'émotion; ce qui touche, c'est son effort pour s'accomplir à travers les obstacles qui la briment; il est chez les femmes d'autant plus pathétique que la lutte est plus difficile.[13]

> [Freedom alone could not endow them with so many romantic attractions: a pure freedom invites respect but not emotion; what is moving is the effort to achieve freedom despite the obstacles that confront it so aggressively; in women, this effort is all the more moving since the struggle is harder.]

For Beauvoir as a consumer of literature, Stendhal's free female characters simply do not carry the affective punch of his hampered heroines; the self-determining characters that might logically be worthy of her highest admiration do not move her. A few lines later, further light is thrown on the reason why Beauvoir prefers the prisoner-like heroines: 'Il est manifeste que la sympathie de Stendhal pour ses héroïnes est d'autant plus grande qu'elles sont plus étroitement des prisonnières.'[14] [It is clear that Stendhal's sympathy for his heroines is greater the more narrowly they are imprisoned.] Beauvoir's affective investment in the timid heroines would seem to be connected with her belief that Stendhal, like his heroes, favours these characters. Beauvoir assumes, in fact, not only that the male heroes' tastes in women can be identified with those of the author but also that they mirror the reader's preferences:

> Les héroïnes les plus pures n'ont pas conscience d'elles-mêmes. Mme de Rênal est ignorante de sa grâce, comme Mme de Chasteller de son intelligence. C'est là une des joies profondes de l'amant à qui l'auteur et le lecteur s'identifient.[15]

> [The purest heroines are unselfconscious. Madame de Rênal is unaware of her grace, as Madame de Chasteller is of her intelligence. This is one of the deep joys of the lover, with whom the author and the reader identify.]

Even more surprising than the fact that female ignorance is rated more highly here than female self-consciousness, despite the emphasis of existentialist philosophy on lucidity, is the astonishing closing remark, which suggests that the only way readers can view Stendhal's heroines is through the lens of the male lover.[16]

In an article published in 1965, Beauvoir proposes that the specificity of literature lies in its simultaneous affirmation and transcendence of our separation from other people. The reading of what she calls authentic literature involves the hearing of a fascinating and unique authorial voice which emanates from a place that is simultaneously different and familiar, 'un monde singulier qui se recoupe avec le mien et pourtant qui est autre' [a singular world that intersects with my own and that is nevertheless other]. Beauvoir then acknowledges that the notion of identification is central to her understanding of literature: 'Qu'il y ait personnage, ou non, pour que la lecture prenne, il faut que je m'identifie avec quelqu'un: avec l'auteur; il faut que j'entre dans son monde et que ce soit son monde qui devienne le mien.' [Whether there is a character or not, if the reading is going to be successful I need to identify with someone, namely with the author. I need to enter into his or her world and his or her world has to become mine.] Identification, for Beauvoir, is an essentially transformative process: she observes that instead of simply adding to her worldview, as a non-literary work might do, a literary work changes her worldview, at least temporarily, giving her 'le goût d'une autre vie' [the taste of another life].[17] It would appear that an identificatory transformation of the kind discussed in this essay has taken place in Beauvoir's study of Stendhal's heroines.[18]

Beauvoir's affective identification with the male hero and inferred author is only the most surprising instance of a very widespread phenomenon in Stendhal studies. As Kristeva puts it, 'Dans l'univers pourtant réaliste de Stendhal, tout dépend [...] et peut-être plus qu'ailleurs, plus que ne le croit le lecteur naïf, de l'interprétation: de la projection identificatoire demandée au lecteur.' [In the admittedly realist universe of Stendhal, everything depends, and perhaps more than elsewhere and more than the naïve reader believes, on interpretation, that is, on the identificatory projection required of the reader.][19] Philippe Berthier says something similar, but frames his point in terms of love rather than identification: 'Chaque "stendhalien" est intimement persuadé qu'il est le seul à entrer véritablement dans Stendhal et à l'aimer comme il eût aimé être aimé.' [Every 'Stendhalian' is privately convinced that he is the only one truly to enter into Stendhal and to love him as he would have loved to be loved.][20] It is possibly as a result of the strength of such pre-critical dynamics that, even today, many readers of Stendhal seem, like Beauvoir, to be guided in their engagement with his fictions by the intuition that his male heroes express the author's own thoughts and preferences. This has meant that Stendhal's most independent heroines, often careless of masculine pride and rejected in love, tend to be sidelined or otherwise censured by critics, including some feminist critics.

Traditionally, and even often today, criticism has taken the side of Stendhal's meeker females over his audacious ones. Hans Boll-Johansen, for example, writes of his heroines that: 'L'opposition est quasi absolue entre la femme idéalisée, capable de passion généreuse, et la femme néfaste, toute vouée à son égoïsme, marquée par son manque de spontanéité.' [There is an almost total opposition between the idealized woman, capable of generous passion, and the harmful one, entirely devoted to her selfishness and marked by her lack of spontaneity.][21] Leo Bersani writes that while the more vivid heroines exert a certain appeal, 'it's nevertheless important to see that for the young heroes of Stendhal's fictions they never carry the promise of happiness embodied in their less colorful, almost conventual rivals'.[22] It is equally important to ask why it should matter that the colourful heroines do not offer happiness to the heroes, and why it is that their own hypothetical happiness, as well as that of their 'conventual rivals', is so easily dismissed as a focus of interest. Bersani's entire analysis of desire in Stendhal's fiction is premised on an assumption that it is the hero's desire and happiness that count and not the heroine's. Tellingly, he does not consider any of the author's fictions in which a female plays the principal role, and subscribes to the widespread notion that Stendhal identifies with his male protagonist:

> We can describe the relation between the narrator and the hero in Stendhal's fiction as the esthetic realization of a dream of self-creation. The novelist creates, or engenders himself. More exactly, Stendhal splits himself into a narrator-father and a hero-son.[23]

A similar privileging of the male can be discerned in Michel Crouzet's statement that he is less interested in '[les] trop fameuses Amazones' [the too famous Amazons] than in the heroine who 'ne peut être heureuse que par le bonheur de l'autre' [can only be happy by way of the happiness of the other].[24]

Arguably, of course, Stendhal identified with his heroines at least as much as he saw them as fictional love objects. Lisa G. Algazi gestures towards such an argument when she points out that Mathilde may be 'the woman he would have liked to be, but this does not make her the woman he would have liked to love'.[25] While Stendhal does occasionally admit to having fallen in love with a fictional heroine, he also makes the following comment, upon reading the first volume of Madame de Staël's *Delphine*: 'Je me suis senti presque entièrement dans le personnage de Delphine.' [I felt almost entirely inside Delphine's character.][26] Stendhal was, in fact, very aware of the identificatory dynamics involved in reading. In an 1804 letter to his sister Pauline, for example, he claims that readers laugh at a particular episode in Montesquieu's *Lettres persanes* [*Persian Letters*] because they put themselves in the place of the master, Usbek, rather than in the place of his slave.[27] Far from simply offering a reassuring reflection, however, reading was a dialogic process for Stendhal: 'Un roman est comme un archet, la caisse du violon *qui rend les sons* c'est l'âme du lecteur' [A novel is like a bow, the body of the violin *which produces the notes* is the reader's soul] (*OI* II 699; *Vie de Henry Brulard* [*Life of Henry Brulard*]). The active participation of the reader was therefore essential, in other words, to any felicitous literary encounter. For Stendhal, reading constructs the self: 'L'Arioste forma mon caractère' [Ariosto shaped my character] (*OI* II 619; *Vie de Henry Brulard*). The readerly identifications produced in the process of this construction can have both undesirable and salutary consequences: *Le Rouge et le Noir* [*The Red and the Black*] satirizes the influence of literary models on guests at the Hôtel de La Mole, but Stendhal's letters to Pauline urge her to model herself on a range of literary and historical characters as a means of protecting herself from the debasing influence of those who surround her in life.[28] As the violin analogy suggests, reading was conceived by Stendhal as much as a pleasurable activity as a character-building one. Indeed, reading is represented in *Vie de Henry Brulard* as 'one of the highest forms of pleasure and one of the intensest kinds of emotional experience'.[29]

Stendhal was nevertheless always alert to the fact that, however intense the reader's pleasure, including his or her pleasure in identification, it is contingent, like love itself, on his or her social, historical, and individual circumstances. Stendhal notes, for example, in his *Histoire de la peinture en Italie* [*History of Painting in Italy*], that nineteenth-century readers are likely to fall into the trap of believing that the protagonists of medieval literature experience the world as they do:

> En lisant les chroniques et les romans du moyen âge, nous, les gens sensibles du dix-neuvième siècle, nous supposons ce qui a dû être senti par les héros, nous leur prêtons une sensibilité aussi impossible chez eux, que naturelle chez nous.[30]

> [In reading the chronicles and romances of the Middle Ages, we sensitive people of the nineteenth century imagine what the heroes must have felt, lending them a sensibility as impossible for them as it is natural for us.]

The inevitably subjective character of experience is a favourite theme of Stendhal's work. He writes, for example, that 'Chaque artiste devrait voir la nature à sa manière' [Every artist should see nature in his own way], and that 'Il y a peut-être autant de façons de sentir parmi les hommes que de façons de voir' [There are perhaps as many ways of feeling among men as there are ways of seeing].[31] Stendhal's belief in the partiality of perception made him highly suspicious of universal truths and received wisdom. In a passage that occurs towards the end of *Le Rouge et le Noir*, Julien Sorel compares human beings to flies that live for only a day and who consequently never know what night is, and to ants whose home is destroyed by a hunter, without ever understanding that the devastating black body is the hunter's boot, or that the red flames have come from his gun.[32] The union of the two colours of the novel's title in this latter parable might lead us to speculate that the insurmountable partiality of point of view is more crucial to that novel than has previously been understood.

Yuri M. Lotman notes that the multiple points of view expressed within a literary text testify to the fact that 'there is no exhaustive, finite interpretation' either in art or in life.[33] Stendhal's characteristically open-ended fiction illustrates this point particularly well, even if commentators occasionally deny the possibility of any disagreement among readers as to the author's perspective on events.[34] This book will take as its focus Stendhal's fictional representations of freedom rather than the freedom of his readers to disagree with one another; nevertheless, the latter remains a key underlying theme, which will come to the fore again in the conclusion. The primary objective of this study is, in other words, to show how a number of Stendhal's less-loved heroines enact their freedom; a secondary objective is to show that these heroines can be, and indeed increasingly are, well-loved, by readers at least.

Stendhal's own conception of freedom owed much to his reading of recent philosophical works. He found in the work of the sensualist philosophers and the Ideologists, particularly Destutt de Tracy, a powerful assertion of the freedom of the individual in the face of a social order that functioned to constrain individual freedoms.[35] That Stendhal saw Ideology as a philosophy of freedom may be surprising, given the extent to which its proponents considered human behaviour to be a predictable effect of biology, psychology, and social conventions.[36] Nevertheless, it was from the Ideologists that Stendhal derived that scepticism with regard to universal and eternal truths which has already been touched upon here, as well as his belief in the importance of self-invention and resistance to reification, testified for example by the draft scene in which Mina Wanghen inspires her young duke to discover 'un horizon immense, gai, nouveau' [an immense, cheerful new horizon] by peeling away an aristocratic role and title that mercilessly bind him (*Orc* I 1137).

This book will approach Stendhal's work partly through the lens of his own intellectual inheritance, but will also adopt a broadly French existentialist perspective. French existentialism is compatible with Ideology to the extent that both philosophies emphasize the significance of physical and cultural situations, both conceive of the individual as an organic unity guided by a decipherable logic, and both insist upon the close connections between lucidity and freedom. The choice of French existentialism as a theoretical framework has been made for a number of reasons. Firstly, we have already seen that an important early instance of twentieth-century feminist literary criticism was existentialist in emphasis and took Stendhal as its focus; the fact that it was also a strangely androcentric study of his work means that the question of how to read his heroines from a broadly feminist existentialist perspective remains open. Secondly, some of the most influential studies of Stendhal (by, for example, Blin, Brombert, Starobinski, as well as Beauvoir) have drawn on existentialist ideas. Thirdly, the ideas of Sartre and Beauvoir offer a peculiarly appropriate theoretical framework for a study of freedom in literature, on the one hand because this philosophy places the problem of freedom at its centre and on the other because it is closely associated with literary fiction.[37] Finally, because existentialist thought refuses to treat values as given, it offers a fitting backdrop for a study that aims to question some of the received critical wisdom on the subject of Stendhalian values.

The first chapter will begin with a consideration of Stendhal's understanding, influenced by Destutt de Tracy, of the relationship between freedom and happiness. It will go on to examine the representation of freedom in two narratives that were written around the same time as *Le Rouge et le Noir*: *Mina de Vanghel* and *Vanina Vanini*. The second and third chapters, focusing on *Le Rouge et le Noir* and *Lamiel* respectively, will place a more explicit emphasis on existentialist ideas about freedom, in their privileging of notions of authenticity and playfulness. All three chapters will show how the heroines in question take control of the plots of their own lives, and how they do so in a manner that upsets narrative conventions and disconcerts narrators and readers at least as much as it upsets and disconcerts other characters.

Mina, Vanina, Mathilde, and Lamiel are not the only self-inventing heroines in Stendhal's writing. However, the heroines selected for study all enact a particular style of freedom, and it is of a kind that sometimes alarms critics even more often than it shocks lovers. It is easy enough to explain why characters such as Armance, Madame de Rênal, Madame de Chasteller, Madame Grandet, Clélia Conti, Hélène de Campireali, and Valentine Boissaux have been omitted from this discussion. They do occasionally resemble the four Amazons under discussion, but they all lack their joyful egoism, even if some are joyful and others self-centred. It is more difficult to explain, on these grounds, the exclusion of Gina del Dongo from any sustained consideration. Certainly, Gina has joy and selfishness in spades; however, she is intrinsically different from her younger counterparts. Gina's greater maturity means that she is more prone than they to compromise and concession. In addition, and possibly as a result of her greater experience of the world, Gina has almost magical powers of charm. Stendhal leaves us in no doubt as to the extent of Gina's magnetism: tyrants, courtiers, poets, and servants all fall under its spell. So do critics of *La Chartreuse de Parme* [*The Charterhouse of Parma*].[38] Her attractions are different from those of a Lamiel, which are at least partly an effect of her lack of worldly wisdom. Moya Longstaffe notes that Gina's gender and situation oblige her to have recourse to her beauty as an instrument of power;[39] Lamiel and Mina, by contrast, try to diminish their natural beauty by applying a thick paste to their faces, while neither Mathilde nor Vanina is interested in the power offered by beauty. Tellingly,

Prévost does not include Gina among Stendhal's Amazons; he describes her, instead, as a 'catin sublime' [sublime harlot].[40]

Ultimately, Gina has a degree of that hypocrisy which Stendhal wished his sister to acquire, but which is largely absent from the heroines under discussion in this book. In his many letters to his sister Pauline, Stendhal repeatedly urges her to become hypocritical, by which he means that she must learn to be graceful and charming, and to hide her strength and intelligence.[41] The author maintains in those letters that French women in the early nineteenth century are obliged, for their own social survival, to uphold a particularly insipid version of femininity. Stendhal refers his sister to the example of Madame de Staël who, he claims, longed to be loved but who made the mistake of not hiding her superiority and who consequently ended up miserable. The author's advice to his sister anticipates Beauvoir's observation about the traditional choice confronted by a woman:

> Ce n'est pas [...] en augmentant sa valeur humaine qu'elle gagnera du prix aux yeux des mâles: c'est en se modelant sur leurs rêves. [...] De la plus servile à la plus hautaine, elles apprennent toutes que, pour plaire, il leur faut abdiquer. [...] [L]es hommes n'aiment pas les garçons manqués, ni les bas-bleus, ni les femmes de tête; trop d'audace, de culture, d'intelligence, trop de caractère les effraient. Dans la plupart des romans, comme le remarque G. Eliot, c'est l'héroïne blonde et sotte qui l'emporte sur la brune au caractère viril [...]. Être féminine, c'est se montrer impotente, futile, passive, docile.[42]

> [It is not [...] by increasing her worth as a human being that she will increase her value in men's eyes; it is by modelling herself on their dreams. [...] From the most servile to the most haughty, they all learn that, in order to please, they must abdicate. [...] [M]en do not love tomboys, nor bluestockings, nor capable women. Too much daring, learning, or intelligence, too much character, will frighten them. In most novels, as George Eliot observes, it is the silly, blonde heroine who triumphs over the dark-haired female with the masculine character. [...] To be feminine is to appear impotent, useless, passive, and docile.]

Gina del Dongo is hardly exemplary of the impotent, docile heroine evoked by Beauvoir, but her strategic charm marks her out as different from the heroines under consideration here. In addition, it is no doubt largely to the extent that Gina devotes her energies to Fabrice's well-being that she is so popular with critics. Stendhal's heroines often seem to be favoured by critics to the extent that they subordinate their own desires to those of a male hero, and disliked in so far as their first allegiance is to themselves. In any case, Gina has always been overwhelmingly esteemed by critics; she has no need of defence.

This book will focus, then, on four of Stendhal's less popular heroines, whose lack of interest in the traditional female pursuit of being pleasing is emblematized by the green holly paste that both Mina and Lamiel wear to deter unwanted male attention. It will be suggested that the censure such heroines provoke — in other characters, in critics, and even possibly (though far from certainly) in the author himself — is their well-earned badge of honour.

Notes to the Introduction

1. Catherine Rodgers discusses the failure of feminist literary criticism to acknowledge the pioneering status of Beauvoir's studies of literary heroines in her 1949 work. 'Étude féministe de cinq auteurs: cinquante ans de recul', in *Cinquantenaire du 'Deuxième Sexe'*, ed. by Christine Delphy and Sylvie Chaperon (Paris: Syllepse, 2002), pp. 139–42.

2. 'Stendhal et la politique du regard: L'Amour d'un égotiste', in *Histoires d'amour* (Paris: Denoël, 1983), pp. 319–40.

3. See for example Margaret Waller, *The Male Malady: Fictions of Impotence in the French Romantic Novel* (New Brunswick, NJ: Rutgers University Press, 1993), chapter 5; Maddalena Bertelà, *Stendhal et l'Autre: L'Homme et l'œuvre à travers l'idée de féminité* (Florence: Olschki, 1985).

4. *The Resisting Reader: A Feminist Approach to Feminist Fiction* (Bloomington: Indiana University Press, 1978), p. xx.

5. Simone de Beauvoir, *Le Deuxième Sexe*, 2 vols (Paris: Gallimard, 1949; repr. 1976), I, 375–89. Beauvoir's essay on Stendhal occupies a privileged position as the fifth of five literary essays located towards the end of a section devoted to myths of femininity, which closes the first volume of *Le Deuxième Sexe*. The essay had already appeared the same year in the journal *Les Temps modernes*.

6. *Essai sur les sources de 'Lamiel'. Les Amazones de Stendhal. Le Procès de Lacenaire* (Lyons: Imprimeries réunies, 1942). For an analysis of how Beauvoir privileges Stendhal's less independent heroines, see my 'Simone de Beauvoir on Stendhal: in Good Faith or in Bad?', *Irish Journal of French Studies*, 8 (2008), 55–71 (from which some of the following discussion has been drawn).

7. For contestations of Beauvoir's claim that Stendhal demystifies women, see Kristeva, 'Stendhal et la politique du regard', p. 339 and Gita May, 'Le Féminisme de Stendhal et *Lamiel*', *Stendhal Club*, 77 (1977), 191–204 (p. 194).

8. *Le Deuxième Sexe*, I, 382.

9. *Le Deuxième Sexe*, I, 378.

10. Clara Malraux, 'Les Grandes Sœurs de Mathilde de la Mole', *Confluences*, 30 (1944), 262–64. Malraux's article does not feature among the works on Stendhal by which, according to Christof Weiand, Beauvoir's argument was influenced, namely: Maurice Bardèche, *Stendhal romancier* (Paris: La Table Ronde, 1947), André Maurois, *Sept visages de l'amour* (Paris: La Jeune Parque, 1946), Alain, *Stendhal* (Paris: Rieder, 1935). See Christof Weiand, 'Stendhal ou le romanesque du vrai', in *Simone de Beauvoir: 'Le Deuxième Sexe.' Le Livre fondateur du féminisme moderne en situation*, ed. Ingrid Galster (Paris: Champion, 2004), pp. 241–55.

11. *Le Deuxième Sexe*, I, 242.

12. Jean-Paul Sartre, *L'Être et le néant: Essai d'ontologie phénoménologique* (Paris: Gallimard, 1943), p. 635.

13. *Le Deuxième Sexe*, I, 381.

14. *Le Deuxième Sexe*, I, 382.

15. *Le Deuxième Sexe*, I, 386.

16. Elizabeth Fallaize importantly notes, however, that if, 'In [Beauvoir's] chapter on Stendhal, written at the beginning of her work on the book, she explicitly identifies with Julien, the male lover', by the end of *Le Deuxième Sexe* 'she is able to imagine an independent woman in the dominant role, and she perceives all the difficulties inherent in that position'. 'Simone de Beauvoir and the demystification of women', in *A History of Feminist Literary Criticism*, ed. by Gill Plain and Susan Sellers (Cambridge: Cambridge University Press, 2007), pp. 85–99 (p. 94).

17. Simone de Beauvoir et al., *Que peut la littérature?* ([Paris]: Union générale d'éditions, 1965), pp. 73–92 (pp. 82–83).

18. Lucy Garnier has analysed the confusion of authorial voices in Beauvoir's essay on Stendhal, which she contrasts with the more distant tone adopted in the studies of Montherlant, D. H. Lawrence, Claudel, and Breton. 'La Femme comme construction dans la fiction stendhalienne', unpublished doctoral thesis, University of Oxford, 2007, section 3.1.1.

19. *Histoires d'amour*, p. 325.

20. 'Stendhal Club', *Revue des sciences humaines*, 224 (1991), 139–59 (p. 147).

21. *Stendhal et le roman: Essai sur la structure du roman stendhalien* (Aran: Éditions du grand chêne, 1979), p. 61. Yves Ansel problematizes the binary opposition between Stendhal's two female types by drawing attention to a wide range of secondary female characters, mainly venal, that do not belong to either pole. 'Stendhal et la femme "en deux volumes"', *L'Année stendhalienne*, 8 (2009), 139–68.

22. *A Future for Astyanax: Character and Desire in Literature* (Boston: Little, Brown, 1976), pp. 118–19.

23. *A Future for Astyanax*, p. 121.

24. *Le Héros fourbe chez Stendhal ou Hypocrisie, politique, séduction, amour dans le beylisme* (Paris: SEDES, 1987), p. 217. See also Michel Crouzet, *Le Naturel, la grâce et le réel dans la poétique de Stendhal: Essai sur la genèse du romantisme, Tome II* (Paris: Flammarion, 1986), pp. 201–02.

25. *Maternal Subjectivity in the Works of Stendhal* (Lewiston, NY: Mellen, 2001), p. 151. See also Marie-Louise Coudert, 'Mathilde mal aimée', *Europe*, 519–21 (1972), 136–41 (p. 136).

26. *Œuvres intimes*, ed. by Victor Del Litto, 2 vols (Paris: Gallimard, Bibliothèque de la Pléiade, 1981–82), I, 198 (*Journal*, 3 February 1805). Henceforth *OI* followed by volume and page numbers. See also the author's 1837 list of admirable heroines, reproduced in Stendhal, *Le Rose et le Vert, Mina de Vanghel, Tamira Wanghen*, ed. by Jean-Jacques Labia (Paris: Flammarion, 1998), p. 218. On his love of Ariosto's Bradamante, see *OI* II 619 (*Vie de Henry Brulard*).

27. *Correspondance générale*, ed. by Victor Del Litto and others, 6 vols (Paris: Champion, 1997–99), I, 187. Henceforth *Cg* followed by volume and page numbers.

28. For a detailed analysis of the importance to Stendhal of Plutarchan models, for example, see Francesco Manzini, *Stendhal's Parallel Lives* (Oxford: Lang, 2004).

29. Ann Jefferson, *Reading Realism in Stendhal* (Cambridge: Cambridge University Press, 1988), p. 150. On reading as an expression of a form of female agency, see Ann Jefferson, 'Varieties of Female Agency in Stendhal', *From Goethe to Gide: Feminism, Aesthetics and the French and German Literary Canon 1770–1936*, ed. by Mary Orr and Lesley Sharpe (Exeter: University of Exeter Press, 2005), pp. 65–79 (pp. 76–79).

30. Stendhal, *Histoire de la peinture en Italie*, ed. by Paul Arbelet, 2 vols, in Stendhal, *Œuvres complètes*, ed. by Victor Del Litto and Ernest Abravanel, 50 vols (Geneva: Cercle du bibliophile, 1967–74), XXVI–XXVII (1969), II, 327 (chapter 184).

31. *Histoire de la peinture en Italie*, I, 168 (chapter 34); Stendhal, *De l'Amour*, ed. by Henri Martineau (Paris: Garnier Frères, 1959), p. 7 (chapter 1). On the latter point, the notion that love is conditioned by social factors is key to *De l'Amour* and to Stendhal's novelistic practice more generally. See for example Lucy Garnier, ' "La Femme par M. de Stal": *Lucien Leuwen* et la sexualité féminine chez Stendhal', *L'Année stendhalienne*, 9 (2010), 93–119. On the partiality of perception in Stendhal, see especially Georges Blin, *Stendhal et les problèmes du roman* (Paris: Corti, 1954).

32. Ansel notes that similar anecdotes illustrative of the partiality of understanding in Stendhal appear in *Histoire de la peinture en Italie*, II (chapters 68, 91). See Stendhal, *Œuvres romanesques complètes*, ed. by Yves Ansel, Philippe Berthier, and Xavier Bourdenet, 3 vols (Paris: Gallimard, Bibliothèque de la Pléiade, 2005–), I, 1135–36. Hereafter *Orc*. Michel Crouzet notes, without additional comment, that the only place in *Le Rouge et le Noir* where the colours of the novel's enigmatic title are united is in the anthill passage. *'Le Rouge et le Noir': Essai sur le romanesque stendhalien* (Paris: Presses Universitaires de France, 1995), p. 16.

33. *The Structure of the Artistic Text* (1970). Cited in Franco Moretti, *The Way of the World: The 'Bildungsroman' in European Culture* (London: Verso, 1987), p. 97.

34. See for example John Mitchell, *Stendhal: 'Le Rouge et le Noir'* (London: Arnold, 1973), p. 10.

35. See Michelle Chilcoat, 'Idéologie et romantisme: Habitude et réflexion', *L'Année stendhalienne*, 4 (2005), 41–66 (p. 40).

36. On this point, see Bardèche, *Stendhal romancier*, p. 17.

37. It should also be noted that Sartre was a great admirer of Stendhal. See Yves Ansel, 'Sartre' in *Dictionnaire de Stendhal*, ed. Yves Ansel, Philippe Berthier, and Michael Nerlich (Paris: Champion, 2003), pp. 653–54.

38. As F. W. J. Hemmings observes, 'The most extravagant of dithyrambs have been sung for Gina.' *Stendhal: A Study of his Novels* (Oxford: Clarendon Press, 1964), p. 195.

39. 'Le Dilemme de l'honneur féminin dans l'univers masculin du duel: Le Crime de la duchesse Sanseverina', *Stendhal Club*, 75 (1976–77), 305–19.
40. *Essai sur les sources de 'Lamiel'*, p. 9. The term was used by Stendhal to describe his former lover, Angela Pietragrua.
41. See for example *Cg* I 180, 259, 276, 525–26, 253–54, 469, 590; II 134.
42. *Le Deuxième Sexe*, II, 97–98.

CHAPTER 1

Mina, Vanina, and the
Logic of the Strange Step

The Art of Happiness

As a child, Henri Beyle lusted after his freedom. Forbidden to play with children his own age, and constantly monitored by a family he considered tyrannical, he resorted to what he presents in the autobiographical *Vie de Henry Brulard* as the tactics of a slave: 'le mensonge' [lying] or 'une dissimulation profonde' [heavy dissimulation] (*OI* II 624, 700).[1] For example, with the complicity of the family's cook, the young Beyle would take a detour by the Jardin de Ville on returning from his drawing classes, in order to be, if only for a short time, among (though not too close to) the children of Grenoble. One night he even managed to slip into a meeting of the Jacobin Society while ostensibly going to meet his beloved aunt Élisabeth. His instinctive Jacobinism was such that he rejoiced at news of the execution of Louis XVI and was delighted by the guillotining of two priests in Grenoble, was fascinated by political assassins, and even conspired to shoot a tree carrying an inscription that he found offensive, for unremembered reasons. The young Beyle's clandestine readings of books stolen from his grandfather's study are presented in *Vie de Henry Brulard* as participating in the same logic of resistance to authority. It was these readings that gave rise to a long-held ambition to 'vivre à Paris en faisant des comédies comme Molière' [live in Paris while writing comedies, like Molière] (*OI* II 699).

   Pauline Beyle was her brother's main correspondent for some years after he left the family home in late 1799. In his letters to Pauline, Henri urges her repeatedly to read the work of various authors. The author he recommends most insistently is Destutt de Tracy. Beyle, or Stendhal, was passionate in his admiration for Tracy, to the extent that many of his own key ideas echo those articulated in *Éléments d'idéologie* [*Elements of Ideology*] (1801–15). For example, the novelist prized highly the ability to determine the direction of one's own life; Sheila Bell notes of *Vie de Henry Brulard* that 'the question from which all others flow' is '"ai-je dirigé le moins du monde ma vie?" [did I manage my life in the slightest way at all?]'[2] The author frequently insists in his writing on the importance of formulating one's own independent judgements rather than simply believing or seeing what one is told.[3] And an understanding of human behaviour was, for him, 'un grand pas vers le bonheur' [a great step towards happiness] (*OI* I 31; *Journal,*

10 December 1801).[4] All of these ideas lead back to the work of Tracy and his fellow Ideologists.

The first three volumes of Destutt de Tracy's *Éléments d'idéologie* had appeared by 1805. The most consistent reason that Beyle gave for recommending Tracy's work to his sister, from 1804 onwards, was that it would help her to make sound judgements and avoid errors. His letters suggest, in addition, that her study of Ideology will add to her stock in the eyes of intelligent society; that it offers a defence against tyrants and charlatans; that it will amuse her and relieve her boredom; that it will help her to tolerate her lot; that it will help her to discover what she wants out of life; and that it will ultimately add to her measure of happiness.

Ideology is defined by Tracy as the science of the formation, expression, and combination of ideas; he also defines it, even more succinctly, as the study of our ways of knowing.[5] The science of Ideology is, Tracy claims, closely connected with what he calls 'l'art d'être heureux' [the art of being happy].[6] Happiness is the reward of sound judgement, for Tracy, and sound judgement is always grounded in the accurate observation and recollection of our perceptions. However, if the judgements we formulate on the basis of our sensibility can lead us to happiness, they also give rise to desires upon whose satisfaction our happiness depends. The 'volonté' [will], or unsatisfied desire, to which our judgements give rise causes us pain, but it also motivates us to satisfy our desires. Our *volonté* is therefore intimately linked to our happiness, for Tracy: 'nous sommes toujours heureux ou malheureux par elle' [we are always either happy or unhappy because of it].[7]

Freedom was at least as intrinsic as happiness to the thinking of Ideologists like Tracy, Volney, and Cabanis, as might be expected given their Enlightenment inheritance and the fact that they came to maturity around the time of the French Revolution. If, for Tracy, 'le bonheur est le but de l'être voulant' [happiness is the aim of the desiring being], freedom is 'le bien unique de l'être voulant' [the only possession of the desiring being], the greatest good of all and the one that contains all others. Happiness is then the ultimate goal, while freedom is the ability to achieve it.[8] Freedom constitutes the highest value for the living being because its absence implies the disappearance of all possibility of happiness.[9] The two are intrinsically linked and even virtually identical because our happiness is always equal in measure to our freedom, that is, to 'notre pouvoir de satisfaire nos désirs' [our power to satisfy our desires].[10] According to Tracy, each individual has both the right to achieve happiness by satisfying his desires and the duty to use his freedom for this purpose.[11]

In the fourth volume of *Éléments d'idéologie* — from which some of the preceding discussion has been drawn, but which was not published until 1815 — Tracy evokes a number of means of attaining happiness, or at least of escaping 'la *souffrance de la contrainte*' [the *agony of constraint*]: the surmounting of obstacles to the satisfaction of one's desire, the achievement of a compromise position which permits the satisfaction of one desire but at the expense of other desires, and the outright renunciation of one's desire, along with the suffering it brings with it.[12] Henri Beyle's letters to his younger sister, written in the first few years of the nineteenth century, seem in some respects to anticipate Tracy's system.

Pauline might, for example, act on her desire to leave the family home and embrace an independent existence. The young Henri had himself made this choice, devoting himself to the study of mathematics with a view to leaving his controlling family behind him and beginning a new life in Paris as a student. Repeatedly, Henri proposes that Pauline come to join him and his friends in Paris or Marseilles, possibly earning her living by working in a bank (although the presence within this fantasy of a hypothetical or, later, real husband detracts a little from the dream of independence). However, when Pauline tells her brother of her wish to flee from their father, his disapproval is categorical: such an action would reduce her 'au rang des filles perdues' [to the level of debauched women] (*Cg* I 202) and would put paid to any hope of finding a husband.[13] Henri repeatedly warns Pauline of the fate of his childhood friend Victorine Bigillion, whom he portrays as having been confined and treated as mad on account of her desire for independence.[14] He also alludes to the terrible difficulties experienced by his current lover, Mélanie Guilbert, after she left her family home (see *Cg* I 345). In Henri's eyes, any direct refusal by Pauline of the constraints placed upon her would be detrimental to her long-term happiness, even if it procured pleasure in the short term.[15]

A second possible means of achieving happiness is strongly urged by Henri's letters: the exercise of 'une liberté modérée' [a moderate freedom] (*Cg* I 204). This strategy recalls the methods that he had adopted during his own earlier youth, when he had had recourse to ruse in order to effect a partial escape from the tyranny of his family and tutors. While Henri was extremely concerned when he heard of Pauline's walks around Grenoble, disguised in men's clothing, and warns her that such behaviour will reduce her chances of marriage and therefore happiness, he does frequently propose that his sister adopt a different strategy of dissimulation. He advises her to hide her brilliance from others in order to remain charming to them, even while cultivating her mind and her intellectual freedom through her reading: 'C'est un magasin de bonheur toujours sûr et que les hommes ne peuvent nous ravir' [It is a store of happiness that is always reliable and that men cannot take from us] (*Cg* II 38). He regrets that prevailing prejudices make it impossible for a strong, intelligent woman to find any kind of happiness in early nineteenth-century French society except by way of hypocrisy. He repeatedly advises Pauline to learn to exercise influence over others in the interest of her own desires, in view of the fact that women of the time were not in a position to act upon their own desires. Influence, or indirect action, offered women the only possibility of achieving happiness, according to Beyle. Marriage, in his view, could offer women the possibility of exercising such indirect action, while also conferring a certain freedom upon them: 'Le rôle d'une demoiselle, dans nos mœurs, est l'immobilité, la nullité, toutes les négations. On accorde à une femme mariée une liberté qui va jusqu'à la licence' [The role of a young lady, according to our mores, is immobility, uselessness, everything negative. A married woman is allowed a freedom that borders on licentiousness] (*Cg* I 622). Reading and marriage are therefore held up as the only viable keys to happiness available to Pauline in the early part of the nineteenth century.

Henri never explicitly recommends that Pauline renounce her desire for independence. In fact, he continues to try to stimulate her desire for freedom, for example by encouraging her to use her married and child-free state to her advantage by travelling.[16] However, his letters do also emphasize, from the beginning, the need to minimize her suffering or *ennui* — defined by him as 'l'absence du désir' [the absence of desire] (*Cg* I 239) — by aiming for an unambitious degree of happiness. He advises Pauline, for example, to read in order to forget her boredom, to acquire the habit of tolerating her 'chagrins' (*Cg* I 451), and to aim for 'un état heureux, une sagesse qui apprenne à éviter les peines' [a happy state, a wisdom that might teach the avoidance of sorrows] rather than for 'le bonheur extrême' [extreme happiness] (*Cg* I 497). He also insists that she should not hope for passion in a marriage, but rather for 'un contentement raisonnable' [modest happiness] (*Cg* I 589). In brief, Henri advised Pauline to resign herself to a conventional life because he wanted to protect her from the almost inevitable suffering that she would encounter were she to choose a freedom forbidden to women of her day.

However, this is precisely the kind of freedom chosen by a number of Stendhal's fictional heroines.[17] More generally, in the writings he intended for publication, far from promoting compromise and renunciation, Stendhal frequently complained that his compatriots were lacking in *faculté de vouloir* [the ability to want] and in energy. He believed that most of his contemporaries resembled the impassive being briefly imagined in Tracy's *Éléments d'idéologie*, a creature ruled by habit rather than by will.[18] Guests at the Hôtel de La Mole, where 'la moindre idée vive semblait une grossièreté' [the tiniest bright idea seemed crude] (*Orc* I 576), lack energy on account of their submission, for fear of ridicule, to a litany of social codes, codes that produce an all-pervasive *ennui*, or state of desirelessness.

Nevertheless, Stendhal believed that a melancholic, desireless state, if properly exploited, could itself be productive of passion, or of the kind of ambition that leads to greatness.[19] Victor Brombert describes Stendhalian boredom as 'almost the prime condition of fervor'.[20] If Stendhal presents the restrictions imposed by social codes of behaviour as potentially destructive of energy, therefore, constraints in general, at least to the extent that they are felt to be oppressive, are also represented by him as potentially productive of energy, as paradoxically constructive of character. He repeatedly suggests, in his letters to Pauline, that the difficulties encountered by an individual make him or her more admirable.[21] He also repeatedly expresses the view that the character of entire societies depends upon the presence or absence of repression and danger, with the result that despotic regimes can be perversely conducive to the preservation of desire, or the *faculté de vouloir*, in its subjects.[22] Stendhal claims that in the France of his time it is only members of the lower classes who still experience suffering and deprivation, and who consequently preserve 'la faculté de sentir avec force et constance' [the ability to feel with strength and constancy]; it was not by accident, for the author, that it was the petite bourgeoisie that produced Adrien Lafargue, the murderer on whom the character of Julien Sorel was partly modelled.[23]

For Stendhal as for Destutt de Tracy, desire is intrinsically connected with happiness; but if, for Tracy, the frustration of the ability to act on one's desire leads to unhappiness, for Stendhal the existence of constraint can itself give rise to desire and, by extension, to the possibility of achieving happiness through the exercise of the freedom to act on that desire.[24] In this respect, Stendhal's conception of *vouloir* brings him closer to Sartre than to Tracy. While Tracy places freedom and constraint in opposition to one another, Sartre emphasizes their interdependence. He argues for example that the freedom to walk the streets at night is effectively meaningless in the absence of any actual or potential prohibition on walking the streets at night.[25] Accordingly, Brombert's study of Stendhalian freedom, informed by French existentialist ideas, argues for the energy-creating role of constraint in his work: 'Social forces are seen as tyrannical; yet they fail to constrict the Stendhalian hero. Instead, they unleash an energy, which is in turn converted into fervor.'[26]

If Stendhal's heroines are extraordinarily energetic, it is no doubt because, regardless of their social position or nationality, they are all subjected to social structures that tyrannically contrive to deny them the opportunity to choose their own futures. All are prone to *ennui* and frustration. Stendhal frequently returns, in his letters and other writings, to the theme of the restrictions placed on women of his time, and to their consequent lack of happiness. For example, the author of *De l'Amour* [*On Love*] lambasts his own society for approving of young women who enter loveless but financially lucrative marriages and for denouncing other young women who enter into loving sexual relationships outside of marriage, thereby denying them what can be the only form of happiness available to them.[27] He is especially scathing in this work about the very limited education offered to young women of his time, which he claims operates to keep them in slave-like ignorance, confine them to unthinking activity, and ultimately deny them happiness.

The Civil Code of 1804 had put an end to any hope, inspired by the French Revolution, that women might be recognized as the equals of men. Married women were placed by the Code in a state of effective financial and legal dependence on their husbands: a woman was obliged to obey her husband, obtain his permission if she wanted to work outside the home, and pay a heavier legal penalty than he for adultery. As might be expected, then, a woman's destiny was usually understood in Stendhal's time as marriage followed by maternity, and her influence on public life was seen by many as being ideally limited to the early education of her male children. So heavily policed was female desire that the *droit d'aimer* [right to love] was one of the key demands made by and on behalf of women in and beyond the 1830s. George Sand, Marie d'Agoult, and Hortense Allart all wrote about women's right to sentimental freedom. And in two early heroine-centred works by Stendhal, as will be shown in this chapter, the female protagonist is motivated, at least in part, by her will to choose her own lover rather than submit to someone else's marriage plans.

But sentimental rights were only one aspect of the struggle waged by French women in the first half of the nineteenth century. Happiness, certainly, was demanded, in line with Destutt de Tracy's emphasis on happiness as the goal of freedom; so were the right to equal education, the right to equal working conditions, and the right to political representation. Like the educated men of the French lower classes, from whose ranks Stendhal believed that great men would henceforth come, many women of his time were only too aware of the extent to which society had immobilized them, and some, as already suggested, were energetic in their refusal of this state of affairs. In 1832, for example, the journalist and Saint-Simonian Claire Démar published a sharp critique of the Civil Code, in which she defended women's right to freedom and happiness. When, shortly afterwards, she committed suicide in despair, she left a text entitled *Ma loi d'avenir* [*My Law of the Future*], still defending women's rights, which was later published by Suzanne Voilquin, director of one of the feminist periodicals established in the wake of the July Revolution in 1830. In this work, Démar argues for the right of each woman to formulate her own precepts for the future, instead of being confined by an externally imposed 'loi d'avenir' [law of the future].[28] As Démar's position here suggests, while female literary authors of the time certainly enjoyed a high level of recognition, women's authorship of their own destinies was widely considered a masculine prerogative in the France of her time. This explains the reproach formulated by one woman to another, in Balzac's *Mémoires de deux jeunes mariées* [*Memoirs of Two Young Married Women*]: 'Tu te fais le destin, au lieu d'être son jouet. [...] Tu t'es faite homme' [You make your own destiny, instead of being its plaything. [...] You have made yourself a man].[29]

The fate of Victorine Bigillion was, as we have seen, held up by Henri Beyle as an example of the horrors that would surely befall his sister were she to act on her desire for independence; he does not put in writing the account given him by his friend Félix Faure, who had heard that Victorine's behaviour had been so violent that she was now being held in an asylum in Avignon, with straw for a bed and a blanket for clothing. The young Beyle nevertheless had intense admiration for his old friend, describing her as being, along with Pauline, one of the very few kindred souls he had met in his twenty-one years of life.[30] He conceived of Victorine's madness as an effect of her superior strength of mind and feeling. While it has been argued that Stendhal's independent heroines never achieve lasting happiness, and are therefore effectively punished for their refusal to compromise on their desire for self-authorship, the author never bestowed Victorine's unequivocally grim fate upon his free female creations.

These latter heroines assert their freedom to choose their own romantic partners and generally the right to elaborate their own futures, even where it means that they end up inspiring contempt in their lovers. Stendhal repeatedly represents their desire for self-authorship as a kind of counter-plot, that is, as a reaction against the constraints imposed by the plans and plots of others. As is suggested by Stendhal's adaptation of Tracy's ideas in his letters to his sister, as well as by French existentialist thinking later on, there can be no easy harmony between happiness and freedom; but the novelist's self-inventing heroines are never content to compromise on either, however high the cost.

Plots, Counter-plots, and the Female Protagonist

Mina de Vanghel and *Vanina Vanini* were both written in the period immediately following the publication of the *Promenades dans Rome* [*Walks in Rome*] in 1829, and before *Le Rouge et le Noir* appeared in late 1830.[31] Both narratives feature young women who share striking similarities with Mathilde de La Mole as well as with some of the Roman women described in the *Promenades*. For Maurice Bardèche, indeed, Vanina, Mina, and Mathilde de La Mole are all versions of the same character, expressive of 'une forme de l'exigence envers soi-même' [a kind of demand placed on the self] and 'un mode d'énergie chez la jeune fille' [a form of energy found in the young woman], a character that he notes is present already in the *Promenades*.[32] All three wish to become the authors, rather than the passive observers, of their own destinies; all actively seek out and take the initiative in their love affairs; all are audacious and unpredictable to the point of improbability and even ridiculousness (a trait often imbued with positive value in Stendhal's writings);[33] all display a level of energy rarely found, according to the novelist, in the elevated social class from which they issue;[34] all prefer the role of autonomous subject to that of beautiful object; all subscribe to a moral order that is fundamentally incompatible with the one that governs their peers; and all are single-minded in pursuit of their happiness. Unlike Armance and Madame de Chasteller, who obey social rules even where these rules are inimical to their happiness, Vanina, Mina, and Mathilde tend to ignore or reject social barriers to their happiness.[35] And while the arrival of an attractive young man has the power to prompt the previously retiring Madame de Rênal and Clélia Conti to energetic action, Vanina, Mathilde, and Mina are predisposed to exercise their freedom long before the chosen male has presented himself.

It is clear from a very early point in both *Mina de Vanghel* and *Vanina Vanini* that the heroines will resist inscription into the plots proposed for them by other characters.[36] However, the expression of freedom on the part of these young heroines is more than a simple gesture of refusal. What becomes evident as the narratives advance is the extent to which the protagonists not only avoid the course of their lives being plotted by others, but also actively plot their own destinies.[37] The compulsion to over-write one's default narrative with a story of one's own invention is of course present in Stendhal's male protagonists also, most notably Julien Sorel and Lucien Leuwen, but it is far more surprising in the case of young heroines such as Mina, Vanina, and Mathilde, because of the extent to which female destinies, both real and fictional, were circumscribed in the time and place in which these characters were created. Two analytical plot summaries will serve to highlight the insistence with which the heroines not only refuse plots, but also elaborate counter-plots.

Plotting in Mina de Vanghel

In *De l'Amour*, Stendhal writes that Germany is the country where marriages begin most happily, because young people are allowed to choose their spouses;[38] he makes a similar comment in *Mina de Vanghel* (*Orc* I 302), and develops it at greater length in *Le Rose et le Vert* [*The Pink and the Green*] (*Orc* II 1047–48). Nevertheless, the German Mina de Vanghel is initially presented as a sixteen-year-old heiress whom others would readily absorb into their chosen plots: the mention of the feelings she inspires in young men suggests that she will be married off to one of them at the earliest opportunity. However, 'le caractère romanesque et sombre' [the romantic and sombre character] that sometimes shines from her eyes and makes them so attractive (*Orc* I 297) gives us pause for thought; and we are informed early on of the girl's closeness to her independent-minded, philosophical father, a Prussian general who had retired from the army for ethical reasons after a brutally won victory.

Mina's prolonged mourning after the death of her beloved father prompts the friends of her mother to produce a tragic narrative for her: they imagine her to be a victim of tuberculosis. A Prussian prince has a very different though equally sinister plot in mind for Mina: he requires her presence at his court so that he can reward one of his courtiers with a lucrative marriage. Mina is aware, from her reading of the novels of the German author Auguste Lafontaine, that a rich heiress at court is wont to be seduced by a young colonel, and is horrified by a scenario in which love and happiness are made conditional upon money. Her mother, despite recognizing the difficulty of reconciling Mina 'aux idées de son âge' [to the notions of her age] (*Orc* I 298), seems intent on such a plot, hoping that her daughter will get married, and perhaps even find love, in Germany. Mina vehemently rejects, however, the idea of remaining in Prussia, remembering the constant police surveillance to which her father was subjected by the very country to whose glory he had devoted twenty years: 'Non, maman, plutôt changer de religion et aller mourir religieuse dans le fond de quelque couvent catholique!' [No, mother, I would rather change religion and go and die as a nun in the depths of some Catholic convent!] (*Orc* I 298) This alternative narrative, which anticipates in certain respects (self-transformation, retreat from society, death) her actual plot, is clearly perceived by Mina as one of resistance rather than defeat, implying as it does an escape from the tyrannical forces that had persecuted her father.

Proving herself to be far from the tragic victim imagined by her mother's friends, Mina's response to the efforts of the prince to assimilate her into his plot is to seek a way to leave Prussia. She hatches her own alternative plan to disguise herself as a man and go to live in England. With this end in mind, Mina experiments with modifications to her complexion and has male clothing made in preparation. Her awareness that the prince's police are watching her serves only to intensify her zeal. Mina eventually escapes with her mother from the prince's territory thanks to a ruse devised by his mistress.

Upon her arrival in Paris, efforts continue to be made to integrate Mina into a marriage plot, in both senses of the term: various suitors present themselves to her, and a story circulates about the efforts of German diplomats to prevent her fortune being snapped up by a French seducer. Nevertheless, Mina feels relatively free in this anonymous city, where she can become more properly the author of her own story. As well as enjoying the balls and shows that Parisian life offers, she seeks out the house where her father once lived, replaces its existing tenant, and has philosophy tutors visit and foster her inherited love of the subject; as often elsewhere in the story, Mina's great wealth permits the easy satisfaction of her desires. Then, while at a royal hunt in Compiègne, Mina is enchanted by the ruins of Pierrefonds, so persuades her mother to stay with her for several nights in the village. While gazing at the rain falling, during her stay there, she sees an advertisement of land for sale, and fifteen minutes later is arranging its purchase. Unlike the entirely conventional marriage narrative to which others, including her mother, would still like to see Mina subscribe, the plot she elaborates for herself is, at this point in the text, unpredictable and non-end-oriented, governed by the logic of her own impulses. The land she buys belongs to the handsome but vulgar Count de Ruppert, whose financial difficulties inspire in him an unrequited passion for Mina.

After the sudden death of her mother, Mina is informed by one of her new friends that it will now be necessary for her either to return to Germany or send for a German lady's companion to accompany her until she finds a husband in France. The 'il faut' [it's imperative] to which Julien Sorel will react so negatively appears three times in the friend's words of advice. Unsurprisingly, Mina refuses her friend's pragmatic solution, though she will eventually produce her own ironic version of the second option. After a year spent wasting away, she attends a dinner where she meets the much vaunted Madame Larçay, a woman reputed for her wealth and charm, whose character Mina nevertheless finds disappointingly common and prosaic. By contrast, she is charmed by the conversation and manner of her husband, 'un homme fort simple' [an extremely unaffected man] (Orc I 303), veteran of Napoleon's failed Russian campaign and of the Greek war of independence; he is the first Frenchman to strike Mina as utterly sincere. The narrator describes the character of Alfred Larçay as 'inflexible, froid, positif, assez enjoué, mais dénué d'imagination' [inflexible, cold, pragmatic, quite cheerful, but devoid of imagination] (Orc I 303), and therefore as the antithesis of Mina's character. His radical difference only increases his attractiveness to her: 'Ces caractères font un effet étonnant sur les âmes qui ne sont qu'imagination' [These characters make an astonishing impression on souls that are all imagination] (Orc I 945).[39] After a day of imaginative embellishment that recalls the process of 'cristallisation' [crystallization] outlined in De l'Amour,[40] Mina realizes that she loves Alfred, a married man. Single-minded in the pursuit of her happiness, she puts her initial remorse aside and two weeks later follows him to Aix-les-Bains, where he is holidaying with his wife. Having arranged for a lady's companion to come from Germany, Mina now very convincingly plays the role of servant to her servant. The alleged Madame Cramer treats 'Aniken' badly in public and apparently sacks her. Using the pretext of a family drama that would prohibit her return to Germany and a desire to learn French, Mina bribes her way into the servant quarters of the Larçay household.

Despite this victory, Mina is initially anxious about her 'sort' [fate], realizing that her plot is highly unlikely to bring about any real union with Alfred (Orc I 306). Mina's self-designation as author of her own life-story is indicated by her interior monologue on her first evening as a servant. In the course of a moonlit walk in the garden, by a lake that carries exquisite music to her from a small boat, Mina explicitly states her dissatisfaction with the situation into which 'le destin' [destiny] has thrown her and expresses her desire for authorship over her own destiny: 'je me fais une destinée en rapport avec le feu qui m'anime' [I am making a destiny for myself that will match the fire that burns inside me] (Orc I 306). She appears to see no contradiction between traditionally masculine attributes such as courage, honour, and heroism, on the one hand, and her own gender, on the other, although she does acknowledge that her servant's guise might argue against her heroism. Mina also refers in this episode to the fact that it is 'la recherche du bonheur naturelle à tous les hommes' [the pursuit of happiness, natural to all men] that has led her to 'cette étrange démarche' [this strange step] (*Orc* I 307). While this formula suggests a degree of gender blindness on Mina's part, it also constitutes a tacit textual acknowledgement of the pressure that her gender puts on her self-authored plot, the natural desire for happiness giving rise, in a woman, to behaviour that appears absurd. That Mina is alert to the distorting implications of her gender for her plot becomes clear when she goes on to compare her servant's disguise to that of her crusading ancestors; she concludes that 'Le courage qui les animait me jette, moi, au milieu des seuls dangers qui restent, en ce siècle puéril, plat et vulgaire, à la portée de mon sexe' [The courage that animated them throws me right into the only dangers that remain, in this childish, dull, and vulgar century, within reach of my sex] (*Orc* I 307). The repetition of the adjective 'bizarre' within the same passage — to describe first the shapes of the clouds as they pass in front of the moon and then Mina's servant's costume (*Orc* I 306) — has the effect of implying a connection between the eccentricity of her self-authored plot and the weirdness of a scene that brings to mind some of the more gothic paintings of the German Romantic painter Caspar David Friedrich. The clichéd and exaggerated Romanticism of the scene is itself an aspect of its strangeness, Stendhal ordinarily having little truck with what Berthier calls 'l'obscénité du *rubato* et l'usage intempérant de la pédale' [the obscenity of the rubato and the intemperate use of the pedal] (*Orc* I 940). The fact that the narrative has not shown any previous signs of hyperbole or pathos suggests that it is the sheer force of Mina's *volonté* or 'feu' [fire] (*Orc* I 306), the central theme of her interior monologue, that is pulling the prose out of the control of its narrator.[41]

The thought of her own authorship over her destiny and of the 'bonheur' [happiness] of seeing Alfred every day gives Mina courage (*Orc* I 307). It is ultimately her belief in the prerogatives of her own happiness (the word 'bonheur' features four times in her monologue) that reconciles Mina to the outwardly odd plot that she is forging for herself:

> 'Et ne faut-il pas, se dit-elle enfin, que chaque être accomplisse sa destinée? Malgré les hasards heureux de la naissance et de la fortune, il se trouve que mon destin n'est pas de briller à la cour ou dans un bal. J'y attirais les regards. Je m'y suis vue admirée, et mon ennui, au milieu de cette foule, allait jusqu'à la mélancolie la plus sombre! Tout le monde s'empressait de me parler et moi, je m'y ennuyais... Depuis la mort de mes parents, mes seuls instants de bonheur ont été ceux où, sans avoir de voisins ennuyeux, j'écoutais de la musique de Mozart. Est-ce ma faute si la recherche du bonheur, naturelle à tous les hommes, me conduit à cette étrange démarche? [...]' (*Orc* I 307)

> ['And must not every being realize its destiny?', she asked herself at last. 'Despite the happy accidents of birth and of fortune, it happens that my destiny is not to shine at court or at a ball. I was the centre of attention. I could see I was admired, and my boredom, amidst that crowd, turned to darkest melancholy. Everyone was keen to talk to me, but I was bored... Since the death of my parents, my only moments of happiness have been those when, free of irritating company, I could listen to Mozart's music. Is it my fault if the pursuit of happiness, natural to all men, leads me to this strange step? [...]']

Mina's reflection, here, on individual destiny as the pursuit of happiness testifies to her great merit from a Stendhalian perspective. The heroine's boredom at playing the default role of the beautiful heiress, queen of the ball, is shared by Vanina and by Mathilde, who choose alternative roles and plots that are no less strange than hers. Interestingly, Mina's reference to her self-disguise as a strange step echoes Vanina's description of her betrayal of Missirilli as 'une étrange démarche' [a strange step] (*Orc* I 259). In each case, what is at stake is a departure from the expected plot that is far more radical and unexpected than that 'premier pas' [first step] which, according to Nancy K. Miller, is also a 'faux pas' for so many eighteenth-century heroines.[42]

Mina's self-authored plot does bring her happiness, at least partly because she never feels excessively constrained by it; she even allows herself to experience the occasional thrill of slipping dangerously out of role, laughing at her own occasional aristocratic reflexes. It is suggested in the text that the reason why she does not take too seriously 'les devoirs de ce nouvel état' [the duties of her new condition] is that 'Mina n'était nullement agitée par les idées de *devoir* ou par la crainte du ridicule' [Mina was not at all bothered by notions of *duty* or by fear of ridicule] (*Orc* I 307–08).[43] Worried only about not raising the suspicions of Madame Larçay, Mina is described during this period as 'Absorbée dans son bonheur' [Absorbed by her happiness], as experiencing 'des moments de bonheur et d'exaltation' [moments of happiness and rapture] (*Orc* I 308) in Alfred's presence, and as performing her job with a natural enthusiasm. Because of her achievement of happiness, Mina has, in a sense, lost the plot, which is after all a plot centred on the achievement of happiness: 'Voir et entendre à chaque instant l'homme dont elle était folle était l'unique but de sa vie: elle ne désirait pas autre chose, elle avait trop de bonheur pour songer à l'avenir' [To see and hear at every moment the man she was mad about was her only aim in life: she desired nothing else, and was too happy to think of the future] (*Orc* I 309). Her application of a deforming green holly paste to her face serves as an impediment to the development of any love story between servant and master. Mina's happiness does away, at least provisionally, with any need for further narrative development. The natural end of Mina's pursuit of happiness would seem then to be a forgetfulness of plots.

The impetus for further plot development after the happiness found by Mina in Alfred's presence comes only from the latter's decision to make an advance on her. She repels him, apparently because of a falseness she perceives in his behaviour, and forgives him only after he has kept his distance for what she considers an acceptable period of time. Mina's respite from plotting her happiness was only temporary: despite her resistance to Alfred's attempted seduction, she gradually stops concealing her beauty and the two declare their love for one another. Mina decides against revealing her identity and her wealth to Alfred on the basis that to do so would be to remove those social obstacles that she hopes will spur him on to the 'démarches étranges' [strange steps] that she considers necessary to their happiness, namely a change of religion, wife, and country (*Orc* I 312) — her desire for a lover capable of strange, energetic actions recalls her reference to her own self-disguise as 'cette étrange demarche' [this strange step] (*Orc* I 307). The narrator observes that Mina's newly formulated plans are not at all hampered by any moral qualms:

> Ce grand mot *illégitime* ne venait pas se placer comme une barrière insurmontable devant les nouveaux projets de Mina; elle croyait ne pas s'écarter de la vertu, parce qu'elle n'eût pas hésité à sacrifier mille fois sa vie pour être utile à Alfred. (*Orc* I 312)

> [That great word *illegitimate* did not install itself like an insurmountable obstacle before Mina's new plans. She believed she was not leaving the path of virtue, because she would have unhesitatingly sacrificed her life a thousand times to be of use to Alfred.]

It is implied here that Mina (like Gina and Mathilde) adheres to a moral code that is very different from the standard, a code that involves heroic sacrifices and demonstrations of virtù rather than an adherence to social rules and Christian virtues.

When Alfred begins to keep his distance from Mina on account of his wife's suspicions, the young woman attends a costume ball incognito, purely for the 'bonheur' [happiness] of seeing him (*Orc* I 313). However, she is recognized by the Count de Ruppert, who claims to have been seeking her out across the holiday resorts of Europe. Mina realizes that to prevent the count from revealing the secret of her identity to Alfred and his wife she will need to invent some 'fable' [tale] (*Orc* I 314). Consequently, the next evening she arranges a meeting with Ruppert and offers to marry him in one year if he will accept a divorcee as his bride; this fiction has the advantage of holding the count at bay for a while and of procuring his protection, supposedly while the divorce is being arranged. So as not to find herself at the mercy of the Count de Ruppert's tale-telling, therefore, Mina elaborates a decoy marriage plot that has the reverse effect of putting him at her mercy: she procures his agreement to obey her 'comme un enfant' [like a child], and even like a slave (*Orc* I 315).

The count will, as a result of this hoax narrative, be made amenable to participation in a plot elaborated by the heroine to counteract the story being told about her by the jealous Madame Larçay. The latter accuses her maid of being 'une aventurière' [an adventuress] (*Orc* I 312), on the run from the law, who arranges clandestine meetings with men in the home of her supposedly estranged employer, Madame Cramer. Mina's efforts to elude wealth-inspired love have thus ironically given rise to a story in which she plays the role of gold-digger. Madame Larçay's accusation, and her husband's passivity while it is being made, prove a turning-point for Mina. She not only denies the accusations but begins to conceive 'le projet de sa vengeance' [the plan for her revenge], a plot that gives her hope, and therefore happiness, once again: 'Le bonheur qu'elle ressentit en ce moment la sépara pour toujours de la vertu' [The happiness she felt at that moment separated her from virtue forever] (*Orc* I 317).

When Alfred pleads with Mina to find a solution that will allow them to spend time with one another, she begins to despise his lack of resourcefulness; however, she finds consolation in his faith in her 'pouvoir d'agir' [power to take action] and assumes responsibility for their mutual happiness (*Orc* I 318). Mina persuades the Count de Ruppert to appear infatuated with Madame Larçay, and relocates to the one-time home of Jean-Jacques Rousseau in Chambéry, from where she continues to plot a revenge designed to procure her own future happiness. On one of her returns to Aix she witnesses, with Alfred, a scene that she has choreographed and that is designed to convince the latter that his wife is having an affair with the Count de Ruppert. The ruse is successful, resulting in a duel that confines the count to a period of bed rest, in the separation of Alfred and his wife, and in the happy union of Alfred and Mina.

Reunited with Alfred, Mina once again achieves a kind of plotless happiness, though her elation is now diminished by her sense of guilt. After one blissful month travelling around Lake Maggiore, Alfred laughingly asks Mina who she really is, telling her that regardless of her true identity he would ask for her hand in marriage were Madame Larçay to die. Mina finally reveals her real name to him. While this news is initially received with great happiness, over the following months, when they travel in the guise of husband and wife, Alfred becomes melancholic and Mina becomes remorseful about the Ruppert deception, which she finds increasingly difficult to keep secret from her lover. Despite her feelings of guilt, Mina is extravagantly happy and in love, finding 'un bonheur délicieux à faire tout ce que désirait Alfred' [a delicious happiness in doing everything Alfred desired] (*Orc* I 328), just as Livio Savelli in *Vanina Vanini* is 'ivre de bonheur' [drunk with happiness] when he is able to carry out his fiancée's wishes (*Orc* I 262). The abdication by Mina of her role as master plotter is inseparable from her achievement of happiness, but it is also the cause of her plot's unravelling, as she no longer takes the necessary care to hide her innate superiority from Alfred. Eventually, her exaltation leads her unwisely to forget the need to conceal her intellectual and general superiority from Alfred: 'Sa manière de chercher le bonheur, non seulement devait paraître singulière à une âme vulgaire, mais encore la choquer' [Her way of seeking happiness was bound to seem unusual to an ordinary soul, but also shocking] (*Orc* I 328).

When Alfred is on the point of changing his religion to allow him to divorce his wife and marry Mina, and consequently just as the heroine's desired ending seems close to realization, he finally asks her about the fateful night in Aix. Mina admits her role in the event. Alfred promptly abandons her, the narrator commenting only on the coldness of his tone of voice and its note of 'amour-propre piqué' [wounded self-love] (*Orc* I 329). Acknowledging that this is the danger to which 'les grandes âmes' [great souls] expose themselves, the heroine watches her lover's departure from a window. When she can see him no longer, she goes into his bedroom and kills herself with a bullet to the heart. Her suicide is despatched in one short sentence, and is followed by three even shorter sentences of commentary on the part of the narrator:

> Quand il eut disparu, elle alla dans la chambre d'Alfred et se tua d'un coup de pistolet dans le cœur. Sa vie fut-elle un faux calcul? Son bonheur avait duré huit mois. C'était une âme trop ardente pour se contenter du réel de la vie. (*Orc* I 329)

> [Once he was out of sight, she went into Alfred's bedroom and killed herself with a bullet to the heart. Was her life a miscalculation? Her happiness had lasted eight months. Hers was too passionate a soul to be content with the realities of life.]

Mina's pursuit of happiness has reached its natural end: a final loss of plot.

Plotting in Vanina Vanini

Vanina Vanini, set in Italy in the 1820s, opens with a sumptuous Roman ball to which only the prettiest women have been invited. Among these beauties, Princess Vanina Vanini is popularly judged to be the most ravishing, 'la reine du bal' [the queen of the ball] (*Orc* I 247). After dancing with two or three German royals at the request of her father, she accepts the invitations of some noble English men, before dancing with Livio Savelli, 'le jeune homme le plus brillant de Rome, et de plus lui aussi était prince' [the most brilliant young man in Rome, and moreover he too was a prince] (*Orc* I 248). Savelli is in love with Vanina but she has reservations about him: 'Si on lui eût donné à lire un roman, il eût jeté le volume au bout de vingt pages, disant qu'il lui donnait mal à la tête. C'était un désavantage aux yeux de Vanina' [If he had been given a novel to read, he would have tossed the volume away after twenty pages, saying that it made his head ache. This was a drawback in Vanina's eyes] (*Orc* I 248). Despite the heroine's autonomous streak being indicated by her negative assessment of the prince and by the 'orgueil singulier' [unusual pride] (*Orc* I 247) announced by her bearing, Vanina's compliance is suggested by her apparent acquiescence to the demands of her father.

Vanina's inscription into a social system over which she has no control is suggested by the impersonal focalization of her presentation: in the first paragraph she is simply 'une jeune fille' [a young woman] (*Orc* I 247), even if she stands out among many beautiful women in the eyes of the privileged guests. The theme of the subordination of individual freedom to the collective will is evoked by the statement that even kings 'sont obligés d'inviter les grandes dames de la cour' [are obliged to invite the highborn ladies of their courts]; only wealthy bankers like the Duke de B★★★ can choose their guests with impunity (*Orc* I 247). This theme is also suggested by the de-personalizing and impersonal structures used in the two opening paragraphs to evoke the gaze of the crowd: 'tous les regards la suivirent' [all eyes were on her]; 'On voyait les étrangers qui entraient frappés de la magnificence de ce bal' [Foreigners, as they entered, were seen to be struck by the magnificence of the ball]; 'Parmi tant de femmes remarquables il fut question de décider quelle était la plus belle' [There was some discussion about which of the many extraordinary women was the most beautiful]; 'la princesse Vanina Vanini [...] fut proclamée la reine du bal' [Princess Vanina Vanini [...] was declared the queen of the ball] (*Orc* I 247).[44] The omnipotence of the collective 'on' [one/ they] is indicated by the manner in which a sensational event is recounted at the ball: when the news arrives that a young political rebel has escaped from prison and, 'par un excès d'audace romanesque' [with a surfeit of romantic bravado], has attacked the prison guards with a dagger, this produces 'assez d'effet' [some impression] but is, at least for Livio Savelli, a mere 'anecdote' that '*on* racontait' [people were telling] in the background while he talks to Vanina (*Orc* I 248, my emphasis). An act of individual rebellion is thus diminished in significance, not only by its insertion into the collective narrative, but also by the manner in which the individual is represented within that narrative as weakened and out-numbered: 'mais il avait été blessé lui-même, les sbires le suivaient dans les rues à la trace de son sang, et on espérait le ravoir' [but he himself had been wounded, the police henchmen were following his trail of blood in the streets, and it was hoped that he would be caught] (*Orc* I 248; our emphasis).

Vanina, however, is struck by the man's action, telling the lovelorn Savelli that this young Carbanaro would win her affections, because 'au moins celui-là a fait quelque chose de plus que de se donner la peine de naître' [at least he has done more than simply take the trouble to be born] (*Orc* I 248). This man, in other words, has not simply resigned himself to his socially ordained fate, as Lucien Leuwen will later reproach himself for doing. The reference to the young man's surfeit of bravado, which has left him wounded and vulnerable, not only opposes him to the novel-hating Livio Savelli, and makes him instantly attractive to Vanina, but implies again the moderating, normalizing thrust of a collectivity that judges his energy to be excessive. The narrator informs us shortly afterwards of the annoyance of Vanina's father at the fact that his only daughter does not wish to marry, having refused 'les partis les plus brillants' [the most excellent matches] (*Orc* I 248); like the Carbonaro, she clearly wishes to do more than simply accept her default situation. Despite the anger of Vanina's father, he himself has something *romanesque* about him, with his apparently carefree spirit, his resemblance to 'un vieux comédien' [an old actor], and the fact that both of his sons were Jesuit priests who lost their minds before dying (*Orc* I 248). The stage has been set for a conflict between passionate idealism and obedient conformism.

Vanina, like Mina, is an originator of plots whose ultimate goal is her own happiness.[45] The next day, intrigued by her father's uncharacteristic care in locking a door, she notices from outside her family's palace a third-floor window that has, unusually, been left open. Finding her way to the terrace garden outside this window, she glimpses a young woman inside, who has evidently been injured; over a number of days, she is repeatedly drawn back to peer through the window, and learns that her father is hiding the young woman and bringing her food. Two days after being discovered by the object of her fascination, Vanina learns that her new friend, to whom she has expressed her devotion, is actually the escaped Carbonaro, Pietro Missirilli, in disguise. Her first action is to call for a doctor, thereby overruling the young man's pleas for secrecy. The heroine keeps a degree of distance from him for only a few days before starting to visit him again, drawn by an instinct for happiness more powerful than her sense of propriety or pride, and then encouraged in her love by Missirilli's strategic reserve. The two young people spend four extremely happy and intimate months together, but when Missirilli is finally granted his 'liberté' [freedom] (*Orc* I 253) by the surgeon, his thoughts turn again to the liberation of Italy. He tells Vanina that he plans to leave for Romagna within a few hours, to rejoin the struggle for national independence. In response, the astonished Vanina calmly offers her lover money and weapons; he stays two further days in her father's apartment. Over the course of these two days, Vanina offers Missirilli her hand in marriage in order to further his patriotic ambitions. However, the man who is now her lover refuses her offer on the grounds that he must remain faithful to Italy.

Momentarily affronted by this refusal, the proud Vanina then counters with a plan to leave Rome for a family residence conveniently situated in Romagna, so that she can be with Missirilli. At the agreed moment of his departure, Vanina again overwrites his plan by requesting that he remain in the apartment for a further three days. When he finally does get to Romagna, Vanina does not immediately join him; elected leader of a conspiracy, he consequently decides to devote himself entirely to the struggle for freedom rather than to his love affair. However, thwarting Missirilli's plans once more, Vanina shows up, explaining that her father had postponed her departure with a view to arranging her marriage to Savelli. It soon becomes clear that their love is threatened by Missirilli's political passion, to the extent that 'elle se surprit à maudire la liberté' [she was surprised to find herself cursing liberty] (*Orc* I 257). Nevertheless, Vanina uses her wealth to support Missirilli's patriotic plots. Realizing that she is no longer his primary passion, she makes plans to return to Rome, revelling in her projected overturning of his expectations: 'Elle jouissait de sa surprise douloureuse quand il la chercherait en vain auprès de lui' [She thought with pleasure of how painfully surprised he would be when he looked around in vain for her] (*Orc* I 257). Vanina then has the idea of overturning Missirilli's plot in an even more dramatic way, and of inducing him to leave his patriotic struggle behind. She writes a note to betray his co-conspirators just before a particularly well-planned insurrection. Her own plan is perfectly executed, its clandestine character reflecting the style of her lover's own plots. However, her ruthless actions in defence of her own happiness, and in defiance of Missirilli's own political passion, promise to be counter-productive, because of the guilt that suddenly begins to weigh on her: 'en lui parlant d'amour, il lui semblait qu'elle jouait la comédie' [while talking about love with him, she felt as though she was acting a part] (*Orc* I 259). Vanina is subsequently surprised by her lover's disappearance and a written note in which he explains that he is giving himself up to the authorities in solidarity with his fellow conspirators and in which he exhorts her to destroy the traitor. Devastated, Vanina privately vows to punish the culprit — herself — but she departs from Missirilli's plot by deciding first to arrange his release from jail.

From the moment that she receives Missirilli's note, Vanina's primary objective is her lover's release from prison. She agrees to marry Livio Savelli and then deploys her fiancé in the service of her espionage activities, for example by having him procure her access to the office of his uncle, the Minister of Police, and by requesting that he secure posts for her family's servants in strategically important locations. She also mobilizes her confessor in the service of her plot to free Missirilli, and visits the Minister of Police in his home, disguised as a footman, on the pretext that she is saving his life by telling him that he must spare Missirilli's life. Vanina's plot, mounted against the law in its most literal sense, is successful to the extent that her lover's life is saved (though the Pope has already decided to spare Missirilli even before the Minister of Police has a chance to request his pardon); but her plot does not achieve his liberation.

When eventually confronted by her lover in a prison chapel at the end of the novella, Vanina wonders who could have swaddled him in his chains. The implied answer is surely that she herself placed his chains on him, through her plot against his co-conspirators.[46] Missirilli, whose political fervour is now underpinned by religious principles, rejects Vanina's love despite not knowing about her betrayal, and advises her to marry 'l'homme de mérite que votre père vous destine' [the worthy man whom your father has chosen for you] (*Orc* I 268), so that he himself might give himself over fully to the cause of his country. Furious, the heroine reacts by telling him firstly of all she has done to secure his pardon and then of her betrayal. After Missirilli, in a blind rage, attempts to kill her, 'Vanina resta anéantie' [Vanina was crushed]; we read in the next sentence that she subsequently returned to Rome, and that the newspaper has announced her marriage to Livio Savelli (*Orc* I 269). The marriage plan that Vanina had initially resisted has evidently now been accepted; but she has made of it the ending of her own freely chosen plot, and possibly even, in view of the story's circular structure, the beginning of another.

The Ambiguity of Endings

For Michel Crouzet, the heroines of Stendhal's shorter narratives not only dominate those stories but are more powerful than those we generally find in his novels.[47] The fact that Stendhal's shorter narratives tend to end in the death (*Le Coffre et le Revenant, Mina de Vanghel, Les Cenci, L'Abbesse de Castro*) or conventional marriage (*Ernestine, Vanina Vanini*) of the female suggests, in itself, the reason why strong heroines might be better suited to shorter forms: in the conventions of nineteenth-century narrative, female independence can only ever be short-lived. In Stendhal's longer stories, the independence of his heroines tends to be more consistently compromised: for example, Gina's freedom is continually undermined by a love that makes her dependent upon the good will of tyrants; and while the heroine of *Le Rose et le Vert* has much in common with Mina de Vanghel, including her first name and place of origin, a more complex narrative development sees her delegating her natural authority to a mother and a female cousin, even if the narrative makes it clear that this deference is only provisional. The short narrative form may, therefore, have permitted Stendhal the possibility of creating freer heroines than would otherwise be possible.

However, this form, by its very concentration, places a greater emphasis on the symbolism of endings, and these endings have often been understood to symbolize the final capitulation or defeat of Stendhal's heroines. If Stendhal's fiction is usually understood to be more indulgent towards convention-defying females than was the society in which he lived, that fiction is nevertheless widely perceived to be ultimately disapproving of such heroines. For Jacqueline Andrieu, for example, all of Stendhal's rebellious young heroines 'perdent à la loterie, et le seul remède est la mort réelle pour Mina et Lamiel, mort virtuelle pour Vanina et Mathilde' [lose in the lottery, and the only cure is actual death for Mina and Lamiel, and virtual death for Vanina and Mathilde].[48] An important implication of this dominant position is that the moral message of these texts is ultimately a conservative one. In other words, the fates of heroines such as Vanina, Mina, and Lamiel have been widely interpreted as evidence of the author's ultimate censure of the self-determining female figure and preference for the self-abnegating heroine.

There is an obvious counter-argument. If it is true that Stendhal's audacious heroines tend to die or otherwise retire from the headlines at the end of their narratives, it must nevertheless be acknowledged that virtually all of his male protagonists (along with heroines like Madame de Rênal and Clélia Conti) also end their novels either unfulfilled in love or dead. Beauvoir comments as follows on the fact that both Lamiel and Julien commit crimes and die at the end of their stories: 'Il n'y a pas de place pour les grandes âmes dans la société telle qu'elle est: hommes et femmes sont logés à la même enseigne.' [There is no room for great souls in society as it is. Men and women are treated equally in this respect.][49] However, when Stendhal's male protagonists die or are otherwise punished by society at the end of their stories, their fates tend to be interpreted by critics as proof of their superiority rather than as proof of fault or failure.[50] Moya Longstaffe, who argues in one article that heroines such as Vanina, Mina, and Mathilde seem 'prédestinées à l'échec de l'amour ou à la catastrophe' [predestined for failure in love or for catastrophe], does not dwell in a different piece of work on the negative in the context of Octave, Julien, Fabrice, and Lucien: 'None of them will finally achieve worldly success. Yet it is precisely their failure which is the sign of their election, their salvation.'[51] If Stendhal's male protagonists can be understood to triumph over society even as they are punished by it, while the endings met by Mina and Vanina are interpreted in more purely defeatist terms, this is no doubt because of unacknowledged gender assumptions.

Endings: Mina de Vanghel

According to Margaret Higonnet, an act of suicide, particularly when performed by a female subject, has a potentially fragmenting effect on texts, forcing the reader to become a producer of narrative by filling in the gaps created by this scandalously subversive gesture.[52] This appeal to the reader's ingenuity is explicit in the final paragraph of *Mina de Vanghel*. Not surprisingly, then, Mina's suicide at the end of the novella has been interpreted in a number of ways by critics. In one sense, the reasons for her suicide are straightforward enough. She has been abandoned by her beloved Alfred, who now regards her, with a good deal of justification, as a scheming liar. In addition, Mina can no longer live without the illusions and idealizations upon which life with Alfred critically depended. If the ostensible reasons for Mina's suicide are relatively clear, however, the symbolic meaning of her gesture is somewhat less so.

For some critics, the ending of *Mina de Vanghel* highlights the impossibility of reconciling the ideal and the real, the Romantic and the pragmatic. Pierre Laforgue, for example, argues that Mina's suicide signals the triumph of pragmatic Realism over passionate Romanticism.[53] Mina's suicide is certainly compatible with her Romantic character. Like Goethe's Werther, Mina loses in love, and like Madame de Staël's Delphine, she is described as too exalted to be reconciled to the realities of life.[54] For one reading, then, Mina's death is symptomatic of her Romantic *mal du siècle*. After all, even prior to the duel between Alfred and M. de Ruppert, Mina had decided to drown herself in the event of Alfred's death, recalling the death by drowning of Shakespeare's Ophelia, a heroine privileged by the Romantics. Mina's suicide, like many other similar fictional acts, is thus deeply enmeshed in intertexts, as are all literary suicides according to Higonnet: 'The puzzling indeterminacy of the act lends special importance to literary intertexts, which provide lenses through which the act can be read.'[55] Reading Mina's suicide through the lenses offered by *Delphine* and *Werther*, then, permits us to interpret it as a Romantic rejection of a disappointing reality.

According to a second popular interpretation of the text's conclusion, however, it is not the heroine's Romanticism that is revealed, but rather her moral failings. For critics of this persuasion, the climax of the narrative represents the just defeat of an excessively manipulative character, too much in control of her own plot.[56] Arnaldo Pizzorusso presents an interesting variant of this position; for him, Mina undergoes 'une conversion libertine' [a libertine conversion] after which her pursuit of happiness becomes calculated, end-orientated, and ultimately doomed to failure.[57] It is true that happiness is resistant to calculated pursuit in Stendhal's fiction but, as his letters to Pauline repeatedly show, he believed, with the Ideologists, in the importance of applying one's faculty of reason to the business of living a happy life, and more generally in the value of exercising authorship over one's own life. It is interesting to note that Julien Sorel's death is not often ascribed to his excessively zealous plotting of his life, and that Fabrice del Dongo is rarely if ever criticized for the selfishness of his planned abduction of Sandrino. A heroine's single-minded pursuit of her own happiness seems less acceptable to many readers than a hero's uncompromising pursuit of the same goal. Stendhal himself seems to have been all too aware of this double standard as it operated in his own time: he recommended to his sister that she must never seem to be calculating, must always give the impression of acting 'par sentiment' [on feeling] rather than on reflection, even while she plans and manages her own happiness carefully (*Cg* I 534). To the narrator's ultimate question, 'Sa vie fut-elle un faux calcul?' [Was her life a miscalculation?], the answer, for critics unsympathetic to a heroine too fixated on the preparation of her own happiness, is yes. According to this pessimistic interpretation, the narrator's remark that her happiness had lasted eight months implies that Mina's happiness was too ephemeral to make her life a success.

However, for another reading of the conclusion, compatible with its coding as Romantic though not with any emphasis on defeat, eight months of happiness is not to be sniffed at. Mina herself states, towards the end of the text, that death would not be too high a price for the happiness she has experienced during the period of her intimacy with Alfred: 'La mort et mille morts arriveraient demain, se disait-elle, que ce n'est pas trop pour acheter ce qui m'arrive depuis le jour où Alfred s'est battu' [If death and a thousand deaths were to come tomorrow, she thought, they would not be too high a price to pay for my life since the day Alfred fought his duel] (*Orc* I 328). To the narrator's concluding question, then, it is legitimate to reply that Mina did not miscalculate, that in fact she played the hand she was dealt very well, and that her suicide in no way diminishes the rightness of her choices. According to an optimistic reading of the text, the heroine's suicide is, as Laforgue maintains, a lucid choice rather than 'un acte désespéré' [a desperate act].[58] For Berthier,

Mina's death is a noble protest against, rather than a defeat by, 'l'insuffisance constitutive du réel' [the constitutive inadequacy of the real] (*Orc* I 942). Stendhal himself notes in *De l'Amour* that an 'admirable' suicide is possible, but that it risks being interpreted as absurd.[59] Less than two decades after the completion of *Mina de Vanghel*, Charles Baudelaire would associate suicide with the beauty and heroism peculiar to modern life.[60] Certainly, there is heroism in the calmness and poise with which Mina confronts her own death, comparable to the 'grand sang-froid' [great cool-headedness] demonstrated by the Duchess de Palliano in the story that bears her name.[61] The heroine's suicide would thus signify, for this heroic reading of the ending, not her personal failure, nor the failure of idealism in general, but rather the failure of a society incapable of accommodating characters such as hers.[62] Mina's suicide can therefore be interpreted as a final assertion of her authority over her own story, and of her refusal to submit to the narrative that external forces would devise for her.

In her study of fictional female suicides, Higonnet discusses the figure of Roxane in Montesquieu's *Lettres persanes*, a text often referred to as an intertext for *Mina de Vanghel* on the basis of their shared use of the device of the foreigner's perception of Paris. For Higonnet, Roxane's self-poisoning is expressive of 'A heroic thirst for systematic autonomy' at least as much as it is a negation of self.[63] While Mina's situation is very different from Roxane's, her suicide too can be interpreted as an act of self-authorship. Mina's act is particularly subversive because of its unexpected quality. If the apparent reproduction of a Romantic stereotype and gender cliché at the conclusion of *Mina de Vanghel* — whose heroine, like Madame de Staël's Delphine and Chateaubriand's Atala, kills herself for love — seems, in one sense, far from innovative, both Mina and Stendhal handle the act of suicide in an abrupt, dispassionate manner, as if both were seeking ironic distance from the pathos associated with Romantic suicide. Indeed, for a heroine to shoot herself rather than take poison is already to depart from the Romantic gender stereotype. The startling but anti-melodramatic quality of Mina's act can be interpreted as a means of subverting Romantic cliché and of confirming her status as an individual free to choose her own destiny.

If the ending of *Mina de Vanghel* presents a tacit affirmation of the heroine's freedom, this is continuous with her tendency throughout the narrative to determine the direction of the plot. Jean-Jacques Labia notes that 'tout appelle le lecteur à suivre le récit comme l'œuvre de Mina en personne' [everything invites the reader to follow the story as though it were Mina's personal handiwork].[64] The heroine's authorship of her own plot is insistently highlighted by a narrative that not only repeatedly shows her moulding her own destiny, as we have seen, but that also refers to her various projects in writerly terms: the narrator describes Mina's self-disguise as a maid in order to gain access to Alfred as a 'roman' [novel] (*Orc* I 305); she uses the word 'fable' to describe the story that she will need to tell Count de Ruppert in order to allay his suspicion (*Orc* I 314); the count refers to the resulting story as 'un roman désagréable' [a disagreeable novel] (*Orc* I 315); Madame Larçay questions 'le conte de la brouille apparente' [the story of the apparent quarrel] (*Orc* I 316), which she (correctly) claims has been concocted by Mina. The heroine is twice described as 'romanesque'; and, as Laforgue comments, 'En effet, la jeune fille ne cesse d'échafauder des romans.' [It is true that the young girl never stops constructing novels.][65] It should be noted that the phenomenon of female literary authorship was closely identified, in the French popular imagination of the 1830s and 1840s, with the idea of female freedom.[66]

The ambiguity of Mina's concluding act is compatible with the ambiguity that surrounds her motivations throughout the text. The narrator often does not explain the actions of a heroine characterized by 'l'énergie et la soudaineté de ses réso-lutions' [the energy and suddenness of her resolutions] (*Orc* I 300). This means that the reader is frequently obliged to deduce Mina's motivations from her behaviour. Unlike the Balzacian narrator, who wraps his characters' actions in swathes of knowing commentary, Stendhal's narrator often seems uncertain of his protagonists' motivations. When, for example, Mina attends a masked ball in order to observe Alfred, the narrator seems unsure why she has chosen to wear her diamonds:

> Elle demanda des masques, des dominos; elle avait apporté de Paris des diamants qu'elle prit, soit pour se mieux déguiser aux yeux d'Alfred, soit pour se distinguer de la foule des masques et obtenir peut-être qu'il lui parlât. (*Orc* I 313)

> [She ordered masks and domino cloaks. She had brought diamonds from Paris, which she put on, either to disguise herself better in Alfred's eyes, or to mark herself out from the host of masks and perhaps get him to talk to her.]

As if warned by the example of the count, whose attempts to discover Mina's secrets provoke her laughter and whom she entreats to obey her orders unquestioningly, the narrator seems disinclined to explain her motivations. A number of striking ellipses further underline the narrator's bewilderment. For example, when Mina initially moves to Aix, it is left to the reader to deduce that the recently arrived middle-aged lady and the chambermaid named Aniken are in fact the heroine and her newly hired servant. When Mina leaves Aix to live in Chambéry with her lady's companion (and ostensible employer) Madame Cramer, not only does the narrative omit to state that Mina has left the employ of the Larçay household, it also fails to explain that Mina has Madame Cramer pretend to be ill so that she herself can consult doctors about a skin disease that might plausibly explain, in Alfred's eyes, why her complexion improved so drastically after she stopped applying holly paste so assiduously. Instead, the narrator states that Madame Cramer, believing herself to be ill, invites the best doctors in town to her bedside, during which time Mina consults them about a skin disease that sometimes has a darkening effect on her skin. And when Alfred turns up in Chambéry, proposing that Mina become a virtuous form of kept woman, she refuses on religious grounds; again, her actual reasoning is not illuminated by the narrator, though it might be speculated that Mina hopes her resistance will induce him to leave his wife. It is more difficult to explain why, when her planned revenge against Madame Larçay begins to take effect, Mina informs Alfred that he has no right to accuse his wife of adultery, given that he has already neglected and betrayed her; once again, the narrator neglects to explain the young woman's intentions.

Despite the fact that one of the key features of Realism is its insistence upon causal sequences, relations between causes and their effects are thus not always apparent in *Mina de Vanghel*. The most important instance of narratorial reticence is the ambiguous response to the question provoked by Mina's closing gesture: was her life a miscalculation? The narrator's equivocal response to this question directly reinforces the semantic ambiguity of her act but also its existential ambiguity, that is, its non-predetermined, incomprehensible quality. As an ambiguous act, Mina's act of suicide becomes a statement of irreducible and absolute human freedom.

The open-ended, ambiguous quality of the question posed in the final paragraph of *Mina de Vanghel* recalls the similarly unanswered one that features in its first paragraph: 'Un peuple a-t-il le droit de changer *la manière intime et rationnelle suivant laquelle un autre peuple veut régler son existence matérielle et morale?*' [Does a nation have the right to change the innermost and rational way by which another nation chooses to arrange its material and moral existence?] (*Orc* I 297) Apart from the fact that neither question is answered, and the fact that each is positioned at an outer limit of the text, a parallel between the two questions is suggested by the fact that in both cases what is at stake is a surprisingly sudden retreat on the part of a strong character, and by the fact that the characters in question, namely General de Vanghel and his daughter, are closely linked to one another. Both questions, furthermore, probe the wisdom of the characters' respective decisions and both suggest a conflict between two systems of values, the pacific and the aggressive in the first instance, and the passionate and the prosaic in the second. The implication of the parallel is that Mina and her father each subscribe to a value system that is incompatible with their individual situations. Indeed, the novella, and even Mina herself, repeatedly link her difference from Alfred to an insurmountable incongruence between their respective nationalities: 'Elle avait besoin de s'expliquer par la différence de nation ce qu'elle était obligée de ne pas admirer en lui' [She needed to invoke national differences to explain to herself what she felt compelled not to admire in him] (*Orc* I 328). Unanswered questions that gesture towards irreconcilable differences feature then at the beginning and end of this narrative, and at the heart of each question is the problem of how best to live one's life.

The narrator's concluding question implicitly asks whether the manner in which a life ends should dictate its greater or lesser measure of success. From an existentialist perspective, Mina's suicide could not in itself be indicative of the failure of her project; for Sartre, freedom is not defined by the successful achievement of one's goals but rather by the fact of pursuing a goal or goals: 'La formule "être libre" ne signifie pas "obtenir ce qu'on a voulu", mais "se déterminer à vouloir (au sens large de choisir) par soi-même". Autrement dit, le succès n'importe aucunement à la liberté.' [The formula 'to be free' does not mean 'to get what one wanted', but 'to decide to want (in the broad sense of choosing) by oneself'. In other words, success has nothing at all to do with freedom.][67] Simone de Beauvoir, similarly, remarks that 'la notion de révolution se désagrège si l'on n'attache d'importance qu'aux résultats auxquels elle aboutit' [the notion of revolution falls apart if we only attach importance to its end results].[68]

To argue that Mina's eventual abandonment and death prove the failure of her choices in life is to assume that the value of a project is conferred by its outcome, that is, by its success or failure. Stendhal's text itself suggests that the pursuit of happiness has a value independent of the outcomes to which it leads. Mina herself is happiest when she chooses to live in the moment, oblivious of consequences. In the initial period of her service in the Larçay household, her only 'but' [aim] is to see and hear the man she loves (*Orc* I 309); she has no desire to achieve any result beyond her present happiness. Mina herself upholds the view that 'la recherche du bonheur' [the pursuit of happiness] is worth whatever dishonour it may lead her to (*Orc* I 307). On three occasions, Mina even sees her own death as a solution to an imagined negative twist in her plot, whether it is Alfred's death (*Orc* I 321, 324) or a backfiring of the plot to discredit Madame Larçay in his eyes (*Orc* I 322). This lack of regard for outcomes is typical of Stendhal's heroes and heroines, characterized for F. W. J. Hemmings by a 'Readiness to experiment and to adventure, a recklessness of the future, a contempt of caution'.[69]

If Mina shows a certain disregard for plot outcomes, despite her own habit of plotting, the logic of the narrative itself is not end-oriented. Firstly, its ending is strikingly undramatic and even anti-dramatic in style, despite its potentially very dramatic content. Unlike Julien Sorel's choice of execution and unlike Octave's suicide, Mina's death does not produce any repercussions in the plot. Secondly, when the 'secret' of Mina's identity, which has served as the motor for much of the plot by constituting the pretext for all of her deceptions, is finally revealed to Alfred, the scene is something of an anticlimax: it produces no immediate change in the couple's relationship, and indeed a sentence describing their subsequent happiness is immediately followed by a reminder that this bliss is incomplete because of the continuing existence of another secret, that of the false adultery scene. The anticlimactic quality of the revelation is reinforced by the fact that its circumstances suggest the pointlessness of the secret: Mina had withheld her name from Alfred, even after their union, in order to provoke him to divorce his wife, change his religion, and marry her, but none of these strange steps would seem to have been effected or even promised by the time Mina declares her identity. Indeed, she decides to tell Alfred who she is immediately after he has made the typically moderate promise that if Madame Larçay were to die he would ask for Mina's hand in marriage the next day. The revelation of Mina's identity would undoubtedly have provided the dramatic dénouement of a Balzacian text, governed by a robust teleological system. But in Stendhal the endings of narratives, where they do occur, are characteristically anti-climactic and unpredictable. It is only Mina's second confession, this time of her plot to discredit Madame Larçay, that precipitates her sudden abandonment by Alfred and her suicide. If the confession of the revenge plot brings about the end of the novella, the account of that plot within the novella itself contains a warning against interpreting narratives in an end-oriented way: in the scenario that Mina choreographs to convince Alfred of his wife's adultery, it is the conclusion of this sequence, namely the count's sudden departure from the bedroom, that is decisive for the husband's erroneous interpretation of events.

If *Mina de Vanghel* is not end-oriented, then, it nevertheless prioritizes a particular goal. Was her life a miscalculation? Not if happiness rather than self-preservation was her goal.

Endings: Vanina Vanini

Vanina's initial resistance to her father's marriage plot takes the form of an affair with a young political rebel; her subsequent resistance to her lover's plot takes the form of a betrayal which leads her back to her father's initial plot. In other words, Vanina's various counter-plots perversely result in apparent adherence to the original, socially sanctioned narrative: marriage to Livio Savelli. For Xavier Bourdenet, the heroine's marriage is 'une sorte de suicide quotidien' [a kind of everyday suicide].[70] But her 'suicide' is as ambiguous an act as Mina's. Does it indicate Vanina's ultimate decision to obey her father? Does it represent her compliance with Missirilli's exhortation to punish his traitor and/or with his later wish that she might marry the man chosen by her father? Or is it an act of defiance against her former lover, who would prefer to see her dead by the end of the story? Prévost highlights the disconcerting character of the ending of *Vanina Vanini*, which neglects to throw any light on the heroine's motives or feelings. He notes that the marriage is presented 'comme un on-dit' [like a third-hand piece of news].[71] As a result, the manner in which the marriage is announced almost irresistibly returns us to the beginning of the narrative, where the impersonal 'on', as we have seen, reigns supreme.[72]

Early in the narrative, the narrator states that the reason for Vanina's refusal to marry is 'la même que celle de Sylla pour abdiquer, *son mépris pour les Romains*' [the same given by Sulla for abdicating: *his contempt for the Romans*] (*Orc* I 248). The proud Vanina is therefore, from the outset, associated with both power and its abdication. Her non-compliance with her father's wishes is likened to a dictator's haughty withdrawal from his duties; but it is her eventual compliance with those wishes that strikes many readers as an abdication. The fact that the marriage is recounted in the text by way of a reported newspaper announcement implies that the heroine has given up on her individual freedom, and finally allowed her plot to be written by the collective, homogenizing 'on'.

However, the very uncertainty of Vanina's motives at the end of the novella suggests that her apparent concession merely continues her story of resistance. This is, after all, the heroine described by Henri-François Imbert as 'la première des grandes réfractaires stendhaliennes' [the first of Stendhal's great resistant heroines].[73] The ambiguity of Vanina's concluding action is reinforced by the fact that, when she initially agrees to her father's arranged marriage, provoking his astonishment and the reader's surprise, her intentions turn out to be different from what they seem. Like Mina, Vanina is consistently presented as an unpredictable character, with often hidden motivations; her plot against Missirilli's co-conspirators is described with a minimum of authorial intervention, its conception being conveyed only obliquely, by way of a short but suggestive interior monologue: 'Les carbonari ont reçu de moi plusieurs milliers de sequins. On ne peut douter de mon dévouement à la conspiration' [The Carbonari have had several thousand sequins from me. My commitment to the conspiracy cannot be doubted] (*Orc* I 258). Her declaration to her fiancé, only a few days after agreeing to marry him, that she has no intention of becoming his wife is not expected either by him or the reader. In fact, this volte-face is itself revealed shortly afterwards to be a mere ruse, designed to ensure the young man's cooperation in her scheme. A similar deferral of explanation occurs in the episode concerning Vanina's visit to the residence of the Minister of Police, when the latter, surprised not to find his usual servant, undresses before noticing a man's shape behind the curtain. The young man who reveals himself, armed with a pistol, turns out to be the heroine, but the reader obtains this confirmation only at the same time as the minister.

The most significant ellipsis in the text, of course, relates to Vanina's marriage to Savelli. In the absence of any narratorial elaboration, the most obvious interpretation is that the conclusion announces the definitive and humiliating end of the heroine's career. However, as his letters to Pauline indicate, Stendhal himself does not seem to have viewed marriage as an end to a woman's freedom, and marriage certainly does not put an end to the autonomous activities of a Gina or a Madame Grandet. At the conclusion of *Ernestine ou la Naissance de l'amour* [*Ernestine, or the Birth of Love*], the eponymous heroine is married to a wealthy old man, despite being in love with Philippe Astézan, but she is nevertheless represented as intensely happy; it is she who has refused to continue to play her role in the latter's seduction plot, around which the entirety of Stendhal's narrative has revolved. Earlier in the story, we read that Ernestine's ability to perceive 'toutes les conséquences d'une idée' [all of the consequences of an idea] may be at the origin of 'le rôle si brillant' [the so brilliant role] that she plays in society in her later life (*Orc* I 38). By analogy with this earlier story, the ending of *Vanina Vanini* may in fact signal a new beginning. It is nowhere unequivocally stated in the text that Vanina actually dislikes her prince, the most eligible bachelor in Rome, and it is clear that she will marry him with all of her natural advantages intact: her great intelligence, wealth, youth, and beauty. Worse punishments have been imagined.

Any interpretation of Vanina's consent to her father's marriage plot as a defeat may well be just as hazardous as Livio Savelli's reading of Missirilli's surrender as a consequence of 'la sottise' [stupidity] (*Orc* I 261). Missirilli's eventual surrender to the authorities is presented by the text as much as an act of defiance as a defeat, just as his comprehensively chained body in the closing scene connotes his continued opposition as much as it suggests his punishment. Crouzet's reading of Vanina's ultimate marriage, while defeatist in emphasis, nonetheless acknowledges the ambiguity of the novella's conclusion: 'Vanina a (ou semble avoir) tenu son serment, elle s'est faite l'artisan d'un anéantissement volontaire.' [Vanina has — or seems to have — kept her oath, she has designed her own voluntary self-destruction.][74] Jean Peytard emphasizes the questions that are left unanswered in the last paragraph of the novella, but does state that the ending gives a categorical answer to one question that he considers crucial to the text's meaning: 'À quel homme Vanina appartiendra-t-elle? le texte pose, avec insistance, la question. Est-ce à Savelli? Est-ce au carbonaro? Est-ce à la volonté paternelle?'[75] [To which man does Vanina belong? The text asks this question insistently. Is it to Savelli? Is it to the Carbonaro? Is is to the father's will?] My own analysis has tried to show that, regardless of whether the ending of the novella is interpreted as defeatist or defiant, it is Vanina's own *volonté*, own will, that is at the centre of the text. The heroine ultimately belongs to nobody but herself.

As in the case of *Mina de Vanghel*, then, the ending of the text opens the narrative up to multiple interpretations. And as in that other narrative, endings are stripped of their usual decisive importance. Even the subtitle of *Vanina Vanini* seems to undermine the very idea of closure: the word 'dernière' in the phrase 'particularités sur la dernière vente de carbonari découverte dans les États du pape' [particulars concerning the last Carbonaro cell to be uncovered in the Papal States] (*Orc* I 245) could mean 'final' but the context allows us to understand that it actually means 'latest'. This qualified finality is further mitigated when it is understood that the meeting may not even be the most recent one to have occurred, just the one that has been most recently discovered. The plot itself undermines the conclusiveness of endings. Vanina refuses all of the neatly organized endings with which Missirilli presents her. When he initially tries to put an end to their amorous idyll, by telling her of his intention to leave her father's palace immediately, she persuades him to stay another two days, during which time she offers him her hand in marriage and then, upon being refused, tells him that she will join him shortly in Romagna. After Missirilli has again said his goodbyes to Vanina and is already walking downstairs on his way to rejoin the struggle for Italy, she asks him for another three days; he concedes. Later, she joins him in Romagna, but belatedly, and only after he has decided to forget her and concentrate on winning Italy's freedom; again, his planned ending is foiled. When Missirilli once again says his 'adieu', or final farewell, in a note that he later leaves for Vanina before surrendering to the authorities (*Orc* I 260), she pledges to arrange his release. Just before the end of the story, bound in chains, Missirilli yet again bids Vanina a would-be definitive 'adieu', and once again she refuses the conclusion that he wishes to give to their story:

> Adieu, Vanina; promettez-moi de ne jamais m'écrire, de ne jamais chercher à me voir; laissez-moi tout à la patrie; je suis mort pour vous: adieu.
> — Non, reprit Vanina furieuse, je veux que tu saches ce que j'ai fait, guidée par l'amour que j'avais pour toi. (*Orc* I 268)

> [Farewell, Vanina. Promise me you will never write or try to see me. Leave me to give my all to my country. I am dead for you. Farewell.
> 'No', Vanina furiously retorted, 'I want you to know what I did for love of you.']

It is perhaps not surprising, then, that the ending of *Vanina Vanini* is not neat or unequivocal in the style favoured by Missirilli. The announcement of Vanina's marriage is open to multiple interpretations, seeming by its impersonal tone to return us to the beginning of the story, but also referring us back to other points in the novella — to Vanina's vow to avenge the betrayed conspirators, for example, or to her casual consent to her father's arranged marriage, or to the definition of heroism formulated late in the text by Missirilli: 'Le devoir est cruel, mon amie; mais s'il n'y avait pas un peu de peine à l'accomplir, où serait l'héroïsme?' [Duty is a cruel master, my friend, but if there were no pain in doing it where would be the heroism?] (*Orc* I 268) The open-endedness of the outwardly defeatist conclusion, like the ambiguity of the ending of *Mina de Vanghel*, suggests the continuing resistance of the heroine to the closure that others would give to her story.

The logic of all narrative plots, according to Peter Brooks, is one of resistance to closure: 'It is the role of fictional plots to impose an end which yet suggests a return, a new beginning: a rereading.'[76] The plot structures and conclusions of *Mina de Vanghel* and *Vanina Vanini* make this resistance to definitive conclusion unusually blatant.

The difficulty of interpreting Mina's and Vanina's behaviour, which occasionally seems opaque even to the narrator, is a trait that they share with some of the Italian women whose stories figure in the *Promenades dans Rome*, such as Francesca Polo, whose tale is described therein as 'inintelligible' [incomprehensible] for her countrymen, or Clara Visconti, whose lover reacts with incomprehension when she arrives at his door after her escape from her convent.[77] While it is certainly true that, as Simone de Beauvoir notes, it is absurd to describe the actions of a fictional character as free or unpredictable in literal terms, it is nevertheless also a fact that Stendhal's protagonists seem unusually independent of their author.[78] Unpredictability, and therefore existential ambiguity, is characteristic of Stendhal's protagonists, according to Blin, while Brombert notes that the undefined and unpredetermined quality of his characters 'helps explain why Stendhal has been so dear to the Existentialist generation'.[79]

Mina's death can be interpreted as a heroic act of defiance and as an insistence by the heroine on her own self-authorship. Vanina's marriage to Livio Savelli can, similarly, be read as a defiant response to Missirilli: he attempted to kill her, but she will marry a prince who is described as the most 'brillant' [brilliant] young man in Rome (*Orc* I 248), and who by the end of the narrative has proven himself an able executor of her various plots. The endings of both *Mina de Vanghel* and *Vanina Vanini* can also be considered final acts of resistance on the part of the heroines in the sense that these outwardly conventional conclusions defy the reader's expectations, signalling a subversion of traditional plot resolutions on the part of characters that repeatedly resist conventional plotting. Mina's eventual suicide and Vanina's eventual marriage are despatched so quickly and undramatically by the respective texts that they seem like artificial devices. As Labia notes of the endings of *Mina de Vanghel* and *Vanina Vanini*, 'Le dénouement claque.' [The conclusion thuds.][80] The abrupt and unexpected quality of each ending seems to disturb the logic of cause and effect that is so central to narrative structure, and particularly to Realist narratives. As a result, the endings of these narratives seem to lack verisimilitude, or textual plausibility, as befits texts governed by the logic of the strange step. In Balzac's fictions, according to Roland Barthes, 'tout se tient' [everything holds together] and all is legible: the structure is closed.[81] By contrast, illegible elements in some of Stendhal's narratives, including the illegibility of their endings, create a more open structure. The open-ended quality of the endings of *Mina de Vanghel* and *Vanina Vanini* means that, whether they are regarded as capitulatory or defiant, they do not need to determine the meaning of the texts. Neither *Mina de Vanghel* nor *Vanina Vanini* conforms to the hermeneutic code that, for Barthes, is characteristic of the Balzacian text; in other words, neither text formulates an enigma whose solution it then works towards as its climax. These narratives are not end-oriented; there is no great enigma at their heart, to which only their endings can provide answers.

For Barthes, truth in the 'classic' or Realist text is habitually revealed only at the end of a narrative that has striven to defer its appearance (via the hermeneutic code) even while the characters' actions (via the proairetic code) bring the moment of revelation ever closer. According to Margaret Cohen, the 'feminine social text', which flourished alongside the Realist novel during the July Monarchy, establishes no such tension between hermeneutic and proairetic codes, actions serving to illustrate a pre-stated truth rather than threatening always to reveal a truth that the narrative strives to defer. Because of the 'overcoding of hermeneutic and proairetic', or more specifically because the motor driving the plot of the feminine social text is one of emphasis rather than revelation, Cohen notes: 'Whatever their length, the novels end abruptly. As the back cover approaches, the heroine either finds happiness or, more commonly, withdraws from society through retreat, madness, or death.'[82]

Mina de Vanghel and *Vanina Vanini* would seem to have much in common with the feminine social text as analysed by Cohen. The endings of the two texts examined here are nothing if not abrupt, and both involve a form of withdrawal, even if one presents what appears to be a withdrawal into rather than from society. However, by contrast with the plots of feminine social or sentimental texts, which instantiate the preordained truth of female victimization for Cohen, the plots of Stendhal's two narratives strongly suggest that women can escape their victimization and indeed, somewhat less gloriously, become themselves agents of victimization.[83] In less gender-specific terms, both texts suggest that the individual has the freedom to decide whether to accept or transform his or her prescribed destiny.

Happiness or Freedom?

Freedom and happiness are often virtually synonymous in *Vie de Henry Brulard*: the young Beyle envies the '[e]xcès de bonheur' [superabundant happiness] of children who '*jouissaient de la liberté*' [enjoyed their freedom], and considers the restraints placed upon him by his family to be the source of all his unhappiness (*OI* II 608). The liberation of the self from other people's plots is inextricable from the pursuit of happiness in Stendhal's universe. Beauvoir is consequently right to point out that 'C'est non seulement au nom de la liberté en général, c'est au nom du bonheur individuel que Stendhal réclame l'émancipation des femmes.' [It is not only in the name of freedom in general, but also in the name of individual happiness, that Stendhal demands women's emancipation.][84] However, any equivalence between happiness and freedom is inherently problematic, as Beauvoir herself observes elsewhere in her text, happiness often relying upon an abdication of one's freedom:

> Les femmes de harem ne sont-elles pas plus heureuses qu'une électrice? La ménagère n'est-elle pas plus heureuse que l'ouvrière? On ne sait trop ce que le mot bonheur signifie et encore moins quelles valeurs authentiques il recouvre [...]: ceux qu'on condamne à la stagnation en particulier, on les déclare heureux sous prétexte que le bonheur est immobilité.[85]

> [Are the women of a harem not happier than a female voter? Is the housewife not happier than the female worker? It is not known exactly what the word

happiness means and still less what authentic values it conceals [...]. Those in particular who are condemned to stagnation are often pronounced happy on the pretext that happiness is stillness.]

To the extent that happiness and freedom can be separated, in Stendhal's world, it is usually assumed that happiness represents a higher value than freedom. The fact that Julien and Fabrice experience their greatest happiness in prison cells is often interpreted as indicative of this order of values. Unlike Sartre and Beauvoir, who privilege freedom over happiness, Stendhal would seem to give his own priority to happiness.[86]

However, there are also strong indications to the contrary. Happiness cannot be sustained in Stendhal's fictional universe without freedom; for Stendhal as for Destutt de Tracy, freedom is 'la première condition du bonheur' [the first condition of happiness].[87] Prévost observes that his novels habitually have two endings, 'la première selon le rêve, et la seconde selon les forces extérieures' [the first following the dream, and the second following external forces].[88] It can be argued that the second ending arises from an internal force, namely an instinct for freedom. The joy shared by Alfred and Mina during their months together in Italy is both conditional upon and worm-eaten by the limits they each place on their free communication, limits that eventually rupture under the pressure of his desire to know and her desire to unburden herself. Vanina's act of betrayal is prompted by her dissatisfaction with the severe constraints that Missirilli's own will to freedom has placed on their happiness. Julien could choose the possibility of extending his life and his happiness with Madame de Rênal, but he opts instead for the guillotine. After three years, Fabrice del Dongo can no longer be entirely happy in his relationship with Clélia as long as he is forbidden to see her during the day and unable to have full access to his child. Stendhal's most admirable characters may, then, choose happiness over freedom, but the need for freedom is more enduring than happiness, and, as both Mina and Fabrice discover, that need is itself destructive of happiness. Happiness is the goal towards which all of Stendhal's free characters strain, but the need for freedom, even if it is just the freedom to pursue a greater share of joy, always jeopardizes their happiness. It is for this reason that happy endings are, as Franco Moretti notes, 'inconceivable' in Stendhal's novels.[89]

If, for Stendhal as for Destutt de Tracy, happiness is the goal of freedom, it is also notoriously resistant to the logic of goals. The more carefully happiness is planned, the less complete it often turns out to be in Stendhal's work. The fulfilment of Julien's social ambitions, when he becomes both Mathilde's fiancé and the Chevalier de la Vernaye, does not bring him the yield of happiness that he had expected, while Mina and Vanina discover that their deceptions of Alfred and Pietro, in the interest of their own happiness, ultimately detract from that happiness. Similarly, the narrator of *Vie de Henry Brulard* evokes his youthful disappointment when, after years of planning his escape from Grenoble to Paris, he did not find happiness where he expected it to be. Instead, he found it where he did not expect it to be, namely on the scenic road to Italy with Napoleon's army. Happiness tends, in Stendhal's work, to be found in the intervals of the chase rather than at its end. What Moretti says of the classical *Bildungsroman* is at least partially true of Stendhal:

'Happiness is the *opposite* of freedom, the *end* of becoming. Its appearance marks the end of all tension between the individual and the world; all desire for further metamorphosis is extinguished.'[90] If freedom involves plot development, happiness is a plotless condition in Stendhal's writing. When Vanina is happy in Missirilli's arms, 'Toutes les idées d'avenir' [All thoughts of the future] disappear (*Orc* I 255). The resistance of happiness to narrative organization is an often remarked feature of Stendhal's fiction: most famously, the three years of divine happiness enjoyed by Fabrice and Clélia, towards which the narrative of *La Chartreuse de Parme* leads, are entirely skipped over by the text. Happiness is found in moments that have nothing to do with its pursuit: Octave and Armance walking among the trees in Andilly, Julien chasing butterflies in Vergy or finding intimacy with Madame de Rênal in his prison cell, Mina ironing clothes while Alfred tends to his plants, Fabrice gazing at Clélia through iron bars, Lucien walking with Madame de Chasteller near a café in the woods. All of these moments of happiness exist in a space outside of plot; they do not further the plot, and the characters, as they inhabit these moments, give little thought to the future. Freedom, by contrast, tends in Stendhal's work to involve a constant self-extrication from the plots of others and the elaboration of counter-plots: the tactics of self-disguise, plot redirection, and ruse enable characters like Julien, Mathilde, Mina, Vanina, Fabrice, and Lamiel to map out their own journeys through life instead of being manipulated by others. Freedom and happiness are therefore never analogous, in Stendhal. But they are intimately linked, because the freedom to act is a necessary condition of happiness in his work, while also being destructive of that happiness.

Both Mina and Vanina are driven by the force of their desire for happiness, as if to illustrate Jean-Jacques Rousseau's dictum that 'L'homme qui a le plus vécu n'est pas celui qui a compté le plus d'années, mais celui qui a le plus senti la vie' [The man who has lived the most is not he who has counted the most years, but he who has most felt his life].[91] Shoshana Felman points out that Stendhal's heroes prioritize 'la folie' [madness] over contentment, at great risk to their own lives, and remarks that all of Stendhal's (male) protagonists, except Lucien Leuwen, are tragic heroes who gamble their lives on a mad roll of the dice.[92] Mina and Vanina, both associated by their respective narratives with 'la folie', pay a high price for their pursuit of happiness and all the strange steps they take along the way: the single-mindedness and ruthlessness of their quest lose them the love of the person who means most to them and also alienate many readers. Mina knowingly embarks on an affair with a married man and self-servingly and viciously frames his wife as an adulteress. Vanina self-interestedly betrays her lover and his allies, indirectly sentencing them to imprisonment. While neither heroine is universally likeable, then, and while both are ultimately spurned by their lovers, they are nevertheless admirable characters, from both a Stendhalian and an existentialist perspective. Each, in the end, assumes responsibility for her choices and her errors, Mina through her eventual confession and suicide, and Vanina through her attempted liberation of Missirilli, and also possibly through her marriage. The heroines of both *Mina de Vanghel* and *Vanina Vanini* choose not to let their narratives be written for them by external agents or forces. Each experiences, like Mina Wanghen after them, 'le plaisir si doux de faire sa volonté' [the delightful pleasure of following her own will] (*Orc* II 1060). The strange plots that they elaborate are dictated by the *faculté de vouloir*, or will to happiness, of each heroine. In each case, the heroine is represented as author of her own destiny. This makes her a typical representative not only of Stendhal's Amazons, but also of his freedom-loving protagonists more generally.

Notes to Chapter 1

1. See also *OI* II 682, 789. Philippe Berthier refers to Stendhal's 'exceptionnelle capacité de rébellion et de ruse' [exceptional capacity for rebellion and ruse], and describes the *Vie de Henry Brulard* as '[une] chronique donnée comme exemplaire d'une auto-libération' [[a] chronicle offering itself as an example of a self-liberation]. *Stendhal et la Sainte famille* (Geneva: Droz, 1984), pp. 116, 119.
2. *Stendhal: 'Vie de Henry Brulard'* (London: Grant and Cutler, 2006), p. 77. The cited passage is from *Vie de Henry Brulard* (*OI* II 531).
3. See for example *Cg* II 135; Stendhal, *Histoire de la peinture en Italie*, I, 248 (chapter 62), II, 335 (epilogue); Stendhal, *Promenades dans Rome*, ed. by Victor Del Litto (Grenoble: Millon, 1993), p. 143 (25 January 1828).
4. Stendhal writes elsewhere that 'Le génie est un pouvoir, mais il est encore plus un flambeau pour découvrir le grand art d'être heureux' [Genius is a power, but more than that it is a light for revealing the great art of happiness]. Stendhal, *De l'Amour*, p. 216 (chapter 61). I have written about the relationship established by Stendhal between historical knowledge, happiness, and freedom in Maria Scott, 'Stendhal's Heroines: Escaping History through History', *Nineteenth-Century French Studies*, 37.3–4 (2009), 260–72.
5. Antoine Louis Claude Destutt de Tracy, *Élémens d'idéologie*, 5 vols (Paris: Courcier, 1817–18), III (2nd edn), 125.
6. *Élémens d'idéologie*, V (2nd edn), 518.
7. *Élémens d'idéologie*, I (3rd edn), 68.
8. *Élémens d'idéologie*, III, 380; IV (2nd edn), 98. Stendhal had previously come across the idea that happiness was the ultimate good in Helvétius, whom he began to read in late 1802. See Victor Del Litto, *La Vie intellectuelle de Stendhal: Genèse et évolution de ses idées (1802–1821)* (Grenoble: Presses Universitaires de France, 1959), pp. 39–41.
9. *Élémens d'idéologie*, IV, 104.
10. *Élémens d'idéologie*, IV, 101.
11. *Élémens d'idéologie*, IV, 123–24.
12. *Élémens d'idéologie*, IV, 102–03.
13. On the significance of gender difference in Stendhal's advice to his sister, see in particular Lucy Garnier, '"On ne naît pas femme, on le devient": Les Lettres à Pauline et la condition féminine', in *Lire la correspondance de Stendhal*, ed. by Martine Reid (Paris: Champion, 2007), pp. 11–25.
14. See *Cg* I 203–04. On Victorine Bigillion's affliction, see Jacques Félix-Faure, 'La Douloureuse Destinée de Victorine Bigillion', *Stendhal Club*, 1 (1958), 9–14 and Marie-Rose Corrédor, 'Aux sources du discours clinique: La Correspondance avec Félix Faure et François Bigillion (mai 1805 à février 1806)', in *Lire la correspondance de Stendhal*, ed. by Martine Reid and Elaine Williamson (Paris: Champion, 2007), pp. 57–63.
15. On the general importance of placing long-term interest above pleasure, see *Cg* I 312–13.
16. On the relationship between motherhood and freedom in Stendhal, see my 'Stendhal's Rebellious Mothers and the Fight Against Death-by-Maternity', in *Birth and Death in Nineteenth-Century French Culture*, ed. by Nigel Harkness and others (Amsterdam: Rodopi, 2007), pp. 139–51.
17. As Richard Bolster puts it, 'si le rôle de frère oblige à une certaine prudence, celui d'auteur donne plus de liberté' [if the role of brother requires him to be careful, that of author confers more freedom]. *Stendhal, Balzac et le féminisme romantique* (Paris: Minard, 1970), p. 86.
18. *Élémens d'idéologie*, IV, 63. See also IV, 56–57, 81–82. If Stendhal's *faculté de vouloir* has close links with Tracy's ideas about will and desire, it also anticipates Nietzsche's will to power. See

William R. Goetz, 'Nietzsche and *Le Rouge et le noir*', *Comparative Literature Studies*, 18.4 (1981), 443–58.

19. See for example Stendhal, *De l'Amour*, p. 133 (chapter 39 (3)); *Cg* I 77–79, 225, 270.

20. *Fiction and the Themes of Freedom* (New York: Random House, 1968), p. 78. Francine Marill-Albérès attributes Stendhal's positive interpretation of boredom to his reading of Helvétius. See *Le Naturel chez Stendhal* (Paris: Nizet, 1956), p. 40.

21. He says of a friend of Pauline, for example, 'Comme elle a de plus grandes difficultés à vaincre que toi, elle a plus de caractère, c'est tout simple' [Because she has greater difficulties than you to surmount she has more character, it is as simple as that] (*Cg* II 590). See also *Cg* I 225, 270–71, 277.

22. See for example Stendhal, *Promenades dans Rome*, p. 231 (9 June 1828); Stendhal, *Rome, Naples et Florence*, ed. by Pierre Brunel (Paris: Gallimard, 1987), p. 385; Stendhal, *Voyages en France*, ed. by Victor del Litto (Paris: Gallimard, Bibliothèque de la Pléiade, 1992), p. 69.

23. *Promenades dans Rome*, p. 401 (23 November 1828). See also *De l'Amour*, p. 139 (chapter 41).

24. For an alternative but compatible perspective on the difference between Tracy's conception of desire (as will) and Stendhal's (desire as passion), see Catherine Mariette, '*De l'Amour*: Essai d'idéologie ou "fragments d'un discours amoureux"', in *Persuasions d'amour: Nouvelles lectures de 'De l'Amour' de Stendhal*, ed. Daniel Sangsue (Geneva: Droz, 1999), pp. 79–88 (pp. 85–87).

25. *L'Être et le néant*, p. 566.

26. *Fiction and the Themes of Freedom*, p. 88.

27. *De l'Amour*, pp. 50–51 (chapter 21).

28. *Ma loi d'avenir: 1833: Ouvrage posthume; suivi d'un Appel d'une femme au peuple sur l'affranchissement de la femme* (Paris: Au bureau de la Tribune des femmes, 1834), p. 23.

29. *Mémoires de deux jeunes mariées* (Paris: Gallimard, 2002), p. 133 (letter 15)

30. See *Cg* I 203. A private note by Stendhal also suggests that he found something heroic in Victorine's insanity: '*My adm[iration] for this noble madness*' (*Cg* I 234).

31. *Vanina Vanini* was probably written in December 1829, the same month as its publication in the *Revue de Paris*. *Mina de Vanghel* was written between December 1829 and January 1830, but was left unpublished by an author who considered it unsuitable for a French readership. It was published only posthumously, in 1853, by Stendhal's friend Roman Colomb. Stendhal attempted to transpose the basic premise of *Mina de Vanghel*, as well as the character of its heroine, into a novel in 1837, but abandoned the text, *Le Rose et le Vert*, after a few weeks. Because of the significant differences between the two narratives, and the somewhat less wilful character of the later Mina, I have chosen to focus on *Mina de Vanghel*.

32. *Stendhal romancier*, p. 215. See also Maria Scott, 'Les Femmes et la faculté de vouloir dans *Les Promenades dans Rome*', in *'Façons de voir': Enquêtes sur les 'Promenades dans Rome'*, ed. by Xavier Bourdenet and François Vanoosthuyse (Grenoble: ELLUG, 2011), pp. 247–64.

33. See for example Stendhal, *Promenades dans Rome*, p. 402 (23 November 1828).

34. In a letter of 17 January 1831 to Adolphe de Mareste, Stendhal explains that the energetic character of Mathilde is far from being typical of her social class: 'Cette vue du manque de caractère dans les hautes classes m'a fait *prendre une exception*' [This perception of the lack of character in the upper classes led me to *select an exception*] (*Cg* IV 19). If wealth is detrimental to energy, it nevertheless facilitates its expression, as suggested by the fact that three of the four energetic heroines considered in this book are born into great wealth and nobility. Vanina Vanini's wealth permits her to move to Romagna to be near Missirilli, to fund his political campaigns and then her own campaign to secure his release. Mina, similarly, is always able to buy the cooperation of minor players; at one juncture, the narrator even states the amount of money that a particular intrigue has cost the heroine (*Orc* I 305).

35. Juliet Flower MacCannell maintains, however, that 'In Stendhal it is always only the men who seek "*le bonheur*". Women in his writing never entertain these illusions'. 'Stendhal's Woman', *Semiotica*, 48.1–2 (1984), 143–68 (p. 160).

36. On the oppositional qualities of Vanina and Mina, see Jacqueline Andrieu, 'De Mina de Vanghel à Lamiel ou Héroïsme, amour et vraisemblance', *Stendhal Club*, 76 (1976–77), 321–31 (pp. 323–24); Bardèche, *Stendhal romancier*, p. 183; Christopher W. Thompson, '*Vanina Vanini* ou la répétition tragique', *L'Année Stendhal*, 4 (2000), 29–36 (p. 34); Kurt Wais, 'Stendhal zwischen Novelle und Roman: Mina de Vanghel und ihre Schwestern', *Stendhal Club*, 96 (1982), 435–49.

37. For previous statements of this key point, see Ellen Constans, 'Les Problèmes de la condition féminine dans l'œuvre de Stendhal', 2 vols (Lille: Service de reproduction des thèses de l'université Lille III, 1978), II, 1134; Ellen Constans, 'Au nom du bonheur: Le Féminisme de Stendhal', *Europe*, 652–53 (1983), 62–74 (p. 70); Lucy Garnier, 'Stendhal's *Mina de Vanghel* and the question of feminism', *Nineteenth-Century French Studies*, 34.3–4 (2006), 252–61 (p. 253).

38. *De l'Amour*, p. 222 (chapter 58). Stendhal would have found an argument for the freedom of young men and women to choose their own spouses in Destutt de Tracy, *De l'amour* (Paris: Les Belles Lettres, 1926), pp. 32–52.

39. See the author's own comment in a letter of 19 April 1805: 'Le seul danger des âmes grandes est de prendre des *secs* pour leurs égales, et de se mettre à les aimer comme elles savent aimer; alors que de douleurs!' [The only danger for great souls is to consider arid souls their equals, and to start loving them as they know how to love. Then what sorrows!] (*Cg* I 275)

40. See in particular Stendhal, *De l'Amour*, chapter 2.

41. Christopher W. Thompson, similarly, observes that Mathilde's obsession with Boniface de La Mole produces distorting textual effects, re-orienting *Le Rouge et le Noir* towards 'le romanesque "gothique"' [the gothic novelistic style]. *'Lamiel': Fille du feu: Essai sur Stendhal et l'énergie* (Paris: L'Harmattan, 1997), p. 34.

42. *The Heroine's Text: Readings in the French and English Novel, 1722 –1782* (New York: Columbia University Press, 1980), p. x.

43. The author notes, in connection with this passage, that 'Un Français, à ce point-ci, manquerait de courage et de constance' [A French person, at this point, would lack courage and steadfastness] (*Orc* I 947).

44. On the constant tension in Stendhal's writing between the individual and public opinion, or the *doxa*, see Jefferson, *Reading Realism*.

45. Jean Peytard suggests that Vanina is a figure of narrative and textual production. *Voix et traces narratives chez Stendhal* (Paris: Les Editeurs français réunis, 1980), p. 91.

46. Xavier Bourdenet observes that Missirilli's repeated chaining and imprisonment are related not just to his political activities but also to his love for Vanina, which has the repeated effect of locking him up. Stendhal, *Vanina Vanini et autres nouvelles*, dossier and notes by Xavier Bourdenet (Paris: Gallimard, 2010), pp. 140–41.

47. 'Stendhal et le récit tragique', in *Stendhal Europeo: Atti del congresso internazionale Milano, 19–21 Maggio 1992* (Fasano: Schena, 1996), pp. 107–62 (p. 124). Crouzet does acknowledge that Mathilde and Gina resemble these tragic heroines.

48. 'De Mina de Vanghel à Lamiel', *Stendhal Club*, p. 327. See also Lisa Algazi, 'Stendhal féministe ?', *L'Année stendhalienne*, 4 (2005), 29–40 (p. 38); Thompson, *'Vanina Vanini'*; Henri-François Imbert, *Les Métamorphoses de la liberté ou Stendhal devant la Restauration et le Risorgimento* (Paris: Corti, 1967), p. 457; Bertelà, *Stendhal et l'Autre*, p. 182; Karl Alfred Blüher, 'L'Amour tragique dans les premières nouvelles de Stendhal', *Stendhal Club*, 96 (1982), 374–87 (p. 376); Crouzet, 'Stendhal et le récit tragique', pp. 120–21.

49. *Le Deuxième Sexe*, I, 388. Garnier makes a similar point. 'Stendhal's *Mina de Vanghel*', p. 256.

50. See for example Bersani, *A Future for Astyanax*, p. 126; John West Sooby, 'Armance: Le Choix d'un destin', *Stendhal Club*, 25.100 (1983), 490–500 (p. 495); Grahame C. Jones, *L'Ironie dans les romans de Stendhal* (Lausanne: Editions du Grand Chêne, 1966), p. 144; Victor Del Litto, 'Stendhal romancier réaliste?', in *Stendhal-Balzac: Réalisme et cinéma: Actes du XIᵉ congrès international stendhalien, Auxerre, 1976*, ed. by V. Del Litto (Grenoble: Presses Universitaires de Grenoble, 1978), pp. 7–12 (p. 10).

51. 'Le Coup de pistolet, le concert et l'audace féminine: La Fin de la chasse au bonheur', *L'Année Stendhal*, 4 (2000), 5–27 (p. 10); *Metamorphoses of Passion and the Heroic in French Literature — Corneille, Stendhal, Claudel*, Studies in French Literature, 35 (Lewiston, NY: Mellen, 1999), p. 206.

52. 'Frames of Female Suicide', *Studies in the Novel*, 32.2 (2000), 228–41. According to Higonnet, 'heroic' suicides tend to be discursively gendered as masculine while suicides evocative of surrender are coded as feminine (p. 232).

53. *1830. Romantisme et histoire* (Saint-Pierre-du-Mont: Eurédit, 2001), pp. 233–42.

54. On these intertextual allusions, see Blüher, 'L'Amour tragique', p. 383; Michel Crouzet, *Nature*

et société chez Stendhal: La Révolte romantique (Villeneuve d'Ascq: Presses Universitaires de Lille, 1985), p. 159. Goethe's *Werther* is very openly referenced in *Le Rose et le Vert* (*Orc* II 1032).

55. 'Frames of Female Suicide', p. 231.

56. See for example Jean Prévost, *La Création chez Stendhal: Essai sur le métier d'écrire et la psychologie de l'écrivain* (Paris: Mercure de France, 1951), pp. 279–80; Jean-Paul Bruyas, *La Psychologie de l'adolescence dans l'œuvre romanesque de Stendhal* (Aix-en-Provence : La Pensée Universitaire, 1967), p. 207; Crouzet, 'Stendhal et le récit tragique', p. 138.

57. 'Mina de Vanghel ou l'antipode de la raison', *Travaux de linguistique et de littérature*, 13.2 (1975), 631–40 (p. 636).

58. *1830. Romantisme et histoire*, p. 240.

59. *De l'Amour*, p. 298 ('Fragments divers', 152).

60. Charles Baudelaire, *Œuvres complètes*, ed. by Claude Pichois, 2 vols (Paris: Gallimard, Bibliothèque de la Pléiade, 1975–76), II, 494.

61. Stendhal, *Romans et nouvelles*, ed. by Henri Martineau, 2 vols (Paris: Gallimard, Bibliothèque de la Pléiade, 1952), II, 729.

62. Nathalie Froger, accordingly, sees the tragic endings reserved for many of Stendhal's strong heroines as indicative of the shortcomings of their respective societies. 'Femme publique, femme privée: La Dialectique impossible de l'héroïne stendhalienne', *Stendhal Club*, 133 (1991), 39–51. For similar arguments, see also Constans, 'Au nom du bonheur', p. 71 and Garnier, 'Stendhal's *Mina de Vanghel*'.

63. 'Frames of Female Suicide', p. 233.

64. Stendhal, *Le Rose et le Vert, Mina de Vanghel, Tamira Wanghen*, p. 56.

65. *1830. Romantisme et histoire*, p. 235. Laforgue discusses the contestatory nature of Mina's various Romantic or poetic plots, which mirrors the contestatory or anti-prosaic character of the plot of *Mina de Vanghel* itself. I have consistently translated 'romanesque' as 'romantic' (distinct from 'Romantic'), but 'romanesque' maintains a much closer link than 'romantic' to the sphere of the romance and the novel.

66. See Margaret Cohen, *The Sentimental Education of the Novel* (Princeton: Princeton University Press, 1999), chapter 4. Kristeva makes the point that women in Stendhal's fiction are often associated with writing and authorship. *Histoires d'amour*, p. 338. However, despite the very real literary and popular success of female authors of his time, Stendhal expresses disapproval of women who publish their writing for any other reason than to feed their families. *De l'Amour*, p. 210 (chapter 55).

67. *L'Être et le néant*, p. 563.

68. *L'Existentialisme et la sagesse des nations* (Geneva: Nagel, 1986), p. 68

69. *Stendhal: A Study of his Novels*, pp. ix–x.

70. Stendhal, *Vanina Vanini*, p. 137. For Bourdenet as for Bertelà (*Stendhal et l'Autre*, p. 170), Vanina's marriage is an act of self-punishment.

71. *La Création chez Stendhal*, pp. 223–24.

72. Crouzet notes that 'l'histoire "romaine" s'achève en histoire mondaine, comme elle a commencé' [the 'Roman' story ends as a society tale, as it began]. 'Stendhal et le récit tragique', p. 121. Peytard also highlights the circularity of the narrative, drawing attention to various parallels between its beginning and ending.

73. *Les Métamorphoses de la liberté*, p. 453.

74. 'Stendhal et le récit tragique', p. 121.

75. *Voix et traces narratives chez Stendhal*, p. 69.

76. *Reading for the Plot: Design and Intention in Narrative* (New York: Knopf, 1984), p. 109.

77. *Promenades dans Rome*, pp. 314, 210.

78. 'Littérature et métaphysique', *Les Temps modernes*, 1.7 (1946), 1153–63 (p. 1156). Madame Grandet presents a particularly striking example of an unexpectedly self-transforming character. See Xavier Bourdenet, 'Mme Grandet, ou comment l'amour vient aux femmes', *L'Année stendhalienne*, 8 (2009), 169–86 and Maria Scott, 'Le Réalisme et la peur du désir? Le cas de *Lucien Leuwen*', *L'Année stendhalienne*, 9 (2010), 35–57. Gérard Genette highlights Stendhal's literary unpredictability, giving a special mention to the ending of *Vanina Vanini*. 'Vraisemblance et motivation', in *Figures II* (Paris: Seuil, 1969), pp. 71–99 (pp. 76–77).

79. See Blin, *Stendhal et les problèmes du roman*, p. 186; Brombert, *Fiction and the Themes of Freedom*, p. 174; see also Bardèche, *Stendhal Romancier*, p. 27. On the unintelligible qualities of Stendhal's characters, and particularly his heroines, see also Christopher Prendergast, *Balzac: Fiction and Melodrama* (London: Arnold, 1978), pp. 139–40; Christopher Prendergast, *The Order of Mimesis: Balzac, Stendhal, Nerval, Flaubert* (Cambridge: Cambridge University Press, 1986), pp. 119–47.

80. Stendhal, *Le Rose et le Vert, Mina de Vanghel, Tamira Wanghen*, p. 57. Blüher writes of these stories, along with *Le Coffre et le Revenant* and *Le Philtre*, that their endings take the form of 'un dénouement extrêmement bref et spectaculaire' [an extremely short and spectacular conclusion]. 'L'Amour tragique', p. 376.

81. Roland Barthes, *S/Z* (Paris: Seuil, 1970), p. 172.

82. Margaret Cohen, 'In Lieu of a Chapter on Some French Women Novelists', in *Spectacles of Realism: Body, Gender, Genre*, ed. by Margaret Cohen and Christopher Prendergast (Minneapolis: University of Minnesota Press, 1995), pp. 90–119 (p. 98).

83. Christopher W. Thompson suggests in the case of *Le Rouge et le Noir* that Mathilde effects just such a shift of position, if only phantasmally: 'her imagination finds a perverse solution to her fears [of revolution] by transferring her allegiance from victim to victor, thus enabling her to fantasize about being herself at the side of those who will be exercising violence in any future revolution'. 'Conflict, Gender and Transcendence in *Le Rouge et le Noir*', *Nineteenth-Century French Studies*, 22.1–2 (1993–94), 77–89 (p. 78).

84. *Le Deuxième Sexe*, I, 388.

85. *Le Deuxième Sexe*, I, 33.

86. On this point, see Paul Desalmand, *Sartre, Stendhal et la morale: ou la Revanche de Stendhal* (Paris: Pocket, 2005), p. 65 and Pierre Deguise, 'Stendhal et Sartre. Du naturel à l'authentique', *French Review*, 42.4 (1969), 540–47 (p. 544).

87. Imbert, *Les Métamorphoses de la liberté*, p. 454.

88. *La Création chez Stendhal*, p. 363.

89. *The Way of the World*, p. 118.

90. *The Way of the World*, p. 23. However, Moretti distances Stendhal from this narrative convention: 'the classical *Bildungsroman* plot posits "happiness" as the highest value, but only to the detriment and eventual annulment of "freedom" — while Stendhal, for his part, follows just as radically the opposite course' (p. 8).

91. *Émile ou de l'éducation* (Paris: Flammarion, 1966), p. 43.

92. *La 'Folie' dans l'œuvre romanesque de Stendhal* (Paris: Corti, 1971), p. 153.

CHAPTER 2

Mathilde and the Paradox of Authenticity

Stendhal's characters often seem at their most free and happy when performing before an audience. We have already seen that the heroine of *Mina de Vanghel* derives great pleasure from playing the role of a servant, not worrying unduly when she occasionally forgets her part. Vanina Vanini clearly revels in the role she plays on her visit to the Minister of Police, first disguised as a manservant and then pretending to be her host's protector. Similarly, assuming the role of 'roi de la maison' [lord of the house] with Madame de Rênal and Madame Derville, Julien is described as 'heureux, libre' [happy, free] (*Orc* I 395). Under Madame de Chasteller's eyes, Lucien 'se crut affranchi de tous les lieux communs [...]. Il osa parler, et beaucoup' [believed himself liberated from commonplaces [...]. He dared to speak, and at length] (*Orc* II 216). In *La Chartreuse de Parme*, Gina is repeatedly represented as an actress, even if it is also noted that she is too spontaneous to play a prescribed role.[1] In *Lamiel* we read that the heroine, 'ravie du rôle que le comte lui faisait jouer dans le monde' [delighted with the part that the count had given her to play in society], is all the more witty because of the 'religieuse attention' [religious attention] that others pay her.[2] Jean Starobinski says the following of such moments in Stendhal's work:

> Il est des moments où la vie jouée et la vie spontanée semblent se rejoindre et se fonder l'une dans l'autre; il est des instants où semble se résoudre l'antinomie du factice et de l'authentique. [...] Et c'est le jeu qui, à force de s'accélérer, fait naître l'authenticité.[3]

> [There are moments when performed life and spontaneous life seem to come together and blend into one another. There are moments when the antinomy of artifice and authenticity seems to resolve itself. [...] And it is the performance that, as it accelerates, produces authenticity.]

Through performance, the Stendhalian self can be simultaneously invented and discovered, its boundaries temporarily unfixed.

The occasional blurring of the distinction between role-playing and naturalness in Stendhal's writing anticipates in some respects the ideas of Judith Butler about the primacy of performance over identity. For Butler, as for Beauvoir and Sartre, 'there need not be a "doer behind the deed", but [...] the "doer" is variably constructed in and through the deed'.[4] However, for both Beauvoir and Sartre, by contrast with Butler, the notion that the authentic self is invented and discovered through action does not apply to the particular action that is role-playing, as the assumption of any pre-defined role is, for them, a form of crutch that enables the inauthentic individual to act in bad faith. In the Stendhalian universe, too, a certain kind of performance very closely resembles the form of acting that Sartre associated with the inauthentic subject, in denial of his or her freedom.[5] However, if it is true that, as Sartre points out, 'on peut devenir de mauvaise foi à force d'être sincère' [one can develop bad faith by dint of being sincere], a passage within *L'Être et le néant* [*Being and Nothingness*] suggests that one might also arrive at good faith via play-acting. Sartre claims that play is a kind of activity that has its origins in human freedom, and even that all manifestations of freedom partake of play.[6] Play is understood here in the broad sense of any non-appropriative, freedom-affirming activity, whose principles are devised by human beings. Nevertheless, the fact that Sartre includes mime artistry, along with sports and games, in his definition is significant, as it suggests the possibility that a certain form of acting is compatible with what he and Beauvoir understood as authenticity. After all, as Sartre observes in another passage from the same study, 'nous ne pouvons rien être sans jouer à l'être' [we cannot be anything without playing at being it].[7] However, role-playing is more usually associated with inauthentic behaviour by both Sartre and Beauvoir, because the individual who identifies with his or her role assumes the position of object for other people rather than that of subject for oneself.

The problem of how to perform in the presence of other people is a particularly strong theme in *Le Rouge et le Noir*. The tyranny of opinion is evoked, for example, in the very first chapter, is highlighted in a discrete passage that appears on a separate page just after the novel's conclusion in the first edition of the novel, and is discussed towards the beginning of the author's draft article of 1832 on the novel (*Orc* I 354, 807, 822–23). Mathilde de La Mole, in particular, is usually held by critics to be in thrall to the opinion of other people. For Grahame C. Jones, for example, the young aristocrat is 'incapable de se libérer du besoin obsessif de vivre à travers ses rôles' [incapable of freeing herself from the obsessive need to live through her roles], and her feelings are a mere 'contrefaçon grotesque du vrai naturel stendhalien' [grotesque forgery of true Stendhalian naturalness].[8] The view of Mathilde as being flawed on account of her theatricality is also adopted by a number of critics who approach *Le Rouge et le Noir* from a perspective informed by feminist history and theory. Richard Bolster's study of Romantic feminism in Stendhal and Balzac praises Mathilde's critical intelligence, courage, and energy, but notes that 'la jeune Parisienne personnifie les aberrations d'une sensibilité théâtrale qui contraste avec celle, naturelle et touchante, de Mme de Rênal' [the young Parisian personifies the aberrations of a theatrical sensibility that contrasts with Madame de Rênal's natural and affecting sensibility].[9] For Michèle Coquillat, arguing from an existentialist perspective, Mathilde's theatricality makes of her a two-dimensional creature, 'une caricature, une actrice, un être totalement dépourvu de vérité, dominé par l'obsession d'atteindre une virilité qui se révèle impossible' [a caricature, an actress, a being totally devoid of truth, dominated by her obsession with achieving a virility that turns out to be impossible].[10]

If the opinion of others is a dominant theme in *Le Rouge et le Noir*, so is freedom. One critic has even claimed that 'freedom is the subject of the novel'.[11] This chapter will argue that Mathilde's theatrical style, far from militating against her sincerity or naturalness, actually frees her to be herself in the presence of other people, just as it allowed Stendhal himself to achieve a kind of paradoxical authenticity. In order to make the argument for the liberating qualities of Mathilde's theatricality, some attention will be given first to Stendhal's creative handling of the problem of other people, both in his writings and in his life. Subsequently, Mathilde's approach to role-playing will be contrasted, as it so often is, with a mode of performance that is generally presented as more authentic and free than hers: that of the hero, Julien Sorel.

Stendhal, Sincerity, and the Problem of Other People

Stendhal's writings repeatedly emphasize the problem posed by the presence, actual or spectral, of other people. Georges Blin observes that the gaze of the other person is as central to the author's world view as it is to that of Sartre in *L'Être et le néant*.[12] In Stendhal's fiction as in his other writings, he repeatedly explores the effects produced on a person by the encounter with the gaze of another person: one has only to think of Julien falling to the floor before the stern gaze of the abbé Pirard or, somewhat less dramatically, of the fact that Stendhal's prisoner heroines, to paraphrase Beauvoir, are constrained by other people's expectations of them as much as by their own expectations of themselves.

Solitude is repeatedly presented, in Stendhal's fiction, as an antidote to the tyranny exercised by other people over a character's attitudes and actions. Julien Sorel is intensely happy when he is alone and unobserved in his mountain retreat. Lucien Leuwen retreats to a hotel apartment to escape his parents ('Ici, je suis libre!' [Here, I am free!] (*Orc* II 687)), while Octave longs to 'vivre isolé' [live in isolation] (*Orc* I 94), yearns for the calmness of monastic life, and fantasizes about having a large room of his own, to which others would not have access. Lamiel escapes to a tower to read forbidden books. Seclusion, then, offers one eminently Stendhalian means of achieving freedom from the watchful gaze of other people. However, the solitary individual is never entirely removed from the outside world, and solitude is not a sustainable solution in the radically social universe of Stendhal's fiction where, as André Gide notes, characters exist only 'dans leurs rapports avec autrui' [in their relations with others].[13]

There is much evidence in Stendhal's work to suggest that interaction with others is necessary to the development of a character, just as for Sartre 'autrui est le médiateur indispensable entre moi et moi-même [...]. [J]'ai besoin d'autrui pour saisir à plein toutes les structures de mon être' [the other person is the indispensable mediator between me and myself [...]. I need the other so I can fully grasp all of the structures of my being].[14] As Starobinski says of Lucien Leuwen:

> C'est en affrontant le monde, c'est en se mettant en expérience au contact des autres qu'il devient lui-même. Il ne se connaît qu'à partir du moment où il a fait l'épreuve de ce qu'il vaut (et cette valeur ne se mesure pas en termes de morale, mais en termes d'action efficace et énergie).[15]

[It is by confronting the world, by entering into the experiment of contact with other people, that he becomes himself. He only gets to know himself when he has put his own worth to the test — and this worth cannot be measured in moral terms, but in terms of effective action and of energy.]

Starobinski, who draws here, as elsewhere in his study of Stendhal, on existentialist ideas, cites *De l'Amour*, where the author writes that 'Avoir de la fermeté dans le caractère, c'est avoir éprouvé l'effet des autres sur soi-même, donc il faut les autres' [To have firmness of character is to have felt the effect of other people on oneself, so other people are necessary].[16]

Solitude is, then, one Stendhalian though always only provisional mode of eluding the inhibiting influence of other people. A second is travesty. The author himself had a pronounced taste for codes and self-travesty. As Paul Valéry notes, his mode of being in the world was intrinsically theatrical: 'La conscience de Beyle est un théâtre, et il y a beaucoup de l'acteur dans cet auteur.' [Beyle's consciousness is a theatre, and there is much of the actor in that author.][17] The author took acting classes as a young man, was attracted to actresses, and fostered lifelong dreams of being a playwright. Around the time when he was taking acting classes, in 1804 and 1805, Stendhal came to a realization of the importance of hypocrisy for social success. Bardèche argues that this realization took place after his reading, in 1803, of Madame de Staël's *Delphine*, a book that convinced him that hypocrisy was a particularly important tool for women.[18] Certainly, in a letter of February 1805 to his sister, the author states that hypocrisy is a necessary strategy of social survival for women and cites *Delphine* as a cautionary tale. Tellingly, he advises Pauline in that letter that lessons in theatrical declamation could help to teach her hypocrisy.

Stendhal subscribed, at least sometimes, to the popular view that any form of acting, or hypocrisy, was inimical to sincerity, militating against emotional authenticity:

Ne jouant plus rien on sent le bonheur de l'amour. Vous jouez un beau senti-ment, frappant, prouvant beaucoup d'amour, menant au but, mais, ce sentiment exprimé, vous ne trouverez plus que sécheresse. Rien dans votre cœur, le bâillement sur vos lèvres. (*OI* I 341; *Journal*, 8 August 1805)

[When we are no longer acting we feel the happiness of love. You act out a beautiful feeling, striking your chest, proving the extent of your love, accomplishing your objective, but, once this feeling has been expressed, all you find is coldness. Nothing in your heart and a yawn on your lips.]

However, if hypocrisy is, by definition, an inauthentic attitude, Stendhal also saw it as a means by which the individual might try to preserve his or her authenticity in a social world where hypocrisy was the norm. As Brombert notes of Stendhal's novelistic treatment of hypocrisy, 'What is at stake is the conservation of the unique qualities of the exceptional individual in the face of the immorality of conformist ethics. Freedom is thus forced to seek refuge in dissimulation.'[19]

Stendhal's fiction suggests, however, that such a refuge could, like that offered by solitude, only ever be highly provisional. The concealment of one's true inclinations is a strategy that is favoured by Stendhal's protagonists, most notably Octave, Julien, Lucien, and Féder; but the disguise is never entirely successful. In Julien's case, the impassive mask he assumes comes close to perfection with his transformation into the joyless Chevalier de la Vernaye, but this facade is suddenly and catastrophically discarded upon the arrival of Madame de Rênal's reference letter. Octave's violent outbursts give the lie to his controlled exterior, while Féder's repressed energies are unleashed in an only slightly more socially appropriate way, when following Rosalinde's advice he indulges in wild and joyful dancing every Sunday. The hypocrite's 'true' self can thus rebel against his or her social self with explosive consequences. Furthermore, the sincere self tends, in Stendhal's fiction, to become confused with, or tainted by, the social persona. This is the case for Lucien Leuwen, who discovers that he cannot adopt the guise of an amoral bureaucrat with impunity; while on a dishonorable political mission, the hero is almost literally scalded by the accusation that his inner self is as filthy as his outer self.[20] Dissimulation, then, permits only a mitigated form of freedom in Stendhal's fictional world. As Jean-Pierre Richard observes of the the latter's writings, 'Ennemie de tout spontané, l'hypocrisie étouffe [...] et crispe; elle rend esclave, au pire sens du mot.' [An enemy of all spontaneity, hypocrisy suffocates [...] and hardens. It enslaves, in the worst sense of the word.][21] The Stendhalian hypocrite comes dangerously close to resembling Sartre's 'serious' individual, who identifies with an inanimate object and thereby chooses to deny his or her own freedom: 'L'homme sérieux enfouit au fond de lui-même la conscience de sa liberté [...]. [L]'homme est sérieux quand il se prend pour un objet.' [The serious man buries deep inside him the awareness of his freedom [...]. Man is serious when he considers himself an object.][22]

According to Richard, who argues that Stendhal's fundamental desire was to escape from the objectifying, analytical gaze of other people, this desire led the author to conceive of three potential solutions to the problem of this immobilizing gaze. The first is the hypocritical wearing of a mask, a strategy presented by Richard as ultimately self-defeating, while the second, evasiveness or *pudeur*, is available to women only. The third strategy is one of provocation, and it is the strategy that Richard claims Stendhal adopted in his life:

> Stendhal adopta [...] le plus souvent une troisième attitude: ni repli pudique ni défense hypocrite, mais offensive scandaleuse. La provocation lui fut une pudeur retournée. Vulgarité complaisante, étalage de soi, grossièreté cynique, plus personne, aujourd'hui ne se laisse prendre à cet art de 'stendhaliser' qui réussit pourtant à éloigner de lui tout un siècle de bien-pensants.[23]

> [Stendhal usually adopted a third attitude: neither modest withdrawal nor hypocritical defence, but scandalous offensive. Provocation was, for him, inverted modesty. Complacent vulgarity, self-display, cynical coarseness, nobody today is fooled by this art of 'stendhalizing'[24] that nevertheless succeeded in distancing him from a century of right-thinking people.]

In Richard's view, Stendhal discovered that instead of having to hide his 'vérité intérieure' [inner truth] from the view of others, he could present that truth to others in a form that would seem exaggerated and implausible to others:

> Tel est *l'égotisme*, moyen d'à la fois se connaître et se dissimuler, de jouir de soi et de défier les autres. La sincérité s'y étale, mais s'y étale un peu trop crûment pour paraître vraiment sincère. À ce piège subtil un Valéry lui-même s'est

laissé prendre: il faut beaucoup aimer Stendhal pour comprendre que la parade
du naturel sert chez lui à sauver la vraie nature, et la sincérité à protéger la
liberté.[25]

[This is *egotism*, a way of both knowing oneself and concealing oneself, of
delighting in oneself and challenging others. Sincerity flaunts itself, but a little
too crudely to seem truly sincere. Even Valéry fell into this subtle trap. You need
to love Stendhal greatly to understand that, for him, the parade of naturalness
works to save the genuinely natural, and sincerity to protect freedom.]

While Paul Valéry's essay on the author, to which this passage refers, expresses
scepticism about the existence of any inner true or authentic Stendhalian self, in fact
Valéry is otherwise in agreement with Richard that Stendhalian egotism crucially
involves the presentation of an exaggerated appearance of sincerity. According
to Valéry, then, this mode of egotism consists in performing one's individuality,
in making oneself 'un peu plus *nature* que nature; un peu plus soi qu'on ne l'était
quelques instants avant d'en avoir eu l'idée' [a little more *natural* than comes
naturally, a little more oneself than one was a few moments before having had the
idea].[26] Essentially, for Valéry Stendhal's implausibly overblown sincerity points to
the failure of his effort to be sincere, and by extension the failure of his effort to be
free,[27] whereas for Richard it presents the happy union of freedom and sincerity.

Those who knew, or claimed to know, Stendhal were just as divided on the
subject of his sincerity. Arnould Frémy accuses the author of having lacked that
naturalness that he so idolized:

Ne pouvant être beau, M. de Stendhal s'en vengea en se faisant bizarre. [...] Il
parlait sans cesse de naturel, et nul homme n'était en apparence moins naturel
que lui, non pas qu'il ne sentît à merveille, mais il craignait surtout d'être lui-
même. Il avait aussi pour maxime favorite: 'Savoir braver le ridicule.'[28]

[Not being capable of handsomeness, Monsieur de Stendhal avenged himself
by making himself bizarre. [...] He spoke constantly of naturalness, and no
man seemed less natural than he. Not that he didn't have wonderful sensitivity,
but he was above all afraid of being himself. He therefore had as his favourite
maxim: 'Know how to face down ridicule.']

By contrast, Prosper Mérimée came to understand, as his friendship with the author
developed, the latter's apparent affectation as an expression of his naturalness:

Quelque temps je l'ai soupçonné de viser à l'originalité. J'ai fini par le croire
parfaitement sincère. Aujourd'hui, rappelant tous mes souvenirs, je suis
persuadé que ses bizarreries étaient très naturelles, et ses paradoxes le résultat
ordinaire de l'exagération où la contradiction entraîne insensiblement. [...]
Les boutades de Beyle n'étaient, à mon avis, que l'expression exagérée d'une
conviction profonde.[29]

[For a while I suspected him of affecting originality. I came to believe him
perfectly sincere. Today, recalling all my memories, I am convinced that
his quirks were very natural, and his paradoxes the ordinary result of the
exaggeration to which contradiction imperceptibly leads. [...] Beyle's witticisms
were, in my opinion, only the exaggerated expression of a deep conviction.]

Despite differences in approach and argument, these commentators do agree on the fact that Stendhalian sincerity bears at least the appearance of falseness. Stendhal himself writes in *De l'Amour* about how sensitive individuals seem less natural than others because less ruled by habit, and how original individuals can seem ridiculous.[30]

The mixture of falseness and sincerity that was characteristic of Stendhal's chosen style of being in the world can be related to what has already been said about the problem encountered by the dissimulator or hypocrite. Just as the allegedly authentic private self cannot be sealed off from and protected by the hypocritical social self, the false or social self also, inevitably, bears traces of the private self. As Blin puts it, 'On ne se trahit peut-être jamais mieux que par la manière dont on revêt un caractère d'emprunt.' [We never betray ourselves better than in the way in which we take on an assumed character.][31] Jules Barbey d'Aurevilly makes a telling observation after the first publication, in 1855, of Stendhal's private letters: he notes that they ultimately fail to reveal the sincere man, the latter having been replaced by a kind of composite of private and social self, 'une sincérité de seconde main' [a second-hand sincerity].[32] But Stendhal's chosen way of being in the world may be best understood not as a merging of private and public selves but rather as running counter to any fixed or idealized notion of the self, be it private or public. It involved, in other words, a rejection of traditional notions of sincerity as much as a resistance to hypocrisy. This strategy can be associated, in the language of Stendhal criticism, with *égotisme*, *pseudonymie*, provocation, or improvisation. It can also be linked, as in this chapter, with the idea of playfulness and performance.

A number of commentators have distinguished between two sorts of acting in Stendhal, the first of which has the effect of undermining the individual's freedom, while the second works in the service of that freedom. Francesco Spandri, for example, makes a qualitative distinction between role-play and 'mimétisme' [imitation], while Francesco Manzini argues for a crucial difference between emulation and imitation.[33] Crouzet, for his part, distinguishes the bad hypocrite from the good player: the good player abandons the self-control so cherished by the bad hypocrite. Instead of jealously guarding the integrity of the self, the player 's'oublie dans son rôle, se laisse porter par lui et consent au mélange de vrai et de faux qui constitue cette nouvelle unité de soi' [forgets himself in his role, lets himself be carried along by it, and consents to the combination of truth and falsity that constitutes this new unity of self].[34] While Crouzet presents Julien Sorel as a hypocrite rather than a player, he does not explore Mathilde's status as a social performer. The next section will attempt to confirm Julien's fundamental hypocrisy, while the subsequent one will examine Mathilde's very different style of being in the world.

Julien: Hypocrite or Player?

Julien Sorel is presented in *Le Rouge et le Noir* as a young man intent on exchanging his modest place in society for a far grander one. In order to further his personal ambition, he has recourse to two kinds of role-play, one public and one private.

To facilitate the social mobility he desires — 'Julien était surtout ambitieux' [Julien was ambitious above all else] (*Orc* I 656) — the hero adopts a strategy of hypocrisy in public, becoming moderately adept at what the narrator calls 'cet art de la faiblesse' [this art born of weakness] (*Orc* I 508). He mimes piety for the purpose of furthering the ecclesiastical career he initially envisages, feigns ignorance in the Besançon seminary for the same reason, and affects an unquestioning acceptance of reactionary values in both the Rênal and La Mole households. Julien's ability to quote lengthy sections of the Bible from memory earns him the admiration of many in his home town of Verrières. The fact that he also quotes profane texts in order to impress various audiences — a Besançon barmaid, the bishop of Besançon, Mathilde de La Mole — implies that his talent for religious hypocrisy is of a piece with his equally impressive talent for seduction. When Julien pretends to be in love with Madame de Fervaques in order to make Mathilde jealous and thereby regain her affection, the latter marvels at the 'fausseté parfaite' [perfect falsity] and extreme 'machiavélisme' [Machiavellianism] that he demonstrates in his apparent seduction of this other woman (*Orc* I 721). It is unsurprising that a character whose mimetic talents transform him into both holy man and seducer should think of Molière's Tartuffe as a 'maître' [mentor] (*Orc* I 641).

As a result of his choice of hypocrisy, Julien is rarely free in the presence of other people. The narrator remarks that even in the company of his closest friend he is not at liberty to be himself: 'son hypocrisie faisait qu'il n'était pas libre meme chez Fouqué' [his hypocrisy prevented him from being free even in Fouqué's home] (*Orc* I 414). What Korasoff flippantly says of the risks that Julien runs in his false seduction of Madame de Fervaques is also more generally true of the hero's strategic simulations: he must always remain on the defensive: 'Je ne vous le cache pas, votre rôle est difficile; vous jouez la comédie, et si l'on devine que vous la jouez, vous êtes perdu' [I won't pretend that your role is not difficult. You're acting a part, and if there's any suspicion that you're acting, all will be lost for you] (*Orc* I 704). The debilitating influence of the hero's hypocrisy on his freedom is implied by the narrator's description of his feigned seduction of Madame de Fervaques as 'ces six semaines de comédie si pénible' [these six weeks of terribly painful play-acting] (*Orc* I 722) and by the remark that 'Ses efforts pour jouer un rôle achevaient d'ôter toute force à son âme' [His efforts to play a part ended up draining all the strength from his spirit] (*Orc* I 721). Julien himself earlier laments the circumstances that have led to his choice of hypocrisy: 'Quelle misère! [...] Ma vie n'est qu'une suite d'hypocrisies, parce que je n'ai pas mille francs de rente pour acheter du pain' [How wretched! [...] My life is nothing but a series of hypocritical acts, because I don't have an income of a thousand francs to buy my bread and butter] (*Orc* I 623).

The second form of role-play in which Julien Sorel indulges takes the form of private identification with personal heroes, most notably Napoleon and Rousseau.

The latter two are the key figures associated with the hero's three most beloved books: the *Mémorial de Sainte-Hélène*, a collection of the bulletins of the Grand Army, and *Les Confessions*. Julien identifies with Napoleon and Rousseau even when he is most fully and radically himself, that is, when he is at his least self-consciously hypocritical. His repugnance at the idea of dining at the servants' table in the Rênal household, his own status as a literate servant (private tutor, private secretary) and seminarian, his display of erudition and bout of compassion while dining in the Valenod household, his occasional escapes to secluded places conducive to reflection, and his relationship with the mature Madame de Rênal all call elements of Rousseau's narrative to mind. Similarly, Julien's social, sexual, and military ambitions stem from a powerful identification with Napoleon. Even when he is most himself, then, Julien emulates his chosen role models.

Critics are generally agreed that there exist strong parallels between Julien Sorel and Mathilde de La Mole insofar as both make identification with their chosen role models integral to the strategy of resistance that they adopt in the face of a conformist society. However, there are certain decisive differences between their chosen approaches. For a start, the nature of their role models is different, Julien's often being considered more appropriate than Mathilde's. Richard remarks, for example, that Julien's penchant for imitation is more excusable than hers by virtue of the fact that Napoleon had far more currency and relevance during the Restoration than did Mathilde's sixteenth-century heroes; this is despite the fact that Stendhal's great enthusiasm for the sixteenth century is a critical commonplace.[35] In addition, Julien's identifications with Napoleon and Rousseau seem less conscious or voluntary than Mathilde's imitations, leading some critics to argue that his mimetic practice is qualitatively superior to hers. Accordingly, Manzini distinguishes between Mathilde's practice of superficial imitation, presented as the vain mimicry of outward appearances, and Julien's allegedly far more successful efforts at emulation, understood as a transformative and less self-conscious process.[36] Thirdly, for many critics Mathilde seems more trapped by her identifications than does Julien. Annie-Claire Jaccard, for example, describes what she calls the heroine's inability to separate from her role as 'une sorte d'infirmité atavique dont Mathilde est la victime malheureuse' [a sort of atavistic infirmity of which Mathilde is the unfortunate victim].[37]

Another significant difference between the two identificatory practices is the fact that Julien's imitations are as covert as Mathilde's are flamboyant. In the next section we will turn to the implications for the latter's freedom of the overtness of her mimetic practice. In the meantime, it can simply be noted that the covert nature of Julien's identifications, dictated at least in part by social circumstances that are very different from Mathilde's, has the effect of constricting him. This is most emblematically demonstrated when, early in the novel, he punishes himself for a moment of spontaneous and public praise for Napoleon by binding his right arm to his chest, thereby recalling the trademark pose of his hero. As this episode suggests, the secretive nature of the hero's emulation of the Emperor is a source of significant discomfort for him. Julien also feels he needs to hide his Rousseauian sensibility from the eyes of the world, for example when he finds himself shedding tears of compassion at a dinner hosted by M. Valenod, or when he discovers that revealing his true sentiments to Mathilde has adverse consequences. From the perspective of his achievement of freedom, then, Julien's private identifications are arguably just as ineffectual as his more public role-playing; they too make demands on his hypocrisy.

The hero does not always succeed in maintaining his hypocritical stance. Sometimes he lets his guard down, as in the example just cited, when he reveals his passionate admiration for Napoleon in the company of Chélan and other priests, or when his would-be love letters to Madame de Fervacques contain careless mistakes; unusually, Julien's discovery of his error in the latter episode provokes him to mirth rather than self-reproach. At other times, Julien's duplicitousness is intuited by other characters, as when Mathilde detects his potential as a revolutionary. Occasionally, in addition, Julien discovers genuine feelings where previously he had feigned them, as in the case of his seduction of Madame de Rênal. The hero takes a break, furthermore, from his hypocritical habits when he finds himself in remote, secluded places: there, he can experience 'son bonheur de liberté' [the happiness of his freedom] (*Orc* I 414).

Nevertheless, while it is true that in his relationships with Madame de Rênal and Mathilde, and in his relations with Fouqué, Chélan, and Pirard, Julien does reveal something of his 'real' self, it is equally evident that he spends most of the novel trying to hide and defend that private self from the gaze of others.[38] His memorization of scripture, his wearing of a black habit, his Besançon studies in dullness and his London lessons in impassivity are just some of the ways in which he attempts to shield his private self from the view of others.

Julien's anxiety about the opinion of others, his 'horreur du mépris' [horror of scorn] (*Orc* I 781), is repeatedly evoked in the text. Richard observes that Julien's defensive mask reduces him to a state of wretchedness: 'N'oublions pas que pour Stendhal Julien Sorel est un héros pitoyable et malheureux.' [Let us not forget that for Stendhal Julien Sorel is a pitiful and unfortunate hero.][39] This is not, however, the viewpoint usually adopted by critics. Interestingly, Richard himself also maintains, somewhat inconsistently, that this pitiful hero is one of Stendhal's sublimely detached heroes, in that he never lets himself be defined by any of his assumed roles: 'Le héros sublime se sent supérieur à tous ses gestes: Julien glisse à travers ses rôles sans se laisser entamer par aucun d'eux.' [The sublime hero feels superior to all his gestures: Julien slips between his roles without letting himself be damaged by any of them.][40] Similarly, for Bardèche, Julien Sorel is 'le contraire d'une âme hypocrite' [the opposite of a hypocritical soul], capable of assuming and discarding his hypocrisy at will and with impunity, while according to Blin Julien remains closer to Rousseau despite his efforts to resemble Tartuffe.[41] Certainly, most critics of the novel would agree with Longstaffe that Julien remains admirable despite his hypocrisy, which she chalks up to 'the arms and the ethical code of the exceptional individual'.[42]

The argument that Julien's deeper self survives his hypocritical tactics hinges on the supposition that he shakes off all his masks in the final chapters of the novel. The most prevalent critical view of the novel has it that Julien's hypocritical exterior shatters when he abandons his Parisian success story and shoots his former mistress in the church of Verrières. To cite just two instances of this dominant reading, Hemmings claims that the 'poetic truth' of the shooting of Madame de Rênal 'lies in the opportunity it provided Stendhal to reveal in the end the authentic Julien', while Roger Pearson writes that 'Julien's development leads from hypocrisy and role-playing to sincerity and authenticity'.[43] The hero's apparent rupture with his false social persona, in the final part of the novel, tends (as here) to be perceived as evidence of the perseverance of his core self throughout the novel.

It is not at all clear that Julien has a stable fictional self, however. In fact, critics from the nineteenth century through to the twenty-first have emphasized the inconsistencies and contradictions of his character.[44] While it is often argued that a more unified and coherent moral self finally reveals itself in the prison cell, Julien is a complex and divided character even at the end of the novel; his sincerity still hovers very close to hypocrisy. For example, just a few hours after he makes an oath of silence in a letter to Mathilde, he breaks this vow by asking his gaoler about what people are saying in Verrières. The answer given by the gaoler (who wants to be paid in exchange for his information), and Julien's response to that answer, are heavily laden with an irony that is oblique to the point of being invisible to readers sympathetic to the hero:

> 'Que dit-on dans Verrières?'
> — Monsieur Julien, le serment que j'ai prêté devant le crucifix, à la cour royale, le jour que je fus installé dans ma place, m'oblige au silence.
> Il se taisait, mais restait. La vue de cette hypocrisie vulgaire amusa Julien.
> (*Orc* I 757)

> ['What are they saying in Verrières?'
> 'Monsieur Julien, the oath I took before the cross, in the crown courthouse, the day I was invested with my office, obliges me to silence.'
> He stopped, but remained standing there. The sight of this vulgar hypocrisy amused Julien.]

The jailer's hypocrisy is certainly vulgar, in that it is perfectly blatant; the hypocrisy of Julien's oath of silence to Mathilde is less vulgar, to the extent that it is far more subtly evoked in the text. If the final chapters are understood to express the hero's continuing vacillation between sincerity and hypocrisy, then the reader must decide whether this duality renders him more or less psychologically authentic. I would argue, though, that — despite the existential angst he experiences in the concluding part of the novel, and despite his sense of the absurdity of existence — in existentialist terms the hero can only be understood as inauthentic.

When his loving former mistress condemns his character and lifts the veil on his hypocrisy, thereby thwarting his intention to marry his current lover, the hero's response is to shoot his accuser. Julien explains his own action to himself as follows: 'J'ai été offensé d'une manière atroce; j'ai tué, je mérite la mort, mais voilà tout. Je meurs après avoir soldé mon compte envers l'humanité' [I was appallingly wronged; I committed murder and I deserve death. That's all there is to say. I'll die after settling my account with humanity] (*Orc* I 757). His attempted murder, described by him as an act of 'vengeance' (*Orc* I 756), might be elucidated by reference to

Sartre's definition of hatred: 'La haine est haine de tous les autres en un seul. Ce que je veux atteindre symboliquement en poursuivant la mort de tel autre, c'est le principe général de l'existence d'autrui.' [Hatred is hatred of all others in one individual. What I want to achieve symbolically by seeking the death of such an other is the general principle of the existence of others.][45] From this perspective, there is a profound continuity, rather than any contradiction, between Julien's shooting of Madame de Rênal and his love for her in the prison cell: when he shoots her he attacks the threat posed by others, in a general sense; when he loves her, he can forget the existence of other people. Visitors to his cell, such as Mathilde, the priest, and his father, irritate him greatly; even a visit from his old mentor, Chélan, leaves him depressed: 'Le pire des malheurs en prison, pensa-t-il, c'est de ne pouvoir fermer sa porte' [The worst misery of prison, he thought, is not being able to shut your door] (*Orc* I 793). He forbids Mathilde and Fouqué to speak of the world outside his prison cell: 'Que m'importent *les autres*! Mes relations avec *les autres* vont être tranchées brusquement' [What do *other people* matter to me! My ties with *other people* are going to be abruptly cut] (*Orc* I 775).

Julien's intolerance of others at the end of the novel is accompanied by a continued need to present himself to those others as fully in control of his actions. He repeatedly insists on the premeditated nature of his attack on his former lover (see *Orc* I 755, 763, 774, 782), even though the text itself gives no indication of his thought processes as he rushes to Verrières and buys his pistols. The fact that the chapter in which he shoots Madame de Rênal is entitled 'Un orage' [A storm], the fact that his usually neat handwriting becomes an illegible scrawl when he tries to write to Mathilde, and the fact that after the shooting he is immobile and unseeing, and defends himself 'machinalement' [automatically] (*Orc* I 754), all suggest that Julien is not thinking clearly either before he commits his crime or in its immediate aftermath. Nevertheless, he chooses to go to his death, and to condemn his child to what he suspects will be a life of neglect, rather than admit to a crime of passion that would rupture the illusion of psychological coherence and consistency to which he cleaves. The Abbé de Frilair is therefore correct in his observation that the hero's death is 'une sorte de *suicide*' [a kind of *suicide*] (*Orc* I 793). Unlike Mina's suicide, however, Julien's is driven by a concern for the opinions of others. His dread of being found wanting is evidenced by his great fear of revealing any personal weakness in the face of death. He worries constantly about how courageous or otherwise he will appear on his way to the guillotine, and what stories will circulate about him after his death. Even Blin, who is broadly sympathetic towards Julien, suggests that the latter's 'angoisse de l'opinion' [anxiety about other people's opinions] perseveres until his death, and asks: 'sa vie se sera, au total, entièrement laissé déterminer par la menace du *qu'en va-t-on penser?*' [will his life finally have allowed itself to be entirely determined by the threat of *what will others think*?][46] While Mathilde chooses, despite some niggling doubts,[47] to see Julien as impervious to that fear of ridicule that she knows to haunt the noblemen who surround her, there is much in the final part of the novel to suggest that Julien is just as prone as they to '[l]a résignation sublime' [sublime resignation], and just as fearful as they of ridicule and the opinions of others, even at the point of death: 'Leur seule peur en mourant serait encore d'être de mauvais goût' [Their only fear, as they died, would still be that of being in bad taste] (*Orc* I 631).

In existentialist terms, Julien's subjectivity or *pour-soi*, now as always previously in the novel, attempts to defend itself against the objectifying gaze of other people by presenting itself as an invulnerable object (*en-soi*). The hero's decision to go to his death, rather than state that his crime was motivated by passion, can be understood both as a vain assertion of his self-control and as a refusal to continue living in a society where his sense of himself is constantly threatened by the presence of other people. Leslie W. Rabine, indeed, argues that it is Julien's reluctance to allow his self to be repeatedly challenged, as it continually is in his relationship with Mathilde, that leads him to choose Madame de Rênal over her younger rival; Rabine suggests that the hero's love for Madame de Rênal is 'more based on vanity' than his love for Mathilde, in that it requires of his partner 'a permanent loss of self'.[48] According to this reading, the hero sees Madame de Rênal less as a subject in her own right than as a kind of mirror or comfort blanket; the hero himself suggests as much when he tells her: 'Je te parle comme je me parle à moi-même' [I'm speaking to you just as I do to myself] (*Orc* I 790). Julien's preference for Madame de Rênal would thus be complicit with his decision to die with a relatively intact and coherent sense of himself rather than confront the uncertainty that he experiences in his relationship with Mathilde.[49]

The main reason why many commentators consider the final section of *Le Rouge et le Noir* to demonstrate that Julien's integrity survives his hypocritical stance is that he finally rejects his false, ambition-driven love for Mathilde and undergoes what Philippe Berthier calls 'la révélation finale du seul amour véritable de Julien' [the final revelation of Julien's one true love].[50] However, the hypothesis of self-revelation tends to necessitate a forgetfulness of the fact that the hero's feelings for his provincial mistress were never particularly profound before. There are numerous mentions of Madame de Rênal in the Parisian section of the novel, but little sense that the hero is suffering terribly in her absence; indeed there is scant enough evidence of genuine depth of feeling even in the part of the novel devoted to Julien's time in the Rênal household. There is a particularly telling moment that takes place in the course of Madame de Rênal's brilliant deception of her husband, when she finds a moment to run to the top of the dovecote and give the agreed signal of success to Julien who, she knows, is walking in the woods with her children. She waits a long time for a return signal from the lover for whom she believes she has sacrificed her eternal soul. She marvels when none comes; and no explanation is offered by the text.

The superficial nature of Julien's attachment to Madame de Rênal is particularly heavily, though subtly, ironized in the part of the novel that describes his initial departure from her home:

> Il était fort ému. Mais à une lieue de Verrières, où il laissait tant d'amour, il ne songea plus qu'au bonheur de voir une capitale, une grande ville de guerre comme Besançon. (*Orc* I 493)[51]
>
> [He was very emotional. But a league from Verrières, where he was leaving behind so much love, he could think only of the happiness of seeing a capital, a great military city like Besançon.]

Returning for a nocturnal visit three days later, Julien is uncomprehending of his mistress's paralysing grief, accusing her of not loving him and rather flippantly commenting that she will now be free of any remorse, no longer visualizing her children in the grave every time they fall ill. After the sardonic account of the hero's emotional obtuseness in this passage, and his subsequently short-lived melancholy — we read that he felt so distressed by his lover's coldness that he looked behind him often for as long as he could see the steeple of the Verrières church — it comes as little surprise that he goes on, in the following chapter, to proclaim 'l'amour le plus violent' [the most passionate love] (*Orc* I 497) for a barmaid who happens to be the first woman he meets at his destination in Besançon. Julien may belatedly discover the strength of his love for Madame de Rênal in the prison cell (ironically located in the city that previously witnessed the weakness of his passion), but this does not mean that he ever genuinely loved her before. Nevertheless, he tells her that he has loved her all along: 'Sache que je t'ai toujours aimée, que je n'ai aimé que toi' [Know that I've always loved you, that I've loved only you] (*Orc* I 789).[52] The sheer hypocrisy, or at the very least bad faith,[53] of this claim suggests that he has not, in fact, abandoned his habit of duplicity.

Certainly, Julien's feelings for Mathilde are as inauthentic, at the outset at least, as his love for Madame de Rênal appears to be upon his departure for the Besançon seminary; but what begins as Parisian pseudo-sentiment transforms into a more intensely passionate love than anything he experiences with his provincial mistress.[54] The text tells us that his affection for Mathilde, described at one point as the 'maîtresse absolue de son bonheur' [absolute mistress, reigning over all his happiness] (*Orc* I 678), overrides his ambition and vanity in a way that his feelings for Madame de Rênal never did: 'Mathilde avait tout absorbé; il la trouvait partout dans l'avenir' [Mathilde had absorbed everything; he found her everywhere in his future] (*Orc* I 701). The detail of the text itself reveals the truth of this statement. When Julien learns that M. de La Mole is to become a minister, he does not turn his mind to the glittering implications of this promotion for his own ambitions; all he can think about is Mathilde: 'à ses yeux tous ces grands intérêts s'étaient comme recouverts d'un voile' [in his eyes, all of these great concerns had been obscured by a kind of veil] (*Orc* I 712; see also *Orc* I 716, 718). By contrast, while participating in the guard of honour assembled in Verrières for the visiting king, an extraordinary honour controversially arranged for him by Madame de Rênal, Julien's happiness knows no bounds, because he imagines himself as one of Napoleon's officers and observes that the eyes of all the women are on him. Nowhere is it stated that he notices the eyes of Madame de Rênal on him, or that any thought of her so much as crosses his mind, even as she races between three venues to admire him.

Admittedly, the two cases outlined above are not perfectly comparable, as Julien possesses Madame de Rênal's love while Mathilde has withdrawn hers, thereby exacerbating his desire to the extent that 'Il se sentait pénétré d'amour jusque dans les replis les plus intimes de son cœur' [He felt permeated by love, right down into the deepest recesses of his heart] (*Orc* I 728). The point is that Julien is very clearly presented by the text as loving Mathilde, such that his denial, in the prison cell, of ever having felt any love for her sheds serious doubt on his integrity at the end of the novel. Indeed, Julien's assertion, upon Madame de Rênal's first visit to his cell, that Mathilde is now his 'femme' [wife] rather than his 'maîtresse' [mistress] seems equally hypocritical (*Orc* I 789); much has been made of Pierre Barbéris's claim that Julien and Madame de Rênal have sexual intercourse, between the lines, in the prison cell;[55] however, references to Mathilde's 'transports' both on her first and subsequent visits, and to moments of 'affreuse volupté' [awful ecstasy], as well as the narrator's description of Julien as 'son amant' [her lover] (*Orc* I 766, 772), all suggest that the hero's alleged sexual continence in Mathilde's presence does not date from long before this first meeting with Madame de Rênal.

Arguably, then, the hero remains a hypocrite until his death: to preserve an illusion of unity and self-mastery he insists that his shooting of Madame de Rênal was premeditated, claims that he has loved only her all along, and feigns impassivity on his way to his death. It is only when he is at his most lucid, in the penultimate chapter, that Julien can admit to himself the deep-rooted nature of his own hypocrisy: 'Je suis hypocrite comme s'il y avait là quelqu'un pour m'écouter' [I am as hypocritical as if there were someone here listening to me] (*Orc* I 799).

If Julien's shooting of Madame de Rênal has the appearance of not being premeditated, despite the length of the journey he undertakes from Paris to Verrières, his eventual execution does have all the appearance of premeditation. From very early in the novel, the hero's destiny has been chosen, and tacitly accepted, as though it were not a choice, as though it were inevitable.[56] Julien's choice of role model for his projected rise in society testifies to his sense of the inevitability of defeat; on our first meeting with him, the hero is reading Las Cases's *Mémorial de Sainte-Hélène*, the post-defeat pseudo-memoirs of Napoleon; shortly after this first meeting, Julien finds a fragment of printed paper in Verrières church (where he will later shoot Madame de Rênal) which references the execution of a man whose name forms an exact anagram of his own; that Julien reluctantly intuits a parallel between his own story and that of Louis Jenrel is made clear by the text. Towards the end of the book, when Julien is in his prison cell, the narrator informs us that 'Toute sa vie n'avait été qu'une longue préparation au malheur' [His whole life had been nothing but a long preparation for misfortune] (*Orc* I 757). In our view, then, Hemmings is correct in his observation that 'Julien does not *invent* himself, he conforms to a borrowed model'.[57]

However, for Peter Brooks, Julien freely invents his own destiny:

> Julien continually conceives himself as the hero of his own text, and that text as something to be created, not simply endured. He creates fictions, including fictions of the self, that motivate action. [...] Julien's fictional scenarios make him not only the actor, the feigning self, but also the stage manager of his own destiny, constantly projecting the self into the future on the basis of hypothetical plots. One of the most striking examples of such hypotheses occurs when, after receiving Mathilde's summons to come to her bedroom at one o'clock in the morning, he imagines a plot — in all senses of the term, including plot as machination, as *complot* — in which he will be seized.[58]

It is true that Julien elaborates narratives of which he imagines himself the hero, but what Brooks omits to mention here is that this hero's overarching plot has been effectively pre-written. In effect, and very literally in the episode cited by Brooks, Julien imagines himself already dead; when Mathilde invites him to her bedroom, he writes a letter to his friend Fouqué, giving instructions that an enclosed 'petit mémoire justificatif arrangé en forme de conte' [short justificatory memorandum, presented as a story] be published in the event of his death at the hands of Mathilde's imagined accomplices (*Orc* I 651). Julien is concerned above all with his posthumous destiny; he does not want to be 'un monstre dans la postérité' [a monster for posterity] (*Orc* I 652). Calling to mind Sartre's serious man, who identifies with a stone,[59] Julien feels goaded on to heroic action by a marble bust of Cardinal Richelieu in his bedroom:

> Ce buste avait l'air de le regarder d'une façon sévère, et comme lui reprochant le manque de cette audace qui doit être si naturelle au caractère français. De ton temps, grand homme, aurais-je hésité? (*Orc* I 650)
>
> [This bust seemed to be looking at him sternly, as if admonishing him for lacking the daring that should come naturally to the French character. In your day, great man, would I have hesitated?]

The hero is petrified not only by fear but also a sense of heroic obligation. Elsewhere in the novel, too, Julien musters courage by binding himself to a heroic model; on his first visit to Madame de Rênal's bedroom, for example, his fear of departing from his role, and his 'idée du *devoir*' [idea of *duty*], mean that he fails to allow himself 'le bonheur qui se plaçait sous ses pas' [the happiness that came his way] (*Orc* I 426). When, thanks to the efforts of the Marquis de La Mole, Julien finally becomes the Chevalier de La Vernaye, and considers that his 'roman est fini' [novel is finished] (*Orc* I 749), his impassive appearance and measured style prompt older officers to think of him as entirely lacking in 'jeunesse' [youth] (*Orc* I 751). The hero is as much, now, a 'soldat de plomb' [tin soldier] as he ever was under the 'petits yeux gris et méchants' [nasty little grey eyes] of his father; but now his own eyes are no longer described as tear-filled but rather as 'sévères et presque méchants' [stern and almost nasty]; they resemble those of his father (*Orc* I 365, 751).

Another point omitted by Brooks is that it is in fact Mathilde who has conceived and stage-managed not only the plot that sees him bravely climb into her bedroom but also, arguably, the plot ending in which Julien heroically loses his head; Michel Guérin even goes so far as to say: 'La mort de Julien, Mathilde l'impose.' [Julien's death is dictated by Mathilde.][60] It is time now to turn to this least doll-like of Parisians.

Mathilde's Role-Playing and Relationship with Others

We have already seen that Mathilde's tendency to act out roles is habitually represented in criticism as a crucial shortcoming in her character. Mimetic behaviour, or the practice of copying models, is in fact one of the primary satirical targets of *Le Rouge et le Noir*. The author of this chronicle of 1830 shows no mercy in his depiction of a society he considered to have become stultified by a universal conformity to rules and models of behaviour.[61] In the first chapter of the novel, we read that all of the gardens of Verrières resemble each other; anyone who dares to diverge from the prototype earns 'une éternelle reputation *de mauvaise tête*' [a lasting reputation for being *wrong-headed*] (*Orc* I 354). Later, we discover that the Besançon seminarians are a homogenous bunch, distrustful of any who distinguish themselves from the herd. Later again, guests at the Parisian salon of M. de La Mole know never to mark themselves out by, for example, wearing boots after half past five in the evening or talking about politics. The second volume of the novel begins with a dialogue between two minor characters, one of whom, Saint-Giraud, initially left Paris because of 'cette comédie perpétuelle' [this perpetual role-playing] that he considers to characterize nineteenth-century civilization (*Orc* I 556), but having found the provinces to be just as hypocritical, he is returning to Paris to find some peace.

Against this backdrop, Madame de Rênal seems refreshingly original to many readers. The novel presents her as never having been exposed to novels, and therefore as oblivious to those models of behaviour that could otherwise afford her an insight into her situation. Jefferson has made a strong case for Madame de Rênal's inadvertent achievement of authentic subjectivity as a result of her ignorance of role models.[62] However, this devoted mother, who becomes a devoted lover of the young hero, does conform, albeit unknowingly, to a social type. The narrator remarks that 'Mme de Rênal était *une de ces femmes de province* que l'on peut très bien prendre pour des sottes pendant les quinze premiers jours qu'on les voit' [Mme de Rênal was *one of those provincial women* who might well strike you as foolish for a fortnight after the first meeting] (*Orc* I 381; my emphasis). In the publicity article that Stendhal wrote subsequent to the publication of *Le Rouge et le Noir*, he makes it clear that Madame de Rênal is representative of a broad social category, namely 'ces malheureuses femmes de province que l'amour a un peu compromises aux yeux de leurs voisines' [those unfortunate provincial women whose affairs of the heart have somewhat compromised them in the eyes of their female neighbours] (*Orc* I 822); she is 'une charmante femme comme il y en a beaucoup en province' [a charming woman, like so many who live in the provinces] (*Orc* I 831). Evidence of Madame de Rênal's lack of originality as a specifically literary character, too, is furnished by Stendhal's review of Claire de Duras's 1825 novel *Édouard*, for the *New Monthly Magazine*, a text from which, according to Alison Finch, he borrowed elements of *Le Rouge et le Noir*. Despite his praise for *Édouard* and its author in a November 1825 piece for the *London Magazine*, in this review, published the next month, Stendhal is caustic about Duras's heroine, whose situation and fate quite closely resemble those of Madame de Rênal:

> Edward, the hero of the story, who is not of noble extraction, becomes passionately enamoured of a widow of high birth. [...] [He] finds a glorious death in the field of battle. The noble widow, on learning his fate, sickens, and dies of love. What a triumph this for the *convenances*! What a lesson for tender and romantic young duchesses to beware of the approach of too captivating plebeians.[63]

That Madame de Rênal approximates a banal literary type is also suggested by a narratorial aside relating to the hero's incomprehension of Mathilde's behaviour: 'Julien, rempli de ses préjugés puisés dans les livres et dans les souvenirs de Verrières, poursuivait la chimère d'une maîtresse tendre et qui ne songe plus à sa propre existence du moment qu'elle a fait le bonheur de son amant' [Julien, filled with prejudices drawn from books and from his memories of Verrières, was pursuing the fantasy of a tender mistress who no longer thinks of her own existence from the moment she has made her lover happy] (*Orc* I 659–60).

Despite the unconscious conformity of Madame de Rênal to a social and literary stereotype, then, and notwithstanding Julien's habits of citation, identification with role models, and hypocrisy, it is Mathilde, of the novel's three main characters, whom critics associate most often with false or inauthentic behaviour. While the literary originality of the young Parisian has always been recognized, her moral character has overwhelmingly been considered derivative. To cite just one powerful proponent of this critical commonplace, Richard argues that the heroine exemplifies 'le *faux sublime*' [the *false sublime*]: she is less noble than Julien because more preoccupied with the imitation of nobility; her mimicry of past heroes is not then ultimately very different from the literary imitations indulged in by the majority of her peers.[64] However, the very thing that makes Mathilde seem so strangely affected, and that inspires such negative reactions, is also what makes her entirely her own invention. Mimicry, after all, defined as 'invention incessante' [incessant invention], is one of the categories of play outlined by Roger Caillois in *Les Jeux et les hommes* [*Man, Play, and Games*]; like Sartre, Caillois maintains that play and freedom are indissociable. His other three categories of play are risk-taking, fear, and competition. Mathilde indulges in all of these forms of activity.[65] Above all, though, Mathilde is a player because she is single-minded in the pursuit of her happiness, and in the exercise of her freedom to achieve that goal.[66]

The first reason why mimicry is an aspect of Mathilde's originality is that, as in Julien's case, the figures with whom she identifies — notably Marguerite de Valois and Stendhal's beloved Madame Roland — are themselves exceptional. The first was a princess and queen renowned for her passionate nature and her scandalous private life, while the second was a leading light of the French Revolution. That Mathilde chooses to associate herself with such extraordinary women is no doubt a result of the fact that, as the narrator archly comments, 'Le mérite personnel était à la mode dans sa tête' [To her mind, personal merit was fashionable] (*Orc* I 745).

A second reason why Mathilde's mimetic practice might be understood to contribute to rather than detract from her originality is a point on which, as we have seen, she is often criticized: her role models are anachronistic or seem otherwise incongruous. Madame Roland's republican politics during the French Revolution make her seem an inappropriate role model for one who identifies so closely with royalty, namely Marguerite, but also, obliquely, Catherine de' Medici, Medea, and even possibly Herodias.[67] Mathilde's Restoration France has, furthermore, almost as little in common with Stendhal's beloved sixteenth-century France, the home of Margot and her mother Catherine de' Medici, as it does with Medea's ancient Greece.

Thirdly, Mathilde emulates her chosen role models in an overt fashion rather than in the hypocritical, covert mode preferred by the male protagonist. It is no secret, for example, that on the last day of April every year the young woman wears black and mourns her ancestor Boniface de La Mole, historically the lover of Marguerite de Valois, who was executed for treason on that day in 1574. Unlike Julien, therefore, who carefully conceals his Napoleonic fantasy from the eyes of others, Mathilde flaunts her close personal identification with Queen Margot. Famously, after Julien's execution she assumes possession of his head, thereby reproducing, in spectacular style (if only for the eyes of Fouqué), the action attributed to her precursor. The theatrical, flamboyant style of Mathilde's identifications with her role models is itself an element of her originality.

Fourthly, as Beauvoir indirectly suggests, Mathilde's loyalty to her role models is unpredictable:

> Si Mathilde de la Mole demeure attachante, c'est qu'elle s'embrouille dans ses comédies et que souvent elle est en proie à son cœur dans les moments où elle croit le gouverner; elle nous touche dans la mesure où elle échappe à sa volonté.[68]

> [If Mathilde de La Mole remains endearing, it is because she becomes muddled in her roles and because often she is at the mercy of her heart at moments when she thinks she commands it; she moves us to the extent that she evades her will.]

In fact, Mathilde emulates women who themselves asserted their freedom by departing from norms or expectations. To copy such women in any meaningful way, that is, in any way that does more than merely replicate 'le fait matériel' [the physical fact] (*Orc* II 371), is also to assert one's freedom from prescribed modes of behaviour. For example, while Mathilde clearly departs from Madame Roland in her political affiliations, thereby adopting a looser relationship with her than one of simple imitation, she resembles her predecessor in her self-respect, natural authority, and intelligence. Mathilde emulates rather than copies her role models;[69] like Marguerite de Valois, the young woman is unusually intelligent and free-spirited, and falls for a man who distinguishes himself from the herd. However, Mathilde's relationship with Julien is far removed from that of her precursor with Boniface, not least because of the very different social and historical circumstances that are in play. And if the young Parisian does seem to copy Margot very directly in commemorating the decapitation of Boniface, and in secreting her own former lover's severed head, the second gesture at least is presented by the text as being itself extraordinary to the point of virtual inimitability; earlier in the text, Mathilde asks Julien: 'Quelle femme actuellement vivante n'aurait horreur de toucher à la tête de son amant décapité?' [What woman alive today would not be horrified to touch the head of her decapitated lover?] (*Orc* I 623) The reproduction of an inimitable deed is not a straightforward act of imitation. What Josiane Attuel says of Stendhal's narrative style could apply equally well to this heroine's style of being in the world: 'Inimitable, certes Stendhal l'est, imitateur non esclave, il l'est également.' [It is true that Stendhal is inimitable; but he is also a non-slavish imitator.][70]

As a result, then, of her choice of both exceptional and inappropriate role models, and of her both public and emulative style of role-playing, Mathilde's mimetic practice is an aspect of her originality. Attuel's stylistic analysis of *Le Rouge et le Noir* leads her to observe that the young heroine always returns to herself after her imitations of others, and dominates 'l'Autre' [the Other] by insisting on her 'moi'

[I].[71] For many critics, however, the heroine is condemned by the simple fact that, as the narrator observes, she needs an audience to play to: 'Il fallait toujours l'idée d'un public et *des autres* à l'âme hautaine de Mathilde' [The idea of an audience, of *other people*, was indispensable to Mathilde's imperious spirit] (*Orc* I 771). This statement is problematized by the text itself, when Mathilde's maid tells Julien that her mistress's ostentatious mourning of Boniface de La Mole is not actually intended to 'attirer les regards' [attract attention]; instead, 'Cette bizarrerie tenait au fond de son caractère' [This eccentricity stemmed from the depths of her character], testifying to her genuine love of La Mole (*Orc* I 622). Even if it were the case that Mathilde needs others to witness her performances, it seems unwise to condemn her character on this basis, particularly in view of Stendhal's own leanings towards the theatrical.

In fact, if *Le Rouge et le Noir* emphasizes the threat posed by other people, it also repeatedly shows that characters develop through their interaction with others. Madame de Rênal is very close to being a nonentity at the beginning of the novel; during the course of her relationship with Julien she discovers a facility for duplicity and a capacity for great passion. Mathilde's understanding of the self-transformation that can be brought about by entering into a relationship with another person is testified by her hesitation before deciding to take the risk of loving Julien. Like a particularly lucid version of the lover as theorized by Sartre, Mathilde realizes that she must impose a limit on her freedom in choosing to love the other person.[72] The manner in which her decision is framed emphasizes both her individuality and her identification with a strong heroine; she knows her 'moi' will survive even the cruellest crushing by another person: 'Quelles ne seront pas ses prétentions, si jamais il peut tout sur moi? Eh bien! je me dirai comme Médée: *Au milieu de tant de périls, il me reste MOI*' [Where will his claims end, if ever he holds me in his power? Well then! I shall say like Medea: *In the midst of so many dangers, I still have MYSELF*] (*Orc* I 645). If an individual's self can survive domination by another person, the novel also highlights the possibility of discovering oneself through interaction with others. Mathilde makes 'des découvertes dans son propre coeur' [discoveries about her own heart] while talking to Julien about her feelings (*Orc* I 664), and when talking to Madame de Rênal in the prison cell Julien has an intensified sense of being truly himself.

We have already evoked the numerous instances in Stendhal's work where the presence of *autrui* [the other person] solicits performances in which self-invention and self-discovery merge, moments of exhilarating performance in which the boundaries of the self become fluid. Julien's courtroom speech would appear to be one such instance. His speech is addressed to, and no doubt partly inspired by, an assembly of predominantly young and pretty females. We read that the hero spends twenty minutes expressing 'tout ce qu'il avait sur le cœur' [everything that weighed on his mind], provoking the women in the audience to tears and causing Madame Derville to faint (*Orc* I 782). Julien claims, in conversation with Mathilde the next day, that this was his first experience of improvisation (*Orc* I 785). While this is a debatable point, it is nevertheless true that the hero is usually guarded in the presence of other people. By contrast, the young heroine improvises almost constantly in the presence of other people.[73] So insistent is she on the spontaneity of her performances in public that she considers it in bad taste to voice her own insights moments after they have occurred to her. During Julien's simulated courtship of Madame de Fervaques, Mathilde surprises herself by asking him an indiscreet question about the nature of his relationship with this other woman; the narrator comments that 'Le hasard tout seul avait amené cette explosion' [Only chance had brought about this outburst] (*Orc* I 727).

Certainly, the clandestine nature of Mathilde's library visits and bedroom activities, along with her decision not to chase the Verrières-bound Julien down a Parisian street and her self-concealment in a gothic pilaster during his later trial, all indicate that she knows just as well as Julien how to elude the gaze of others. However, the pleasure that Mathilde can also derive from being the object of other people's attention testifies to a very different relationship with their gaze. The young heroine enjoys startling onlookers by her behaviour, as is nicely illustrated during the period when she has finally committed herself to Julien: in the evenings, she ostentatiously seeks out his company in a room full of noble guests, and then provocatively and openly discusses the history of revolutions with him. Mathilde is thrilled at the prospect of marrying a man who will place her firmly in the limelight: 'Compagne d'un homme tel que Julien, auquel il ne manque que de la fortune que j'ai, j'exciterai continuellement l'attention, je ne passerai point inaperçue dans la vie' [As the partner of a man like Julien, who lacks only wealth, which I can supply, I'll continually attract attention, I won't go through life unnoticed] (*Orc* I 667). The heroine habitually provokes and scandalizes the gaze of others instead of hiding from it. After confessing her pregnancy to her father, she tells him that should Julien happen to die she will mourn him very publicly, and proclaim herself his widow. Indeed, the narrator also notes that 'Sa grande, son unique ambition était de faire connaître son mariage' [Her great and sole ambition was to have her marriage recognized] (*Orc* I 745). Mathilde is even insistent on making her illegitimate pregnancy public knowledge. She only agrees to her father's order that she marry Julien privately rather than publicly because she knows the strain that poverty would put on their marriage. Instead then of adopting a defensive pose, as Julien habitually does, Mathilde makes a practice of actively soliciting the attention of other people. Darting around the streets of Besançon, Mathilde may not wish to be recognized as the daughter of the Marquis de La Mole, but she nevertheless makes a 'spectacle' of her suffering in the assumed guise of Julien's plebeian lover (*Orc* I 779). The text tells us that she does this partly with a view to whipping up public sympathy for Julien and partly because of her 'besoin secret d'étonner le public par l'excès de son amour et la sublimité de ses entreprises' [secret need to astonish the public by the exorbitant nature of her love and by the sublime character of her exploits] (*Orc* I 771).

One result of Mathilde's innate exhibitionism is that, even when the young woman is at her most sincere, and 'vraiment malheureuse' [truly miserable], she seems to Julien, as well as to many readers, to be acting (*Orc* I 638). While Mathilde's efforts to make a show of her grief in Besançon can be understood ironically to suggest the falseness of her attachment to Julien, there is nothing false about the heroine's self-disguise as Julien's anguished lover in Besançon, other than the circumstantial details of name and social class. After her discovery of Julien's correspondence with Madame de Fervaques, towards the end of the novel, the text repeatedly refers to her love in terms that suggest that what began as a false, ephemeral emotion may have become, for the heroine, something more real and more durable:

> Mathilde finit par s'impatienter de voir si peu l'homme qu'elle était parvenue à aimer réellement. (*Orc* I 745)
>
> [Mathilde ended up losing patience at seeing so little of the man she had reached the point of loving genuinely.]

> Son malaise moral, auprès de Mathilde, était d'autant plus décidé, qu'il lui inspirait en ce moment la passion la plus extraordinaire et la plus folle. (*Orc* I 770)
>
> [His moral unease, in Mathilde's company, was all the more marked because he currently inspired in her the maddest, most extraordinary passion.]

> Sa passion n'eut désormais ni bornes, ni mesure. (*Orc* I 772)[74]
>
> [Her passion henceforth knew no limits or proportions.]

Mathilde may derive a certain pleasure from her exhibitionism, but the suffering she displays is not necessarily negated by this pleasure. Similarly, the fact that Stendhal and his narrator refer to her love as 'amour de tête' [cerebral love] (*Orc* I 670, 836, 837) or 'amour parisien' [Parisian love], and contrast it with Madame de Rênal's 'amour vrai, simple, *ne se regardant pas soi-même*' [true, simple love, *not self-regarding*] (*Orc* I 836), does not mean that her love is null and void. It is true that passages such as the following tempt us to dismiss the possibility of the sincerity of the heroine's love:

> S'il meurt, je meurs après lui, se disait-elle avec toute la bonne foi possible. Que diraient les salons de Paris en voyant une fille de mon rang adorer à ce point un amant destiné à la mort? Pour trouver de tels sentiments, il faut remonter aux temps des héros. (*Orc* I 772)
>
> [If he dies, I'll die after him, she told herself with all possible sincerity. What would the Paris salons say, seeing a girl of my rank so enamoured of a lover destined for death? To find such feelings, you have to go back to the heroic age.]

However, what complicates the habitual assessment of Mathilde's love for Julien as a mere product of vanity is that she does not let any fear of ridicule affect her feelings for him. According to the author of *De l'Amour*, vanity is detrimental to love because it implies an aversion to the possibility of appearing ridiculous;[75] Mathilde is certainly open to that possibility. In addition, as the theorist of amorous *cristallisation*, a phenomenon outlined in *De l'Amour*, Stendhal believed even the most passionate love to have its origins in the mind and even arguably in narcissism.[76] Indeed, in his article on *Le Rouge et le Noir*, as well as expressing great pride in his depiction of what he calls Parisian love (*Orc* I 826, 836, 838), Stendhal remarks that any difference established by the novel between the two kinds of love, namely *amour vrai* and *amour de tête*, will be difficult to appreciate just a short distance beyond the French border, namely in Italy (*Orc* I 836). Stendhal also states that at least one aspect of the Parisian style of love described in *Le Rouge et le Noir*, namely the non-denial of boredom with one's lover, will seem 'tout simple' [very simple] to Italian readers, for whom 'le *naturel* dans les façons, dans les discours' [*naturalness* in behaviour and speech] is 'le *beau idéal*' [*ideal beauty*] (*Orc* I 826).

Just as the author's own air of disingenuousness led Mérimée and others to think of him as insincere, Mathilde's exhibitionist style may mislead us. Keen as she is to astonish other people, she does not worry about conforming to their expectations. As a result, the character in the novel who is most conspicuously attentive to the responses of other people is actually the least persecuted by the opinions of others. Far from being enslaved by others, she creates herself according to her own rules under their fascinated gaze. In other words, leaving aside for the moment Mathilde's great material advantage over Julien, she arguably evades the tyranny of other people far more successfully than he, by playing to them rather than hiding herself from their view.

One effect of Mathilde's (Stendhalian) strategy of provocation is the fact that others very frequently do not know what to make of her. Occasionally Julien sees her as a 'poupée parisienne' [Parisian doll] (*Orc* I 619) but at other times imagines that 'Mlle de La Mole fit exception' [Mademoiselle de La Mole was an exception] among the affected women of Paris (*Orc* I 622). The narrator remarks, early in Julien's relations with Mathilde, that the hero has enough sense to realize that he does not know her character, and that 'Tout ce qu'il en voyait pouvait n'être qu'une apparence' [Everything he saw of it could be mere appearance] (*Orc* I 636). Julien is startled to notice that, even while the heroine plays pious and royalist to perfection, she secretly reads Voltaire. He decides that Mathilde is 'inexplicable', but consoles himself that she is equally so for the man who intends to marry her (*Orc* I 638). The Marquis de Croisenois, indeed, struggles to make sense of his prospective fiancée, trusting in the possibility that her 'singularité' [singularity] might 'passer pour du génie' [pass off as genius] (*Orc* I 608). The hero's habit of misreading Mathilde is suggested at various points in the novel, as for example when he mistakenly decides that the love she seems to have for him has been copied from the actress Léontine Fay, or that her courtship of him is in fact a plot organized by her, her brother, and her lover with the aim of mystifying him and making him look ridiculous; or when he imagines that her supply of ropes and her 'sang-froid' upon his first visit to her bedroom indicate that she is in the habit of inviting men to her bedroom (*Orc* I 654). The narrator also tells us, at a later stage in their relationship, that 'Il ne comprenait nullement le caractère de la personne singulière que le hasard venait de rendre maîtresse absolue de tout son bonheur' [He understood nothing whatsoever about the character of the unusual person whom chance had made his absolute mistress, reigning over all his happiness] (*Orc* I 678).

Mathilde is indeed a very difficult character to comprehend; like Julien, she is presented as contradictory.[77] However, while the hero tends to be interpreted as admirable despite much evidence to the contrary, the heroine is far more often understood by critics to be flawed, despite the text's repeated confirmation of her great merit. A sympathetic reading of Mathilde reveals that occasional narratorial imputations of coldness, prudence, and shallowness to her character tend to be made in contexts that are particularly revealing of her passion, imprudence, and depth of character, and that consequently render such judgements highly suspect. For example, the chapter in which she is accused by the narrator of being 'saturée de [...] prudence sèche' [drenched in [...] arid prudence] (*Orc* I 769) begins with her arrival for the first time in Julien's prison cell, having travelled without a passport, in attention-grabbing disguise, under an assumed name. When Julien tries to send her home to her father in the interest of her future happiness and reputation, she mocks his prudence and explains that, by paying off the prison guard, and then revealing her identity and claiming the status of wife, she has obtained daily access to his cell. Mathilde then spends a week running around Besançon, in disguise, bribing solicitors and seeking an audience with the all-powerful Abbé de Frilair, whom she finally meets, alone in the bishop's palace, despite her initial terror at the very idea of him, all with a view to saving the father of her unborn, illegitimate child from the guillotine. The chapter ends shortly after the passage alleging Mathilde's cold prudence. The next chapter begins with the statement that, on leaving the bishop's palace, she unhesitatingly writes a self-compromising letter to her former pseudo-rival, Madame de Fervaques, asking her to help further Frilair's ambitions in the interest of saving Julien; the narrator remarks that she had the 'prudence' not to tell Julien about the various risks she was taking (*Orc* I 770). It seems difficult, given the textual context, not to see irony or injustice in the narrator's attribution of cold prudence to Mathilde.

Mathilde's resistance to easy categorization is related to her refusal to conform to those models of behaviour prescribed by 'la sagesse vulgaire' [ordinary wisdom] and '[les] idées reçues' [generally accepted ideas] (*Orc* I 643). Ironically, she seems to feel most bound by 'le devoir' [duty] and 'les convenances' [conventions] when she receives Julien in her bedroom for the first time and feels obliged to reward him for his intrepidity (*Orc* I 657). The young heroine far more usually refuses to let her behaviour be predetermined by the expectations of others, as demonstrated by the fact that she has the 'hardiesse si inconvenante, si imprudente' [so unseemly and imprudent boldness] to write love letters to young men of her acquaintance, by her decision to risk 'un déshonneur éternel' [eternal dishonour] in initiating a correspondence with Julien (*Orc* I 645) — who notes that 'Quatre cents salons retentiraient demain de sa honte, et avec quel plaisir!' [Four hundred salons would ring out with her shame tomorrow, and with great pleasure!] (*Orc* I 650) — , and by her delight in finding herself pregnant out of wedlock, despite the obvious risk to her reputation.

Above and beyond her defiance of the restrictions that others would place on her freedom, however, Mathilde is careful not to limit her own future possibilities, feeling disgust at the thought of a too predictable future:

> Je sais d'avance tout ce que me dirait le pauvre marquis, tout ce que j'aurais à lui répondre. Qu'est-ce qu'un amour qui fait bâiller? autant vaudrait être dévote. J'aurais une signature de contrat comme celle de la cadette de mes cousines. (*Orc* I 629)

> [I know in advance everything the poor marquis would say to me, and everything I'd say back to him. What kind of a love is it that makes you yawn? I might as well turn to religion. I would have a ceremonial signing of the contract, like my youngest cousin.]

Mathilde is attracted to the idea that Julien will bring 'l'*inconnu*' [the *unknown*] and '[le] hasard' [chance] into her life (*Orc* I 645, 630; see also *Orc* I 749). It is in the context of her love of uncertainty that we can understand her contempt for prescribed modes of behaviour, such as duels, where 'Tout en est su d'avance, même ce que l'on doit dire en tombant' [Everything about it is known in advance, even down to what you have to say as you fall] (*Orc* I 644), as well as her enthusiasm for 'l'imprévu' [the unexpected] (*Orc* I 631). Mathilde herself is highly unpredictable, regularly surprising Julien in the library, often after entering it through a hidden door.[78] Even Mathilde's susceptibility to fluctuations in her feelings for Julien, a habit that earns her the label of 'cette folle' [that madwoman] from him (*Orc* I 681) and the censure of many literary critics, can be understood as evidence, if further evidence were necessary, of her unwillingness to subscribe to expected models of behavior, or to circumscribe herself within the parameters of a conventional love plot. Unlike Julien, who tries to deny the capricious character of his own amorous attachments by claiming that he has loved only one woman all along, Mathilde openly acknowledges the inconstancy of her early feelings for Julien: 'Je ne vous aime plus, monsieur, mon imagination folle m'a trompée...' [I don't love you any more, sir, my mad imagination has deceived me...] (*Orc* I 678) Mathilde's passion for all that is unexpected is reflected in the fact that a decisive turning-point in her relationship with Julien arises from an accidental event, namely her sudden realization that she has inadvertently drawn a likeness of him. The fact that the portrait produced by accident resembles Julien far more closely than any she subsequently attempts to produce by design enchants her: 'elle y vit une preuve évidente de grande passion' [she took it as clear proof of a great passion] (*Orc* I 669).

Mathilde's love of the unpredictable is further evidenced in the text by her association with the idea of gambling, a theme that is evoked in the novel's title.[79] The epigraph to one chapter evokes the 'besoin de jouer' [need to gamble] that led her role model, Marguerite de Valois, to risk her precious reputation (*Orc* I 630). The narrator informs us that 'c'était l'imprudence que Mathilde aimait dans ses correspondances. Son plaisir était de jouer son sort' [imprudence was what Mathilde relished in her letter-writing. She delighted in gambling with her fate] (*Orc* I 627) and that 'Rien ne pouvait lui donner quelque agitation et la guérir d'un fond d'ennui sans cesse renaissant que l'idée qu'elle jouait à croix ou pile son existence entière' [Nothing could cause her a degree of agitation and cure her of an always resurgent background boredom but the idea that her entire existence was staked on the flip of coin] (*Orc* I 660).

The young heroine's love of risk is inseparable from her passion for danger. She directs her admiration, for example, towards figures who incarnate 'le danger solitaire, singulier, imprévu, vraiment laid' [danger that is solitary, out of the ordinary, unforeseen, and genuinely ugly] (*Orc* I 644), such as Boniface and Marguerite, or the young sixteenth-century woman she has read about, who stabbed her husband to reward him for his infidelity (*Orc* I 623). The narrator describes her eyes as 'étincelants de génie et d'enthousiasme' [sparkling with brilliance and enthusiasm] when she talks about the heroism of the sixteenth century (*Orc* I 623), a time (revered by Stendhal as much as by Mathilde) when 'La vie d'un homme était une suite de hasards' [A man's life was a succession of risks] (*Orc* I 644). Danger is actively sought out by Mathilde primarily as an antidote to her boredom: 'S'exposer au danger élève l'âme et la sauve de l'ennui où mes pauvres adorateurs semblent plongés, et il est contagieux cet ennui' [Exposing yourself to danger elevates the soul and saves it from the boredom that seems to consume my poor admirers; and this boredom is catching] (*Orc* I 627–28; see also *Orc* I 634, 661–62). Even after Julien's supposed subjugation of her, Mathilde 'voulait s'exposer avec témérité à tous les dangers que son amour pouvait lui faire courir' [wanted to confront with temerity all the dangers with which her love might present her] (*Orc* I 735). A need to expose herself to danger is presented by the narrator as foremost in the young heroine's character: 'Le courage était la première qualité de son caractère' [Courage was the foremost quality in her character] (*Orc* I 660).

Like Margot, then, Mathilde feels '*Le besoin d'anxiété*' [The need for anxiety] (*Orc* I 630). The notion of anguish or anxiety is, in fact, frequently evoked in connection with the young heroine: she experiences 'angoisse' [anguish] at the idea of writing to Julien (*Orc* I 645), whom she associates with the dreaded figure of Danton, and feels 'toutes les angoisses de la timidité la plus extrême' [all of the anguish of extreme shyness], and 'de longues incertitudes' [lengthy bouts of uncertainty] when her courage is, unusually, in abeyance (*Orc* I 655, 657). The wilful recklessness of her actions occasionally torments her involuntary sense of feminine modesty, while the conflict between her sense of personal 'devoir' [duty] and the modesty 'qu'une femme se doit à elle-même' [that a woman owes to herself] subjects her to 'la violence affreuse' [terrible violence] (*Orc* I 657, 658). The hero eventually discovers that he can make Mathilde's appetite for anxiety work to his advantage: 'la tenir toujours occupée de ce grand doute: m'aime-t-il?' [keep this great question always hanging over her: does he love me?] (*Orc* I 731) A need for uncertainty is thus the heroine's weakness; but it is also bound up with her choice of freedom. Mathilde's rejection of all that is safe and predictable, and her embrace of 'l'immensité de la difficulté à vaincre et la noire incertitude de l'événement' [the immensity of the difficulty to be overcome and the dark uncertainty of the outcome] (*Orc* I 630), are bound up with her awareness of her fundamental freedom. For Sartre, *angoisse* [angst] arises from the recognition of one's freedom, now or in the future, to overthrow one's current projects, and even one's chosen way of being in the world: '[L]a liberté qui se manifeste par l'angoisse se caractérise par une obligation perpétuellement renouvelée de refaire le *Moi* qui désigne l'être libre.' [The freedom manifested by angst is characterized by a perpetually renewed obligation to remake the *I* associated with the free being.][80] Beauvoir, indeed, notes the presence of angst in Stendhal's heroines, and presents it as testament to their assumption of individual freedom: they experience 'la constante tension d'une liberté sans appui' [the constant tension of a crutchless freedom].[81] Beauvoir only grudgingly includes Mathilde among Stendhal's laudable females, but she does praise her enthusiasm for insecurity: 'Elle risque cette estime de soi à quoi elle tient plus qu'à la vie.' [She risks that self-respect that she treasures more than life.][82] For Stendhal, an openness to risk is closely linked to the *faculté de vouloir* that is so closely linked to freedom in his work: 'Vouloir, c'est avoir le courage de s'exposer à un inconvénient; s'exposer ainsi, c'est tenter le hasard, c'est jouer.' [To want is to have the courage to take a risk; to act in this way is to gamble on chance, and to play.][83]

Mathilde's openness to risk suggests that she is not as vain as she is often understood to be. Vanity connotes, in Stendhal's work, an excessive preoccupation with one's reputation and a fear of other people's opinions; it is in this sense that the author considered vanity to be the unique passion of the nineteenth century, and particularly of nineteenth-century France.[84] Vanity is thus very different from narcissism in Stendhal's textual world. Narcissism is a trait common to several of his male protagonists, which suggests that it is not incompatible with the author's preferred brand of heroism: Fabrice consults his mirror reflection immediately after stabbing a rival to death, Octave's fantasized private space is equipped with three tall mirrors, while Julien takes evident pleasure in glimpsing his effect on women. In addition, as Blin notes, even the least vain of Stendhal's heroines are not immune to 'toute hantise du "paraître"' [all worry about appearances],[85] as testified by Madame de Rênal's instinctual wearing of revealing dresses in Julien's presence.

Narcissism is not in itself a hanging offence, then, in Stendhal's fiction. Vanity is far less appealing because, as already mentioned, it is habitually accompanied by a fear of ridicule. An intimate link between vanity and the fear of ridicule can be seen very clearly for example in the character of M. de Rênal:

> M. de Rênal repris par la vanité blessée se rappelait laborieusement tous les moy-ens cités au billard du *Casino* ou *Cercle noble* de Verrières, quand quelque beau parleur interrompt la poule pour s'égayer aux dépens d'un mari trompé. Com-bien, en cet instant, ces plaisanteries lui paraissaient cruelles! (*Orc* I 462–63)[86]

> [Monsieur de Rênal, seized again by wounded vanity, laboriously recalled all the methods quoted in the billiard room of the *Casino* or *Noble Circle* of Verrières, when some fine orator would interrupt the game to have some fun at the expense of a cuckolded husband. How cruel these jokes seemed to him now!]

Monsieur de Rênal's vanity is qualitatively different from the narcissism that is often found in Stendhal's heroes and heroines, because his vanity is inseparable from a fear of being held in contempt by others.

Stendhal's Amazons care little about being disparaged by others. The fear of seeming ridiculous is certainly alien to Mathilde, who actively seeks out intense emotional experiences. She is far less concerned to win the esteem of others than she is to maintain her own high opinion of herself and to surprise and disorient others, in a manner similar to those artists who would later conspire to *épater le bourgeois*, or shake up middle-class attitudes. Certainly, she wishes to attract attention, but this is less because she wants to be admired by others than because she wants to avoid being '[u]ne fille ordinaire' [an ordinary girl] or 'une poupée' [a doll] (*Orc* I, 667, 668). Similarly, while vanity surely plays a part in Mathilde's relief when she realizes that she will not have to assume the name of Madame Sorel, live in poverty, and be exposed to 'ridicule' (*Orc* I 749), her vanity is not so great that it precludes her from jeopardizing her future standing in society by staying in Besançon during Julien's imprisonment, by visiting him regularly in his cell, by making no secret of her real identity either to the court official or to Frilair, or by pleading Julien's case to 'sa rivale' [her rival], Madame de Fervaques herself: 'la crainte de se compromettre ne l'arrêta pas une seconde' [fear of compromising herself did not hold her back for a second] (*Orc* I 770). Julien is forced to beg her — unsuccessfully — to resign herself to the kind of happiness that can be derived from 'la considération, les richesses, le haut rang' [esteem, wealth, high rank] (*Orc* I 765). But, as she has already told her father, 'Ces plaisirs de considération et de petite vanité sont nuls pour moi' [These pleasures of esteem and petty vanity are non-existent for me] (*Orc* I 745).

It might be argued that Mathilde resembles the vain Madame de Fervaques to the extent that the latter adopts 'une façon de vivre tout ambitieuse d'effet sur le public' [a way of life whose goal was to make an impression on people] (*Orc* I 723); but there are crucial differences between the two. Madame de Fervaques, described by the narrator as being possessed of 'une vanité de parvenue, maladive et qui s'offensait de tout' [an unhealthy, socially aspirational kind of vanity, which takes offence at everything] (*Orc* I 723), lives in constant watchful fear — she is described as 'cette âme *qui craignait tout*' [this soul *who was fearful of everything*] (*Orc* I 723) — of being ridiculed for her bourgeois origins. Mathilde, by contrast, worries only about not respecting herself. In fact, the only 'mépris' [scorn] feared by the latter appears to be Julien's (see *Orc* I 725). Madame de Fervaques puts on an act as a means of controlling how others think of her, while Mathilde performs roles in public for her own pleasure only. Mathilde may have all of the *hauteur* [aloofness] and *orgueil* [pride] that come naturally to the established nobility, but she does not identify so closely with her social class that she cannot depart from her preordained role.[87]

Mathilde's alleged vanity comes to the fore in the chapter entitled 'Quelle est la décoration qui distingue?' [What decoration distinguishes a person?], which is the first chapter in which the heroine's point of view predominates. Here, in what is numerically the central chapter of the novel, the heroine herself is more or less explicitly marked out as distinguished. Her distinction is suggested not just by the fact that she is described therein as 'la plus séduisante personne du bal' [the most attractive person at the ball] (*Orc* I 609), as 'l'une des plus belles personnes de Paris' [one of the most beautiful women in Paris] (*Orc* I 608), and twice as 'la reine du bal' [the queen of the ball] (*Orc* I 605, 610), or even because she is portrayed in that chapter as wittier than all in her entourage, her fiancé observing that 'Mathilde a de la singularité' [Mathilde is unusual] and that she possesses the 'distinction' conferred by 'le génie' [genius] (*Orc* I 608). The heroine distinguishes herself, above all, with her own *bon mot*, in this chapter, about what marks a person out from the herd: 'Je ne vois que la condamnation à mort qui distingue un homme, pensa Mathilde, c'est la seule chose qui ne s'achète pas' [The only thing I can think of that distinguishes a man is the death sentence, Mathilde thought; it's the only thing that can't be bought] (*Orc* I 607). Her witticism inspires the chapter's title and becomes the implied basis not only of her admiration for Julien — perceived by her, at this point, merely as 'pas exactement comme un autre' [not exactly like everyone else] (*Orc* I 603) — but also of much of the admiration that readers direct towards the hero. With this insight, as well as her subsequent meditation on the energy deficit prevalent in the upper classes, the young heroine voices the author's own ideas.[88] While the narrator remarks that the heroine's vanity leads her to revel in her own cleverness, he also informs us of her unwillingness to garner admiration by repeating her witticism aloud:

> Mathilde avait trop de goût pour amener dans la conversation un bon mot fait d'avance; mais elle avait aussi trop de vanité pour ne pas être enchantée d'elle-même. Un air de bonheur remplaça dans ses traits l'apparence de l'ennui. (*Orc* I 607)

> [Mathilde had too much taste to bring into her conversation a witticism prepared in advance; but she was also too vain not to be enchanted with herself. An air of happiness replaced, on her face, the appearance of boredom.]

Mathilde is not vain, then, in the usual Stendhalian sense; more interested in discovering proof of her own brilliance than in impressing it upon others, she is her own greatest admirer. This, then, is vanity as narcissistic self-love, or alternatively vanity understood as pride, rather than the kind of vanity that Stendhal associates with the fear of ridicule. Furthermore, when Mathilde's discovery of Altamira's noble origins drives a large hole through her theory about the impossibility of energy in the upper classes, she laughs at herself, thereby demonstrating a flexibility and self-deprecatory humour that is not ordinarily present in Stendhal's vain characters: 'Je suis donc prédestinée à déraisonner ce soir. Puisque je ne suis qu'une femme comme une autre, eh bien, il faut danser' [So I'm predestined to think nonsense this evening. Since I'm just a woman like any other, well, I'll have to dance] (*Orc* I 610). The heroine's brand of vanity takes the form of a strong sense of her own difference from and superiority over others; her desire to impress this superiority upon others is secondary to her desire to prove that superiority to herself.

There is one moment in this chapter when the heroine seems out of favour with the narrator. When she makes a display of her erudition in front of a disapproving Julien, she is described as experiencing 'la première jouissance de la pédanterie' [the first thrill of pedantry] and as 'ivre de son savoir' [intoxicated with her knowledge]; she is also compared derisively to a misguided 'académicien' [Academician] (*Orc* I 606). However, Stendhal admits in his private writings to his own 'orgueilleuse pédanterie' [proud pedantry] (*OI* I 394; *Journal*, 9 March 1806), which he considers the worst fault conceivable in the France of his time, to the extent that it wounds the vanity of others.[89] He also notes that he must cure himself of his 'pédantisme' [pedantism] so that he might be 'celui de tous les écrivains qui aura le moins offensé la vanité de mes lecteurs' [among all writers, the one who will have least offended the vanity of my readers] (*OI* I 91; *Journal*, 5 July 1804). Pedantry is never presented by Stendhal as an attractive quality; however, it is presented by him less as an effect of vanity than as an assault on the vanity of others.

For this reason, pedantry poses a particular problem for women. The author of *De l'Amour* claims that any man would rather spend his life with a servant than an intellectual woman, and describes the female pedant, defined as a woman who has become conscious of her superiority over other women, as the most disagreeable and degraded creature in existence.[90] If there is irony in these observations, it is very subtle; indeed, Stendhal's letters to his sister repeatedly exhort her to hide her brilliance in the interest of the vanity of others and her reputation in society.[91] Nevertheless, the author expresses scorn, in *Racine et Shakespeare*, for women who, out of fear of being ridiculed for resembling the heroines of Molière's *Femmes savantes*, confine themselves to frivolous pleasures. He also pours high praise on any woman whose lack of vanity leads her to reject these pleasures and brave public ridicule, claiming that such a woman, who seems 'singulière' [singular] to all around her, is 'la seule digne d'être aimée' [the only one worthy of being loved].[92] Thus, in a chapter which begins with a question about how to recognize distinction, pedantry might be understood not as an indictment of Mathilde's character but as yet another sign of her distinction, and even of her lack of vanity.

A small number of characters in *Le Rouge et le Noir* share Mathilde's playful or unserious attitude, to the extent that they do not allow themselves to be circumscribed by any externally imposed rules or values, and give themselves the freedom to change the rules they impose upon themselves.[93] The witty Count Chalvet, for example, a very minor figure encountered in the Hôtel de La Mole and described by the narrator as 'l'homme le plus fin du siècle' [the subtlest man of his century], declares himself politically independent on the basis that he is liable to change his mind: he refuses to be tyrannized by his own opinion (*Orc* I 581). The narrator informs us that the Marquis de La Mole himself is not dominated by but 'campé au milieu de ses richesses actuelles' [lodged in the midst of his current wealth], and that his imagination 'avait préservé son âme de la gangrène de l'or' [had protected his soul from the gangrene of gold] (*Orc* I 746). Mathilde, however, is the character in *Le Rouge et le Noir* who best exemplifies that resistance to serious-mindedness that existentialism associates with freedom.

Certainly, the young heroine is capable of a 'sérieux profond qu'aucune de ses rivales ne pouvait imiter' [profound seriousness that none of her rivals could imitate] (*Orc* I 609; see also *Orc* I 636); however, she is averse to the freedom-denying seriousness that characterizes her peers. It is precisely to avoid prudent or serious role-playing, for example as the wife of the Marquis de Croisenois, that Mathilde chooses to play more exhilarating roles. The antithesis of Mathilde's risk-taking, happiness-seeking attitude is the seriousness that Sartre and Beauvoir associate with alienation, or the identification with inanimate things. Such seriousness is the dominant feature of evenings at the Hôtel de La Mole, 'la patrie du bâillement et du raisonnement' [the land of yawns and tedious arguments] (*Orc* I 565), governed by 'l'asphyxie morale' [mental asphyxia] (*Orc* I 577) and populated by ambitious men, affected women, and 'les jeunes gens graves' [solemn young men] (*Orc* I 581), 'où l'on avait peur de tout, et où il n'était convenable de plaisanter de rien' [where everything was a cause for fear, and where it was not seemly to joke about anything] (*Orc* I 625). The life of the Hôtel's habitués is, according to Mathilde, 'emprisonnée comme une momie d'Égypte, sous une enveloppe toujours commune à tous, toujours la même' [imprisoned like an Egyptian mummy, inside an outer casing that was the same for all, and unchanging] (*Orc* I 644). While Julien's unpredictable temper marks him out, in Mathilde's eyes, from the prudent and predictable men who surround her, he is arguably at least as circumscribed as they by social rules. He is, after all, envied by other fashionable young men for his impassivity, 'cette mine froide et à *mille lieues de la sensation présente*' [that cold look, *utterly removed from present sensation*] (*Orc* I 599). Mathilde notes that even after losing his provincial manner, his conversation retains 'encore trop de sérieux, trop de positif' [still too much seriousness, too much pragmatism], and that 'il regardait encore trop de choses comme importantes' [he still regarded too many things as important] (*Orc* I 602). When he has arrived at the zenith of his career, suddenly finding himself a titled lieutenant, he is admired by others in the regiment for his great seriousness.

Throughout *Le Rouge et le Noir*, Julien's heroic instincts have to struggle against his cautiousness, most explicitly in the war he has to wage with himself when Fouqué offers him a secure job.[94] While critics tend to highlight the impetuous aspect of Julien's character,[95] he is often described by the narrator as prudent, and is in many respects just as prudent as those whom Mathilde disdains, as testified for example by his preference for communicating 'commodément' [conveniently] in person rather than engaging in the 'imprudence abominable' [abominable act of imprudence] of her preferred mode of communication: letter-writing (*Orc* I 648, 649). He demonstrates his 'prudence diplomatique' [diplomatic caution] (*Orc* I 643) by quoting Mathilde's own audacious declaration of love in his written reply to her, and by making a copy of her letter in order to ward off possible public ridicule. He copies her second and third letters also, then hides them in a Voltaire volume in the library and sends the originals to Fouqué along with an explanatory document, to be opened and published in the event of his death. The differing levels of prudence of Julien and Mathilde are illustrated in the account of a heavy bunch of her hair landing on his hands just as those hands attempt to erase any imprint of a ladder on the flower bed below her bedroom; one character makes a deliberate trace of their night together while the other attempts to efface all trace of their meeting. Subsequently, at lunch, Mathilde displays the shorn side of her head for all to see, and even calls Julien her master, while he blushes at her imprudence. Similarly, his later desire to be put to death in order to settle his accounts with humanity, as he puts it, is in marked contrast with Mathilde's view of the death sentence as the only thing that eludes the logic of commerce, a logic associated by Stendhal with bourgeois seriousness and prudence. Julien's seriousness can, of course, be explained in part by his social situation, very different from that of Mathilde, whose wealth and status mean that she enjoys what Ansel calls 'l'immunité sociale' [social immunity].[96] Play, as Caillois reminds us, is an 'activité de luxe' [luxury activity]: 'Qui a faim ne joue pas.' [Hungry people do not play.][97] In blaming his hypocrisy on his poverty, though, as he does (*Orc* I 623), Julien fails to take responsibility for his own choice of strategy.[98] He does not embrace his freedom as Mathilde does.

This chapter has argued that the young heroine of *Le Rouge et le Noir* is the most powerful exponent of Stendhalian freedom in that novel. The next chapter will argue that the young heroine of *Lamiel* presents a similar model of freedom, despite her far more modest social circumstances. While Lamiel's starting position is far closer to Julien's than to Mathilde's, she has none of the debilitating seriousness of her male precursor; her voice can already be heard in the words Stendhal wrote in a letter of 1834 to his friend Romain Colomb: 'Rien ne me semble bête, au monde, comme la gravité...' [Nothing in the world seems as stupid to me as gravity...] (*Cg* V 237).

Notes to Chapter 2

1. See Stendhal, *Romans et nouvelles*, II, 153–54, 257, 420–22.
2. Stendhal, *Lamiel*, in *Œuvres complètes*, ed. by Victor Del Litto and Ernest Abravanel, 50 vols (Geneva: Cercle du Bibliophile, 1967–1974), XLIV (1971), 135. Henceforth *L* followed by page number.
3. *L'Œil vivant* (Gallimard, 1961), pp. 222, 225.
4. *Gender Trouble: Feminism and the Subversion of Identity* (London: Routledge, 1990), p. 142. I have discussed Stendhalian theatricality and explored some of the issues raised in this chapter in 'Performing Desire: Stendhal's Theatrical Heroines', *French Studies*, 62 (2008), 259–70, and 'Comédie et liberté chez Stendhal: Une étude de ses actrices', *L'Année stendhalienne*, 11 (2012), 217–31. In this chapter, as in those articles, the heroines are not considered specifically from the perspective of their (often subversive) performances of gender, though there is much in Stendhal's writing to support an analysis informed by Butler's ideas, as indicated in Catherine Authier and Lucy Garnier, 'Giuditta Pasta, le travestissement et la "féminité" chez Stendhal', *L'Année stendhalienne*, 8 (2009), 117–38.
5. Deguise writes that Sartrean authenticity and Stendhalian *naturel*, while far from being identical, are intimately linked. 'Stendhal et Sartre.'
6. *L'Être et le néant*, pp. 105, 669–70.
7. *L'Être et le néant*, p. 125. Unfortunately, he did not take his analysis of playfulness very far; it appears as a short digression in *L'Être et le néant*.
8. 'Les Murs et l'emprisonnement dans *Le Rouge et le Noir*', *Stendhal Club*, 25.100 (1983), 449–63 (pp. 459, 460).
9. *Stendhal, Balzac et le féminisme romantique*, p. 38.
10. *La Poétique du mâle* (Paris: Gallimard, 1982), p. 362. Coquillat maintains that female readers consequently have no option but to identify with the disappointingly docile Madame de Rênal. In fact, a minority of readers, from Malraux onwards, have expressed strong approval of Mathilde. See for example Michel Guérin, *La Politique de Stendhal: Les Brigands et le bottier* (Paris: Presses Universitaires de France, 1982) and Coudert, 'Mathilde mal aimée'. The critical reception of Mathilde will be the subject of a separate study.
11. Mitchell, *Stendhal*, p. 61.
12. *Stendhal et les problèmes de la personnalité* (Paris: Corti, 2001 [1958]), p. 76.
13. 'En relisant *Lamiel*', in Stendhal, *Lamiel*, ed. by Jean-Jacques Hamm (Paris: Flammarion, 1993), pp. 21–37 (p. 37).
14. *L'Être et le néant*, pp. 276–77.
15. *L'Œil vivant*, p. 221.
16. *De l'Amour*, p. 265 ('Fragments divers', 92)
17. *Variété II* (Paris: Gallimard, 1930), pp. 85–86.
18. Bardèche speculates that it was Stendhal's recognition of the social necessity of hypocrisy that led him to attend the actor Dugazon's declamation classes on a frequent basis. *Stendhal romancier*, pp. 27–28.
19. *Fiction and the Themes of Freedom*, p. 91.
20. See Maria Scott, 'Stendhal's Muddy Realism', *Dix-Neuf*, 16.1 (2012), 15–27.
21. *Littérature et sensation* (Paris: Seuil, 1954), p. 49.
22. *L'Être et le néant*, p. 669.
23. *Littérature et sensation*, p. 49.
24. The word 'stendhaliser' is intended to suggest 'scandaliser' [to scandalize].
25. *Littérature et sensation*, p. 50. Gérard Genette says something similar: 'Le paradoxe de l'égotisme est à peu près celui-ci: parler de soi, de la manière la plus indiscrète et la plus impudique, peut être le meilleur moyen de se dérober. L'égotisme est, dans tous les sens du terme, une parade.' [The paradox of the egotist is more or less this: talking about oneself, in the most indiscreet and shameless way, can be the best way to hide oneself from view. Egotism is, in all senses of the term, a parade.] *Figures II*, p. 157.
26. *Variété II*, p. 102.

27. For Sartre, who quotes Valéry's essay on Stendhal, any attempt to be sincere stems from bad faith, and is incompatible with one's freedom. *L'Être et le néant*, pp. 102–11.

28. Louis Desroches [Arnould Frémy], 'Souvenirs anecdotiques sur M. de Stendhal', *Revue de Paris*, February 1844, reproduced in *Stendhal: Mémoire de la critique*, ed. by Michel Crouzet and others (Paris: Presses de l'Université de Paris-Sorbonne, 1996), pp. 219–37 (p. 223).

29. *HB suivi de XIX lettres à Stendhal* (Geneva: Slatkine Reprints, 1998), pp. 23–24.

30. *De l'Amour*, pp. 96–99 (chapter 32), 139 (chapter 41). On the proximity of ridiculousness and naturalness in Stendhal's heroines, see Pierrette Pavet-Jörg, 'Le Temps des héroïnes stendhaliennes', in *Le Dernier Stendhal 1837–1842*, ed. by Michel Arrous (Paris: Eurédit, 2000), pp. 207–31.

31. *Stendhal et les problèmes de la personnalité*, p. 270.

32. Jules Barbey d'Aurevilly, 'Stendhal' (1856), in Émile Talbot, *La Critique stendhalienne de Balzac à Zola* (York, SC: French Literature Publications Company, 1979), pp. 198–208 (p. 201). Starobinski refers, in his study of Stendhal, to 'un naturel au second degré' [an alternative kind of naturalness], composed rather than disclosed. *L'Œil vivant*, p. 222.

33. Francesco Spandri, *L'Art de Komiker': Comédie, théâtralité et jeu chez Stendhal* (Paris: Champion, 2003), pp. 124–25; Manzini, *Stendhal's Parallel Lives*.

34. *Le Héros fourbe*, p. 95.

35. *Littérature et sensation*, p. 69. For similar criticism of Mathilde's choice of anachronistic role models, see Constans, *Les Problèmes de la condition féminine*, II, 809–10 and John West Sooby, 'La Société et le jeu dans *Le Rouge et le Noir*', in *Stendhal: l'Écrivain, la société et le pouvoir* (Grenoble: Presses Universitaires de Grenoble, 1984), pp. 99–114 (p. 105). For West Sooby, who draws on the ideas of Roger Caillois, Julien is the supreme figure of the player in the novel, while Mathilde is a failed player. On Stendhal's love of the sixteenth century, see Michael Nerlich, 'Renaissance', in *Dictionnaire de Stendhal*, pp. 591–92.

36. *Stendhal's Parallel Lives*, pp. 295–98.

37. 'Julien Sorel: La Mort et le temps du bonheur', *Europe*, 519–21 (1972), 113–27 (pp. 116–17).

38. The inverted commas are intended as a reminder not only that the text is fictional but also that reality and pretence, sincerity and cynicism, are notoriously difficult to distinguish from one another in this novel. On Julien as an actor for whom even naturalness is a role, see Armand Hoog, 'Le "rôle" de Julien', *Stendhal Club*, 78 (1978), 131–42.

39. *Littérature et sensation*, p. 49. Bersani notes that 'Julien's readiness to repel insult is a characteristic worthy of a minor comic figure in realistic fiction'. *A Future for Astyanax*, p. 106.

40. *Littérature et sensation*, p. 70.

41. Bardèche, *Stendhal romancier*, pp. 195; Blin, *Stendhal et les problèmes de la personnalité*, p. 308.

42. *Metamorphoses of Passion*, p. 268.

43. *Stendhal: A Study of his Novels*, p. 127; *Stendhal's Violin: A Novelist and his Reader* (Oxford: Clarendon Press, 1988), p. 187.

44. See for example Hippolyte Taine, 'Stendhal (Henri Beyle)' (1864), in Talbot, *La Critique stendhalienne*, pp. 210–31 (p. 214); Yves Ansel, *Stendhal littéral: 'Le Rouge et le Noir'* (Paris: Kimé, 2001), pp. 50–57.

45. *L'Être et le néant*, p. 483. Felman's reading of the shooting is similar to that proposed here: Julien's 'agressivité' [aggressivity], responsible for both his shooting and his suicide, derives from a desire to kill the Other, because the Other sees him as a 'monstre' [monster]. *La 'Folie'*, p. 205. Crouzet, who describes Julien as 'un être de haine' [a creature of hatred], refers to 'son refus intrinsèque de l'autre' [his intrinsic refusal of the *other*]. '*Le Rouge et le Noir*', pp. 148, 124. Longstaffe presents a useful overview of critical interpretations of Julien's crime, noting that most commentators consider the crime either irrational or out of character, while some see it as 'a rational and deliberate act', and while others again 'see in Julien's act the only line of conduct allowing him to save his honour, the only possible demonstration that he is not the blackguard described in Madame de Rênal's letter'. *Metamorphoses of Passion*, p. 262. Longstaffe subscribes to the third group, arguing that Julien's crime can be understood as a vindication of his honour. See also Yves Ansel's synopsis and bibliography of critical responses to the shooting (*Orc* I 978). None of these more or less psychological interpretations exclude the ontological interpretation proposed here. For a similarly existentialist

though differently nuanced reading of the shooting, see Jones, *L'Ironie dans les romans de Stendhal*, p. 184.

46. *Stendhal et les problèmes de la personnalité*, pp. 65, 67. Laszlo K. Géfin notes that 'Despite his newfound love, Julien remains a hypocrite to the last, a borrowed persona self-consciously looking at himself in Napoleonic terms, even during his walk to the guillotine.' 'Auerbach's Stendhal: Realism, Figurality, and Refiguration', *Poetics Today*, 20.1 (1999), 27–40 (p. 38).

47. 'Peut-être [...] n'a-t-il que les apparences d'un homme supérieur?' [Perhaps [...] he only has the look of a superior being?] (*Orc* I 644)

48. *Reading the Romantic Heroine: Text, History, Ideology* (Ann Arbor: University of Michigan Press, 1985), pp. 103, 99. Josiane Attuel remarks that, in the prison cell, 'Mme de Rênal devient la prolongation de Julien sur terre, un second "moi".' [Mme de Rênal becomes the earthly extension of Julien, a second 'I'.] *Le Style de Stendhal: Efficacité et romanesque* (Bologna: Pàtron, 1980), p. 582.

49. Rabine persuasively argues that the stability of Julien's identity, and consequently the possibility of reader identification with his character, are undermined by his love for Mathilde. *Reading the Romantic Heroine*, p. 98. René Girard makes a very similar, though differently inflected, point. *Mensonge romantique et vérité romanesque* (Paris: Grasset, 1961), p. 96.

50. 'Stendhal entre Julia et Simone', *L'Année stendhalienne*, 8 (2009), 187–95.

51. Interestingly, the author of a study of irony in Stendhal's novels perceives no irony in the presentation of Julien's love for Madame de Rênal, seeing it as 'une passion intense et fatidique comme celle qui liait un Tristan et une Iseut' [an intense and fateful passion like the one that bound Tristan and Iseult]. Jones, *L'Ironie dans les romans de Stendhal*, p. 56. Marie Parmentier observes that in the scene describing Julien's departure from Verrières the narrator is 'ni ironique ni critique' [neither ironic nor critical]. *Stendhal stratège: Pour une poétique de la lecture* (Geneva: Droz, 2007), p. 161. Ironically Parmentier's study argues for the illusory sense of freedom produced by Stendhal's novelistic techniques, and the restrictions placed on the reader's actual interpretative freedom by those same techniques.

52. Rabine highlights the dishonesty of Julien's attempt to erase Mathilde from his script, and also points out that, by contrast with his despair when separated from Mathilde, he forgets Madame de Rênal very quickly when not in her presence. *Reading the Romantic Heroine*, pp. 101–02.

53. Bad faith, as understood by Sartre and Beauvoir, differs from hypocrisy in that the individual who acts in bad faith does so without admitting his or her pretence even to him or herself.

54. On this last point, see Moretti, *The Way of the World*, pp. 100–01. Moretti's more general argument that unnaturalness and parody are fundamental components of modern consciousness is pertinent in the context of this chapter, which holds that Stendhal and Mathilde, unlike Julien, achieve an outwardly false kind of authenticity.

55. 'Qu'est-ce qu'un personnage littéraire au féminin? (à propos de Louise de Rênal)', *HB. Revue internationale d'études stendhaliennes*, 4 (2000), 47–73 (p.49). For a sharp response to this strange essay, see Martine Reid, 'Sur le personnage féminin et Mme de Rênal. Réponse à Pierre Barbéris', *L'Année stendhalienne*, 8 (2009), 197–212.

56. Carol A. Mossman discusses the extent to which Julien's fate is narratologically over-determined. *The Narrative Matrix: Stendhal's 'Le Rouge et le Noir'* (Lexington, KY: French Forum, 1984).

57. *Stendhal: A Study of his Novels*, p. 117.

58. *Reading for the Plot*, pp. 71–72.

59. 'L'homme sérieux [...] s'est donné à lui-même le type d'existence du rocher, la consistance, l'inertie, l'opacité de l'être-au-milieu-du-monde.' [The serious man [...] has given to himself an existence like that of rock: consistency, inertia, the opacity of the being-in-the-midst-of-the-world.] *L'Être et le néant*, p. 669.

60. *La Politique de Stendhal: Les Brigands et le bottier* (Paris: Presses Universitaires de France, 1982), p. 68. Mathilde's assumption, within *Le Rouge et le Noir*, of the role of author is highlighted both in the third chapter of Mossman, *The Narrative Matrix* and in Lane Gormley, '"Mon roman est fini": Fabricateurs de romans et fiction intratextuelle dans *Le Rouge et le Noir*', *Stendhal Club*, 21 (1979), 129–38.

61. For West Sooby, the novel associates obedience to rules and norms with the ludic attitude of the society it depicts. 'La Société et le jeu'.

62. *Reading Realism in Stendhal*, pp. 81–86.

63. Stendhal, *Chroniques pour l'Angleterre: Contributions à la presse britannique*, ed. by Renée Dénier and Keith G. McWatters, 8 vols (Grenoble: ELLUG, 1980–95), V, 360; III, 204. See Alison Finch, *Women's Writing in Nineteenth-Century France* (Cambridge: Cambridge University Press, 2000), p. 23. On the stereotypical nature of the heroine who dies of a broken heart, see Nancy Rogers, 'The Wasting Away of Romantic Heroines', *Nineteenth-Century French Studies*, 11.3–4 (1983), 246–56. For a study of the relationship between Stendhal and Duras and of his borrowings from her work, see Richard Bolster, 'Stendhal, Mme de Duras et la tradition sentimentale', *Studi Francesi*, 107.36 (1992), 301–06.

64. *Littérature et sensation*, p. 69.

65. *Les Jeux et les hommes: Le Masque et le vertige*, revised and augmented edn ([Paris]: Gallimard, 1967), p. 67. On Mathilde's enjoyment of competition or conflict, which is an aspect of her playfulness that this chapter has neglected to discuss in any detail, see in particular Anne Hage, 'Crime et châtiment dans *Le Rouge et le Noir*', *L'Année stendhalienne*, 2 (2003), 179–209 (pp. 185–97).

66. For references to the premium Mathilde places on happiness, see *Orc* I 610, 628, 629, 637, 643, 645, 663.

67. See Gilbert Laurens, 'Le Mythe d'Hérodiade chez Stendhal, III', *Stendhal Club*, 106 (1985), 131–47 (pp. 134–37). As Pearson notes (*Stendhal's Violin*, p. 129), Julien repeatedly compares Mathilde to a queen (*Orc* I 604, 618, 665, 725, 765).

68. *Le Deuxième Sexe*, I, 386.

69. For the opposite point of view, already evoked, see Manzini, *Stendhal's Parallel Lives* (pp. 295–98), from which the antithesis between imitation and emulation has been borrowed.

70. *Le Style de Stendhal*, pp. 60–61.

71. *Le Style de Stendhal*, p. 605.

72. For Sartre, 'l'idéal de l'entreprise amoureuse' [the ideal of the amorous venture] is 'la liberté aliénée' [relinquished freedom]. *L'Être et le néant*, p. 443.

73. For the opposite point of view, see Yves Ansel, *Stendhal littéral: 'Le Rouge et le Noir'*, p. 171.

74. See also *Orc* I 729, 733, 735, 742, 745, 785, 787, 794, 800.

75. In *De l'Amour*, Stendhal describes France as '[le] pays où la plante nommée amour a toujours peur du ridicule, est étouffée par les exigences de la passion *nationale*, la vanité, et n'arrive presque jamais à toute sa hauteur' [the country where the plant called love is always afraid of ridicule, is suffocated by the demands of vanity, the national passion, and hardly ever arrives at its full height] (p. 325, first draft preface). In the same work, he describes Italy as 'le seul pays où croisse en liberté la plante que je décris [l'amour]. En France, la vanité [l'étouffe]' [the only country where the plant [love] I am describing grows. In France, vanity suffocates it] (p. 137, chapter 40). And the narrator of *Lamiel* observes that: 'Les cœurs dominés par la vanité ont une peur instinctive des *émotions*, c'est la grande route pour arriver au ridicule' [Hearts dominated by vanity have an instinctive fear of *emotions*; they are the high road to ridicule] (L 129).

76. See Stendhal, *De l'Amour*, chapter 2. Girard highlights the link between *cristallisation* and vanity, and observes that while *De l'Amour* presents vanity-inspired love as inferior in intensity to passionate love, Stendhal's novels reverse this opposition. *Mensonge romantique*, pp. 26–30. Anne Marie Jaton points out that Lucien's passion for Madame de Chasteller begins as 'un véritable "amour de vanité"' [a genuine 'vanity love']. '*De l'amour* et *Lucien Leuwen*: Une poétique de l'obstacle', in *Le Plus Méconnu des romans de Stendhal:'Lucien Leuwen'* , ed. by Société des études romantiques (Paris: SEDES-CDU réunis, 1983), pp. 89–98 (p. 92).

77. Rabine asserts that 'the novel hardly presents Mathilde as a unified model of anything. Even more than Julien, she is a fragmentary and contradictory character. At times the narrator speaks of her "great coldness of soul" or her "dry prudence," at other times he says: "Courage was the primary quality of her character."' *Reading the Romantic Heroine*, p. 104.

78. See *Orc* I 572, 578, 617, 618, 646, 647, 648, 661, 678, 724.

79. See Crouzet, '*Le Rouge et le Noir*', pp. 17–18.

80. *L'Être et le néant*, p. 72.

81. *Le Deuxième Sexe*, I, 385.

82. *Le Deuxième Sexe*, I, 386.

83. *De l'Amour*, p. 284 ('Fragments divers', 122).
84. In this view he would have been influenced, according to Blin, by Hobbes, Helvétius, and by classical moralists, including Pascal, La Rochefoucauld, de La Bruyère, Vauvenargues. *Stendhal et les problèmes de la personnalité*, pp. 82–83. See also Albérès, *Le Naturel chez Stendhal*, pp. 56–58.
85. *Stendhal et les problèmes de la personnalité*, p. 63.
86. See also *L* 40. On vanity as fear of ridicule, see for example *Cg* I 81; Stendhal, *De l'Amour*, pp. 138–39 (chapter 41), p. 325 (first draft preface); Stendhal, *Racine et Shakespeare (1818–1825) et autres textes de théorie romantique*, ed. by Michel Crouzet (Paris: Champion, 2006), pp. 361–62 ('De la moralité de Molière').
87. On Stendhal's understanding of the distinction between pride and vanity, see Blin, *Stendhal et les problèmes de la personnalité*, pp. 108–11. Crouzet notes that pride entails 'une solidité du moi bien étrangère à la vanité' [a solidity of the self very foreign to vanity]. *Le Naturel, la grâce et le réel*, p. 108. For Sartre, pride is an authentic attitude, in that it is characterized by the 'affirmation de ma liberté en face d'Autrui-objet' [affirmation of my freedom before the Other-as-object]. *L'Être et le néant*, p. 351.
88. Regarding the distinction conferred by a death sentence, Ansel points out that Stendhal himself made a similar observation in a letter to his friend Domenico Fiori, in exile in France from a death sentence in Italy (*Orc* I 1085 n. 12).
89. See *Cg* I 181–82.
90. *De l'Amour*, p. 202 (chapter 54).
91. See for example *Cg* I 134, 160–61, 180, 186–87, 314, 362.
92. *Racine et Shakespeare*, ed. by Crouzet, p. 364 ('De la moralité de Molière'). See Bolster, *Stendhal, Balzac et le féminisme romantique*, pp. 81–84, on Stendhal's passionate interest in improving women's education. Bolster finds, in the writer's letters to his sister, 'un présage de la supériorité intellectuelle que Stendhal se plaira à personnifier en une Mathilde de la Mole' [a presage of the intellectual superiority that Stendhal will delight in personifying in a Mathilde de La Mole] (p. 82).
93. This attitude might be aligned with the lack of political consistency, partisanship, and *coquinerie* (roguery) that characterized Stendhal himself. See Francesco Manzini, 'Stendhal, Imagination and Inconsequentiality: the Dirt of Politics and the Politics of Dirt in the *Vie de Henry Brulard*, *Lucien Leuwen* and *La Chartreuse de Parme*', *Dix-Neuf* (forthcoming). See also Francesco Manzini, 'Work, Idleness, and Play in Stendhal's *Lucien Leuwen*', *Dix-Neuf*, 16.1 (2012), 28–37. What Peter Brooks refers to as eighteenth-century worldliness or theatricality, described in the context of Stendhal as freedom from social fixity, also has much in common with the playful, unserious attitude being evoked here; 'true urbanity' is a disengagement even from worldly codes. See *The Novel of Worldliness: Crébillon, Marivaux, Laclos, Stendhal* (Princeton: Princeton University Press, 1969), pp. 219–78 (p. 263).
94. See in particular *Orc* I 416, 424, 431.
95. See for example Bersani, *A Future for Astyanax*, p. 107; Ansel, *Stendhal littéral: 'Le Rouge et le Noir'*, p. 133.
96. *Stendhal littéral: 'Le Rouge et le Noir'*, p. 103.
97. *Les Jeux et les hommes*, p. 22.
98. As Goetz says of the hero's courtroom speech, 'his words ring false' and his argument 'shows him trying to foist guilt onto the shoulders of a hostile society'. In this, for Goetz, Julien departs from the Nietzschean superior man he otherwise resembles. 'Nietzsche and *Le Rouge et le noir*', pp. 449–50.

CHAPTER 3

On Not Taking *Lamiel* Seriously

An Unserious Novel

In the last chapter, seriousness was associated with submission to other people's rules and expectations and with the hypocritical denial of one's freedom. Like Mina and Vanina, Mathilde has no truck with what Stendhal calls 'prudence' or with what Sartre calls *l'esprit de sérieux* [serious-mindedness]. What the narrator says of Mina could equally easily be applied to her two contemporaries: 'Ces idées de *prudence humaine* étaient bien au-dessous d'elle' [These notions of *human prudence* were very far beneath her] (*Orc* I 307–08). All three heroines rebel against the value system that governs their social world: all refuse to agree passively to the marriages that other characters plan for them, all make a scandalous choice of lover, and all are disrespectful of traditional gender roles and hierarchies. They each possess that *faculté de vouloir* [ability to want] that marks Stendhalian characters out from the crowd. For these characters, the courage to want entails a willingness to embrace risk and playfulness over the security of a serious life.[1] The epigraph to *Lucien Leuwen* suggests that the hero's father, one of the most playful of Stendhal's fictional characters,[2] 'savait vouloir' [knew how to want] (*Orc* II 83); but M. Leuwen also takes great risks with his reputation and finances, risks that culminate in financial ruin. Stendhal's Amazons might be understood to resemble Lucien's father (only) in that they too are players and they too are led by their desire.

The ability to want was in short supply in nineteenth-century France, according to Stendhal, where the dominant passion was, he claimed, vanity and where people were therefore ruled by habit for fear of marking themselves out as different from others and thus ridiculous. The France of his time was consequently characterized by Stendhal as a morose and boring place.[3] By contrast, pre-revolutionary France was, for the author, a place defined by its gaiety. The narrator of *San Francesco a Ripa*, for example, explains that the French character was renowned for its gaiety prior to the French revolution, but that this quality disappeared in 1789, along with the 'insouciance' [carefree attitude] that maintained it (*Orc* II 24).

The joyfulness of Stendhal's early childhood disappeared around the same time. After the death of his beloved and vivacious mother when Henri was only seven, the atmosphere around him turned to prolonged gloom. He was allowed none of the fun that he could see other children enjoying. The occasional presence of the author's uncle, Romain Gagnon, brought some pleasure to an otherwise miserable childhood. The young Henri longed to be free of a city and a father that together inspired in him a deep and instinctive repugnance. In *Vie de Henry Brulard*, he establishes a close connection between the horror provoked in him by Grenoble and the disgust inspired in him by bourgeois seriousness.[4]

We have already seen that, after he had finally left Grenoble behind him, the author wrote many letters to his much loved sister, Pauline, who remained at home, frustrated and oppressed by her circumstances. We have also seen that many of Stendhal's letters urge Pauline to adopt an attitude of compromise, an attitude foreign to all of his Amazons. However, the letters also recommend another strategy, namely humour: 'plaisantons de tout, rions sur chaque chose' [let us joke and laugh about everything] (*Cg* I 139). Criticism of Stendhal has long acknowledged the close relationship in his work between playfulness and freedom. Crouzet, for example, claims that 'la *gaîté*' [gaiety] is one of the cornerstones of Stendhalian ethics and of his notion of freedom, while Jefferson refers to the subversive qualities of the author's 'gay citationality' and notes that 'for Stendhal laughter is a reprieve from the obligation to imitate'.[5] For Beauvoir, Stendhal's heroines achieve a mitigated form of freedom simply by dint of their confinement to the unserious.[6]

It was argued in the last chapter that Mathilde's love of anxiety testifies to her choice of freedom; but so does her joy. She assumes a mocking, irreverent approach to herself and others that contrasts with Julien's habit of taking himself and others seriously. Indeed, Julien is at one point critical of Mathilde's 'yeux riants' [laughing eyes], which he compares negatively to those of 'cette pauvre Mme de Rênal' [that poor Mme de Rênal] (*Orc* I 647). While Mathilde is certainly more than capable of cruel mockery, she is also prone to an innocent kind of laughter, as when she joins Norbert and Julien in laughing at the latter's fall from his horse, or later when the sound of her mirth wakens her mother and a servant, thereby putting both her and her lover at great risk of discovery. If Mathilde, like Mina and Vanina before her, treats the seriousness of the social world with irreverence, Lamiel, Stendhal's last audacious heroine, openly and joyfully derides it.

Lamiel has traditionally been regarded as greatly inferior in importance to Stendhal's other novels. Upon its first (posthumous) publication in 1889, the unfinished work was recognized as valuable largely for the insights it offered into the author's creative processes. While some critics of the time remarked on the appeal of its content, most perceived the novel as intrinsically odd or flawed.[7] Over seven decades later, Hemmings's study of Stendhal's novels omitted to devote a chapter to *Lamiel* on the grounds that this 'most disturbingly perverse work' could shed no light on 'certain distinguishable themes' that are present in the author's other works.[8] Brombert's study of the theme of freedom in Stendhal's novels included no separate chapter on *Lamiel*, despite briefly acknowledging the eponymous character's extreme experiments in self-liberation.[9] Even today, despite significant feminist interest in the novel, the production of two new editions since 1980, with a third one forthcoming, the publication of three important monographs on the text over the last two decades, an international conference on the text in May 2008, and five essays devoted to it in the 2009 issue of the *Revue d'histoire littéraire de la France*, the author of a monograph on the text can assert that '*Lamiel* ne cesse pas [...] d'être un écrit ignoré, snobé par les commentateurs qui ne savent trop comment aborder

un texte inachevé aussi déroutant et inégal, aussi peu "stendhalien" parfois.' [*Lamiel*
is still [...] an unknown work, snubbed by commentators who do not know how to
approach an unfinished text that is so disorienting and erratic, and, sometimes, so
un-'Stendhalian'.][10] It is true that *Lamiel* continues to be considered marginal and
idiosyncratic by many critics, including some of those who do not avoid writing
about the novel, and whose work will be evoked in this chapter.

  Negative critical reactions to *Lamiel* are largely attributable to the fact that it not
only remains incomplete, like *Lucien Leuwen*, but is also radically plural.[11] Casimir
Stryienski, in his 1889 edition of the novel, and Henri Martineau in his subsequent
editions, had effectively melded the different parts of *Lamiel* together so as to produce
a superficial coherence.[12] In 1971, the publication of Victor Del Litto's edition of
Lamiel revealed for the first time the different stages of the text's progress, rather
than attempting to forge a misleading unity out of the disparate packets of text.
While Del Litto himself seems to have shared the negative evaluations of previous
commentators, believing like them that the characters lacked sufficient fixity and
that the novel suffered from 'l'absence d'une idée directrice, d'un fil d'Ariane' [the
absence of any guiding idea, of any Ariadne's thread] (*L* iii) his edition immediately
sparked the interest of critics. Now at least some sense could be made of the text's
plurality.

  Del Litto's edition presents two substantive versions of *Lamiel*, the first of which
('*Lamiel I*') was allegedly written in late 1839 and the second of which ('*Lamiel II*')
was dictated in the early weeks of 1840.[13] While both versions are incomplete,
they are of approximately equal length. The first begins with a description of the
spectacular religious event that occasions the infant Lamiel's arrival in Carville, and
goes on to describe her life in that Norman village and subsequently in Rouen with
her aristocratic lover. It ends during the heroine's time in Paris. The second version
of the story begins with an introduction to Carville and some of its key characters
(the duchess, the Abbé Du Saillard, Sansfin). It ends while Lamiel is still in Carville.
Critics tend to agree that the heroine of 1840 is a more limited creation, both in
terms of her behaviour and her importance to the novel, than her 1839 precursor.
Further notes and fragments, drafted between 1840 and 1842, seem to indicate that
the author intended to push his heroine even further into the shadows, the projected
title of the text even changing in March 1841 from *Lamiel* to *Les Français du King
φιλλιππε* [*The French under King Louis-Philippe*].

  The first reason, then, why *Lamiel* has not been given the attention it deserves
until relatively recently is the incoherence of the text as it was left upon the author's
death in March 1842. A second reason is its insufficiently Stendhalian tonality, and
particularly its insufficient seriousness; the author is, after all, described by Erich
Auerbach as the founder of 'the serious realism of modern times'.[14] Various critics
have emphasized the contrived comicality of *Lamiel*.[15] Both Crouzet and Ansel note
that the 'grotesque' qualities of the text militate against its 'sérieux' [seriousness].[16]
Complicit with the grotesque tonality is a cynical narrative perspective that, instead
of investing the world with significance as Stendhal's other works do, actively
strips human existence of meaningfulness.[17] Ansel, accordingly, points out that
the text is devoid of any representative of traditional Stendhalian ideals, and that it

therefore lacks seriousness. However, as suggested by the gender uniformity of all of the idealists he lists as missing from *Lamiel* (the army surgeon, Fouqué, Altamira, Julien Sorel, all from *Le Rouge et le Noir*, and, from *Lucien Leuwen*, Lucien, Gros, Coffe, the General Fari), the fact that the novel's protagonist is a heroine rather than a hero would seem to have at least something to do with its purported lack of idealism. An authorial note of 17 March 1840, written over two weeks after the dictation of the second version of *Lamiel*, seems to confirm the problems posed by the protagonist's gender: 'Je ne puis travailler à rien de sérieux *for this little gouine.*' [I cannot work at anything serious for this little hussy.][18] Leaving aside the precise meaning and referent of this note, what strikes this reader as interesting is the fact that it has seemed, in the eyes of many critics, so obviously to refer to the heroine of *Lamiel*.[19]

Certainly, Lamiel's gender has, historically, been a source of significant critical dissatisfaction with the novel. Blin, for example, finds himself unable to see through the heroine's eyes or, alternatively, fall in love with her: 'nous ne pouvons cristalliser pour elle' [we cannot crystallize for her].[20] Bardèche goes so far as to express his disappointment that Lamiel's scheming doctor-tutor, Sansfin, does not have his way with Lamiel, and his barely hidden outrage at the fact that she gives her virginity away to 'un nigaud emprunté que Lamiel rencontre par hasard' [an awkward simpleton that Lamiel meets by chance],[21] who is clearly a far less deserving candidate than the author-Sansfin-reader complex. Prévost notes that 'Lamiel tourne à la vulgarité, par excès de traits masculins' [Lamiel becomes vulgar, on account of too many masculine traits].[22] Interestingly, though, both Beauvoir and the female critic Marill-Albérès, both writing at around the same time as these three male critics, write in the most glowing of terms about the heroine, the former (briefly) praising '[l]a liberté de son esprit' [the freedom of her spirit] and the latter referring to her revivifying effect on her society: terms: 'elle fait irruption dans une société corrompue' [she bursts onto the scene of a corrupt society].[23]

Some examples of gendered reading are more subtle than those already cited. Grahame C. Jones, who accords an albeit very short chapter of his 1966 study of irony in Stendhal's novels to *Lamiel*, describes the heroine as one of the most original women of French nineteenth-century literature, but instead of focusing on the ironic talents of the heroine he describes as 'la naïve Lamiel' [the naïve Lamiel], he bizarrely attributes to Sansfin both narrative pre-eminence and ironic superiority, giving him the bulk of his attention and even claiming that his inner life 'devient à bien des égards l'élément le plus important de l'ouvrage' [becomes in many respects the most important element of the work].[24] For Gilbert D. Chaitin, only Stendhal's 'masochistic tendency' towards the end of his life, 'combined with his reduced ego strength, can explain Stendhal's choice of a young girl as the main character of his new novel'.[25] Boll-Johansen claims that the plot suffers from the heroine's deficiencies, pointing to '[l]a pauvreté psychologique du personnage, le manque de forces vigoureuses' [the character's psychological poverty, her lack of vigorous energy].[26]

Jones's downplaying of the heroine's centrality to the text is a feature of some recent studies of *Lamiel* too; much has been made, in particular, of Stendhal's apparent disengagement from his heroine over time, and his seeming shift of emphasis to Sansfin. 'Lamiel II' does make Sansfin a more central character than he is in 'Lamiel I', in which he barely features, though it should be added that the author's earliest plans for *Lamiel* indicate that he was always going to have a more significant part to play than the one given him in the first draft. Stendhal's other modifications and notes from 1840 to 1842 seem to confirm the hypothesis of a reorientation of interest away from the heroine to the extent that they place the doctor, as well as the duchess, centre-stage. John West-Sooby expresses what has now become the dominant point of view in relation to the text's evolution: he claims that Lamiel becomes increasingly confined to a secondary role in relation to Sansfin, who would make her serve his erotic fantasies and political ambitions.[27]

The apparent change of direction may have been only temporary, however: the previously accepted chronology of the text's evolution has recently been revised. Serge Linkès has highlighted the fact that, in October 1841, on the author's final trip from Civitavecchia to France, where he intended to continue his work on the novel, he took along with him, in addition to his notes of March 1841, the text that had been dictated and corrected in 1839 (being a substantial section of what would become known as 'Lamiel I') rather than the one dictated in January 1840 ('Lamiel II').[28] This revelation radically (though indirectly) complicates the argument that Stendhal had intended to reduce the centrality of Lamiel to *Lamiel*.[29]

However, even if we accept the hypothesis that in a virtual text the heroine's importance would have been reduced, she continues to occupy the vast bulk of the text as we know it; as Ansel puts it, a cold-eyed examination of the existing work, including both main versions and all of the author's notes and sketches, proves, indisputably, that in both statistical and structural terms 'l'héroïne éponyme domine, écrase littéralement tous les autres personnages' [the eponymous heroine dominates, literally flattens, all the other characters].[30] Yves Ansel also points out, indeed, that none of Stendhal's developments of Sansfin's character make him any less ridiculous a character, or any better equipped to survive the 1830 revolution, which occurs towards the end of 'Lamiel II'.[31] He is still, in other words, the vain character that, as early as April 1839, the author wanted to include in the novel 'pour accrocher la sympathie des Français' [to attract the sympathy of French readers] (*L* 3).

If Sansfin was initially conceived to secure the sympathy of readers, the author also had a concern, even from the outset, that went in the opposite direction; he wanted to ward off readerly sympathy for his character in order to render him comical. In May 1839, he writes that Sansfin's character is to have 'nulle profondeur' [no depth] (*L* 5). This comment is illuminated by a note of February 1840, made after the writing of 'Lamiel II' in which Sansfin features as a Machiavellian schemer: 'Trop de profondeur dans la description d'un caractère empêche le RIRE./ Donc la plus grande partie de ce j'ai écrit sur le docteur Sansfin restera dans les sub-structions de l'édifice' [Too much depth in the description of a character prevents LAUGHTER./ So the bulk of what I have written about Dr Sansfin will remain in the substructures of the edifice] (*L* 334). Subsequently, in sketches drafted in March 1841, the formidable mentor is reinvented as a more risible character than before. Instead of engineering his own strategic absence from Carville at the precise moment that the outcome of the July Revolution becomes known, as occurs in 'Lamiel II', this newly recreated 'homme sans profondeur, sans plan de conduite' [lightweight man, lacking any plan of action] is caught unawares by the revolution and is reduced to cowering behind the window of a Carville patient, running down streets and climbing a roof to recover hidden savings (L 352, 360–63). In 'Lamiel II' the doctor gives Lamiel valuable lessons in critical thinking, but is represented in later notes, dating from May 1840, as 'incapable de réfléchir à quelque chose d'une façon suivie. (Autrement plus de rire.)' [unable to reflect coherently on a matter. (Otherwise no laughter.)] (L 342). In a draft of February 1840 we read the familiar portrait of a doctor who sometimes refuses to appear in the duchess's castle for an entire month on account of her lack of regard for his vanity (L 330–31) but in Stendhal's notes of March 1841 Sansfin is said to forget 'un *malheur de vanité*' [a vanity-related misfortune] as soon as it occurs (L 347) and to be unable to remember his 'irréussites' [failures] (L 351).

In addition to being redefined as trivial, the character of Sansfin becomes increasingly incoherent as a figure in the author's notes from February 1840 onwards. His reinvention as shallow does not prevent him, in notes of March 1842, from imparting illuminating 'réflexions profondes' [profound insights] to Lamiel, from offering her an education 'donnée avec passion' [delivered with passion] (L 377), or from being animated by a 'rage profonde' [deep rage] at her account of how she lost her virginity (L 379). More superficially, but arguably just as tellingly, in February 1840 Sansfin is given a black beard, while in March 1841 his beard is blonde (L 332, 351); and in March 1841 and March 1842 he becomes poor, despite previously having been presented as rich (L 375, 377). Whether the doctor was clearly enough conceived to form the centrepiece of a redefined version of the novel is certainly open to debate.[32]

Even if we accept that, despite these various inconsistencies, the doctor would have become the most important character of Stendhal's finished novel, it does not follow that the value and significance of *Lamiel*, as currently constituted in its two substantive drafts, should be reduced in any way, or that the second draft should take priority over the first. It is true that Stendhal was not in the habit of retaining the first drafts or manuscripts of his published works.[33] However, the unfinished *Le Rose et le Vert* is not usually considered superior to *Mina de Vanghel* just because it represents a later reworking and development of the same fundamental story. And the original version of *La Chartreuse de Parme* continues to be considered the authoritative one, rather than the modified text that Stendhal produced in response to Balzac's well-intended suggestions. *Lamiel* has been left to us in a state of flux and openness; it is impossible to know how the novel would have looked had it ever been completed. The numerous authorial plans cannot help us in this respect, because as the author himself frequently repeated, plans had the effect of suffocating his imagination; his best work was improvised quickly with only the most minimal of scaffolding, like the two most complete versions of *Lamiel* itself. If plans and notes for new versions of *Lamiel* proliferate after these two drafts were completed, the substantive drafts should nevertheless logically remain the primary focus of our study of the novel.

Lamiel has, then, been an under-rated component of Stendhal's body of work because of its plural plots, its un–Stendhalian comicality and cynicism, and the gender of its protagonist. The remainder of this chapter will argue that the three reasons why the text has not been taken seriously in the past are not only intrinsically interlinked, but also stem from the idea of freedom that is at the novel's centre, and from the fundamental unseriousness that characterizes that conception of freedom. It follows that no argument will be made here for the political seriousness of Lamiel's motivations, a point on which she has been criticized.[34] The heroine does not fight for any other cause than that of her own liberty.[35] The next section will thus propose not that the heroine's way of asserting her freedom is politically serious but that it is so intrinsically playful that it militates against the novel's seriousness. Subsequently, the chapter will argue against the dominant critical wisdom by suggesting that this heroine is no less zealously attached to her freedom in 'Lamiel II' than she is in 'Lamiel I'.

An Unserious Heroine

Lamiel was, from the beginning, a nomadic text. At its origin there was no pre-existing though minimal plot, as there was in the case of *Armance*, *Le Rouge et le Noir*, *La Chartreuse de Parme*, and *Lucien Leuwen*, but rather the memory of a young woman glimpsed in transit. In a plan drafted in May 1839, the author notes of the woman he calls 'L'Amiel' that: 'je l'ai vue de la Bastille à la porte Saint-Denis et dans le bateau à vapeur de Honfleur au Havre' [I saw her between the Bastille and the Porte Saint-Denis and in the steamer from Honfleur to Le Havre].[36] In both instances, the woman would seem to have been glimpsed while both she and the author were moving between two places.

As befits her apparent origin in the sighting of a woman observed in transit, whether on a steamer or, more fleetingly, as she walks down a street, the character of Lamiel was associated in Stendhal's various plans with pure, spontaneous becoming, pure potential. One note of 18 May 1839 states that 'Sa vie désordonnée se passait à marcher rapidement à un but qu'elle brûlait d'atteindre' [Her disorderly life was spent walking rapidly towards an end she was burning to reach] (*L* 7) while another, dated 15 February 1840, describes her as 'la grâce sans projet, comme Gina del Dongo' [grace without plans, like Gina del Dongo], and as doing nothing 'par projet' [according to a plan]: 'elle a bien quelquefois de beaux projets, mais jamais elle ne les exécute; elle n'agit que par un caprice soudain' [she does sometimes have fine plans, but she never executes them; she acts only on sudden whim] (*L* 336). Despite the fact that one quotation suggests that Lamiel does pursue at least one goal while the other indicates that she does not, both notes highlight the fundamental alacrity of her character. What they imply is that what is most important about the heroine is not her destination but her style of moving through the world.[37] Even Lamiel's beauty is dynamic, in process: the duke notes in 'Lamiel I' that her lack of 'embonpoint' [plumpness] is 'un des désavantages de l'extrême jeunesse' [one of the disadvantages of extreme youth] (*L* 86). Similarly, in the Abbé Clément's description of the heroine in 'Lamiel II', he writes that she is 'point encore une beauté' [not yet a beauty] and that 'Sa tête offre le germe de la perfection de la beauté normande' [Her head foretells the perfection of Norman beauty] (*L* 265). An attempt is made, in Stendhal's text, to capture a heroine in the making.[38]

It is not the heroine's story as such, but rather her energy, and her love of energy in others, that are at the heart of the plans that Stendhal drew up in May 1839. In one, Lamiel is imagined to overthrow all of Sansfin's plans, motivated either 'par véritable amour' [by true love] or 'par amour pour l'énergie véritable' [by love of true energy] (*L* 4; see also *L* 9). In another plan, we read that the heroine 'marchait trop vite dans les rues, enjambait les ruisseaux, sautait sur les trottoirs' [walked too fast in the street, strode over gutters, skipped along footpaths], because 'elle songeait trop au lieu où elle allait et où elle avait envie d'arriver, et pas assez aux gens qui pouvaient la regarder' [she thought too much about where she was going and where she wanted to get to, and not enough about the people who could be watching her] (*L* 6). Stendhal habitually gave nuances of character priority over plot, both in his preparation of a novel and in its elaboration.[39] In the case of *Lamiel*, his downgrading of plot is even more striking than usual because the plans suggest that not only will the heroine's style or attitude be prioritized over her story, but her attitude will itself be bound up with a disregard for plot. Given that Lamiel invests as much passion in the selection of a chest of drawers as in a life-changing event, as the plan of 18 May 1839 states, it follows that motivation and plot detail will be of merely secondary importance in her story, the central role being given to the force of her personality. If it matters little, for the author, what motivates Lamiel to overthrow Sansfin's plans, this is because what counts above all is her manifestation of energy.[40]

In an important reading of the novel, to which this chapter will return, Naomi Schor has emphasized the progressive binding of the heroine's energy, particularly in the transition from '*Lamiel I*' to '*Lamiel II*'. However, Lamiel's great vitality is evident in both main drafts of the novel. In each, she is a movement-hungry child oppressed by the constraints imposed on her physical freedom by her adoptive parents (or purported aunt and uncle), and later by the requirement to walk slowly inside the duchess's castle and to be accompanied by one of the duchess's ladies when outside it. In the castle, her natural vivacity reveals itself in her resemblance to 'une gazelle enchaînée' [a chained gazelle] (*L* 35, 226), and in her lively leaps whenever she believes herself to be unobserved.

As soon as she is let go by the duchess, in both '*Lamiel I*' and '*Lamiel II*', she rushes out into the countryside of Carville, free at last to run around in peasant clothing. In both versions of the story, she defies her uncle's objections and only returns to her family home 'à la nuit noire' [when it is pitch dark] (*L* 61, 305). Shortly after this event, '*Lamiel II*' comes to an end. However, in '*Lamiel I*' the heroine spends the months after this event 'dans les champs' [in the fields] (*L* 63), and indeed her first two encounters with the duchess's son, her future lover, take place while she is out roaming the country roads. It is after three days of suffocating confinement in the family home that the heroine runs through the rain to tell the duke that they are going to run away to Rouen together. Impatient to leave, and unwilling to be slowed down by the duke's hesitations, she completes the first two legs of the trip alone; the second is by night. The dangers of such freedom of movement for a woman of the time are revealed when she is obliged to defend herself with a pair of scissors against four travelling salesmen. She is grateful to be taught, later that evening, about the deforming properties of green holly paste, knowledge that she will later use to facilitate forays to the theatre and solitary travel by stage-coach.

After spending some time with the duke, we read that Lamiel loses 'sa tournure de jeune biche prête à prendre sa course' [the bearing of a young doe about to take flight] (*L* 96). However, the heroine's natural vivacity has not been suppressed. She realizes that her boredom in Rouen stems from the constraints the duke places on her movement, and orders him to rejoin his mother for three or four days so that she can run happily around the fields with a maid from the hotel in which she is staying. During the duke's absence, she also attends the theatre in the company of the hotel manageress; Lamiel wears her green holly paste to deflect the attention of potential admirers. Another moment of intense happiness is experienced when Lamiel takes the night coach to Paris, again wearing her holly paste. While staying at Mme Le Grand's hotel in Paris, the other guests are struck by the exuberance of her movements. Lamiel takes dance classes, apparently to learn how to walk in a more restrained way. No longer a chained gazelle, as she was in the castle, Lamiel strikes the count as 'une jeune gazelle' [a young gazelle] liable to leap away from him if he does not ensnare her (*L* 118). When she flees his apartment in the final pages of '*Lamiel I*', she does so 'précipitamment' [hastily], 'sans attendre le bras du laquais' [without waiting for the footman to offer his arm], very much in the manner of a young gazelle (*L* 147).

The heroine's movements are equally precipitous in '*Lamiel II*', where she eludes even Sansfin's all-knowing eye when, having recovered from her apparent illness, she leaves home unexpectedly for the duchess's castle. Similarly, when upset by her aunt's behaviour, she escapes from the Hautemare cottage 'par un mouvement instinctif' [propelled by instinct] (*L* 307), and escapes to the woods by day and the tower by night to read her books. In a later note for a much transformed version of the novel, a rewritten, more ridiculous Sansfin is astonished to see, in the midst of the disarray caused by news of the July Revolution, the girl he thinks to be genuinely tubercular, who 'ne marchait jamais qu'en voiture' [always travelled in a vehicle], coming on foot from the castle to his house (*L* 363); even when her character seems to have been grotesquely diminished both in narrative importance and in life-force, Lamiel's power of locomotion still has the ability to surprise. And it is of course highly possible that the Sansfin of March 1841 has misdiagnosed Lamiel's apparent illness, and that she is as far from being frail as ever she was.

And yet, for many critics, the heroine lacks vitality. According to Bardèche, *Lamiel* and its protagonist are the entirely appropriate end products of Stendhal's creative method, the author being ultimately a maker of 'des poupées mécaniques' [mechanical dolls] who, as his writing matured, became increasingly less interested in the logic of story.[41] What Bardèche objects to, above all, are the plot deficiencies he perceives in *Lamiel*: the various parts of the text offer what he considers to be the mechanical process of the heroine's formation rather than introducing obstacles that would, crucially, vitalize her character. If Lamiel was intended finally to enter into conflict with society, it was only by an accident of plot, namely her encounter with, and attraction to, an outlaw. But the plotlessness of which Bardèche complains is entirely continuous with the particular attitude of its heroine. It is entirely logical, in view of the heroine's characteristic unpredictability, and her habit of disengaging from her present situation, that the novel in which she plays the leading role should lack traditional plottedness. It seems appropriate, too, that Stendhal's famously improvisatory practice of writing should eventually produce a character that is the very incarnation of the spirit of improvisation. Indeed, as Julien Gracq puts it, Stendhal himself 'n'est guère que mouvement' [is nothing but movement], and his texts, governed only by 'la mécanique des fluides' [fluid mechanics], convey 'le sentiment d'allégresse et de liberté né du mouvement sans bride' [the feeling of quickness and freedom arising from unbridled motion].[42]

From Stendhal's earliest attempts at narrative fiction, his characters had the capacity to act in surprising ways, often unexplained by the narrator. We have already discussed, for example, the surprises that Vanina and Mina de Vanghel reserve for us throughout their stories, while Mathilde is defined by her unpredictability. What Brooks describes as the Stendhalian hero's 'slippage from under the exercise of authority'[43] is nowhere more evident than in *Lamiel*, in which the female protagonist repeatedly avoids attempted appropriation by others (her adoptive parents, Sansfin, the duchess, the duke, the count, Mme Le Grand). That the author wanted to be surprised by his creation and to exercise only minimal control over her is suggested by a note made in May 1839: 'À chaque page je vois s'élever le brouillard qui couvrait la suivante' [On every page I see the fog over the next one lift] (*L* 12).

For many critics, the author's lack of authority over his text is a sign of creative failure.[44] The disorderliness of the text can, however, lend itself to a far more positive interpretation. The apparent lifting of authorial self-constraints in the creation of *Lamiel* prompts Jean-Jacques Hamm to describe it as 'un texte de plaisir' [a text of pleasure], 'une œuvre sans angoisse' [an anxiety-free work].[45] According to this interpretation, *Lamiel* was not a tortuous enterprise but rather a pleasure-producing one, and the work of an author at the height of his powers. For Ansel, too, the author's primary concern in writing *Lamiel* was the indulgence of his own pleasure, as testified by the relative paucity of self-censoring notes.[46] Ansel, indeed, attributes what he perceives as the uncharacteristic vulgarity of the text to the author's unaccustomed lack of heed to its intended audience.[47]

To the extent that *Lamiel* was written to serve the author's pleasure and without the latter's usual concern for his eventual readership, it might be understood, in Barthesian terms, as a *texte scriptible* (writable text) rather than a *texte lisible* (readable text), a production rather than a product. *Lamiel* certainly lacks much of the coherence of Barthes's classical readable text, but this lack does not have to be interpreted negatively, as it traditionally has been. Éric Bordas, for example, despite describing the text as a product of pessimism and exhaustion rather than of discovery and invention, observes that the text's great originality resides in its subversion of Balzacian Realism, and even of the particular style of narrative Realism represented by *Le Rouge et le Noir*.[48] To the extent that Realism is inimical to freedom of movement, and particularly to female freedom of movement, as Schor proposes, it may be that the author of *Lamiel* needed to explore another register in order to give expression to the heroine's energy.[49]

That the register of the grotesque lends itself particularly well to the articulation of (female) irreverence and disobedience is suggested by the laundry scene, an episode that has provoked the very special disgust of readers over the years: Gide, for example, writes of this section that 'toute cette animation factice et lourde reste indigne de Stendhal' [all of this artificial, ponderous liveliness is unworthy of Stendhal].[50] The public laundry was a privileged site of female sociability in the nineteenth century; it was also a privileged site of conversation, that mobilizing, subversive element that is so crucial to the logic of *Lamiel*;[51] and indeed, some of the women present at the scene in question are said to be there only to enjoy the very animated conversation. The grotesque, caricatural dimension of the episode is produced by various elements. The unattractiveness of the doctor's physical deformity is echoed by the hideous cotton caps worn by the women. The laughter of derision is at the heart of this scene, the washerwomen pouring their unanimous ridicule over the doctor, insulting his virility while he insults their virtue. In true grotesque fashion, the women's coarse insults target Sansfin's vanity here, as well as that of Mme Hautemare, while the episode culminates in the doctor's ignominious fall into the mud.[52] That these women are redoubtable figures is suggested by the description of several of them as 'grandes, bien faites, construites comme la Diane des Tuileries' [tall and well-made, built like the Diana of the Tuileries Garden] (*L* 196). The reference to the Tuileries, in the context of a scene in which a man will be humiliated, might recall, in a parodic vein, the historical fact that it was in this place that Louis XVI was obliged by revolutionaries to wear their symbolic cap. The same parodic allegory of revolution is suggested by the fact that, subsequent to the scene of conflict between Sansfin and the women, one of them talks of attaching a lock of his hair to her cap, 'comme une cocarde' [like a cockade] (*L* 203).[53] The fact that the laundry scene appears in '*Lamiel II*' argues against Schor's hypothesis that the conservative logic characteristic of Realist texts compels Stendhal to bind female energy as he re-writes, and effectively un-writes, the text of *Lamiel*.

Another episode, this time from '*Lamiel I*', has also been much censured for its alleged crudity; again, female irreverence is at its centre. The scene in question concerns Lamiel's sexual initiation with a young farmhand, Jean Berville, whom she pays to show her what all the fuss is about. Jacques Laurent remarks that while Stendhal may have wished to amuse us with this scene, 'il n'a réussi qu'à nous troubler' [he succeeded only in disturbing us].[54] Why is this passage deemed so offensive by the apparently universal 'nous' [us]?

Various critics have lamented the crudity of the description. However, the physical act itself is evoked only euphemistically in Stendhal's text: 'sans transport, sans amour, le jeune Normand fit de Lamiel sa maîtresse' [without rapture and without love, the young Norman made Lamiel his mistress] (*L* 67). In fact, the only sexually explicit detail in the entire passage is the reference to the heroine wiping away her blood after the act. It is hard to see how the crudeness of the prose could offend.

In addition to the excessively factual and literal nature of the account, Crouzet complains of the absence of desire in the passage, which he contrasts negatively with the scene where Sansfin sadistically persuades the young heroine to kill a bird and then place its blood in her mouth. The critic considers the latter episode far less shocking to the extent that it, at least, provokes an emotional response in the heroine. Lamiel's initiation scene is contrasted by Michel Crouzet with the description of what he calls the 'prise du pucelage' [taking of virginity] in *La Chartreuse de Parme*, a moment that he considers to be loaded with emotion and meaning and in which Clélia's individuality 's'évanouit dans l'absence de "résistance"' [disappears in the absence of 'resistance'].[55] What is interesting about the contrast established by Crouzet between Lamiel's sexual initiation, on the one hand, and both the bird passage and the Clélia passage, on the other, is that in the latter two passages, which he favours, the heroine's will is dominated and her body and emotions foregrounded. By contrast, in the scenes where Lamiel and Mathilde lose their virginity, Crouzet objects that the heroine is 'totalement lucide, volontaire' [totally lucid, deliberate], entirely in control of her emotions and her body, and therefore 'ridicule' [ridiculous].[56] It seems unlikely that many more than half of readers would agree with Crouzet that there is anything ridiculous about the self-control manifested by these heroines during their first sexual encounter. Lamiel's lack of responsiveness, or what Martin Turnell describes as her 'frigidity' (on account of her allegedly peculiar failure to achieve orgasm),[57] is surely not, then, what is most scandalous about this passage.

Those who express dissatisfaction with the account of Lamiel's sexual initiation often draw attention to the negotiation that takes place prior to the sexual act: the fact that the heroine pays Berville for his service suggests, for many readers, her objectification of him.[58] However, the conversation that takes place between Lamiel and Berville shows that he is far from being a passive object or victim of the exchange, and also that she treats him with respect and consideration. The alleged exploitation of Berville by Lamiel can hardly be the most shocking aspect of the episode.

Crouzet's most interesting objection to the initiation scene is arguably the lack of momentousness or 'conséquence' [consequence], for the heroine, of her sexual rite of passage; he observes that '[l]'éclat de rire final conclut une scène risible ou ridicule, explicitement' [the burst of laughter concludes a scene that is explicitly risible or ridiculous].[59] It seems likely that the most scandalous feature of the entire scene is in fact its lack of seriousness, emblematized by Lamiel's laughter, erupting as it does just after an event that is supposed to be of momentous consequence in the life of a nineteenth-century woman:

> Lamiel s'assit en le regardant s'en aller. (Elle essuya le sang et songea un peu à la douleur.)
> Puis elle éclata de rire en se répétant: 'Comment, ce fameux amour ce n'est que ça!' (*L* 68)

> [Lamiel sat down and watched him go. (She wiped away the blood and thought a little about the pain.)

Then she burst out laughing, saying over and over: 'What! This glorious love
is only that?']

Lamiel's laughter does more than just conclude the scene; it is its whole point. As
Dennis Porter suggests, the heroine's sexual self-initiation not only constitutes a
refusal of the passive role conventionally assigned to women of the time, it also
makes 'a mockery of those societal values which invest such significance in a
simple physical act'.[60] As well as demystifying the sexual act, this scene derides
the sacralization of female pre-marital virginity; the enormous value attached to
female virginity by nineteenth-century bourgeois society was the main reason why
young women were denied their freedom.[61] It is on account of the Hautemares's
investment in Lamiel's virginity that the heroine is forbidden even the most vicarious
enjoyment of the village dances. Finally, as well as mocking the gravity with which
her society invests the sexual act, and in particular the great seriousness attached to
the loss of female virginity, Lamiel's laughter also targets male narcissism. It offers
a glimpse of a female perspective on the story of heterosexual relations.[62] Such a
perspective might, for example, challenge the persistent 'belief that sexuality is the
most important aspect of a woman's life',[63] explode myths about female frigidity,
and suggest an answer to the question Lamiel twice asks of Berville — 'il n'y a rien
autre?' [Isn't there anything else?] — very different from the one he offers ('Non pas
que je sache' [Not that I know of]) (*L* 67).

This chapter has suggested thus far that the perceived plot deficiencies of *Lamiel*,
as well as its grotesque register, have their origin in an attempt to bring a supremely
free heroine into novelistic life. This attempt was a career-long one for Stendhal.
Lamiel is only the most free of Stendhal's Amazons: unhampered by the wealth and
social status of Mina, Vanina, and Mathilde, she possesses all of their intelligence,
audacity, and ingenuity. All of these previous independent heroines had given the
author practical experience in the non-pessimistic representation of female agency:
Mina de Vanghel and *Vanina Vanina* take the form of ostensibly tragic though arguably
optimistic *nouvelles*, while *Le Rouge et le Noir* manages to portray an explicitly non-
tragic free female by presenting her as anomalous and bizarre. It is not certain how
the Mina of *Le Rose et le Vert* would have been represented, had the author finished
the novel, though indications suggest that she may have been less central to the
plot than was Mina de Vanghel to hers. The active and central roles accorded to
women in Stendhal's rewritings of sixteenth-century Italian stories are bound up
with the latters' exotic content and anomalous generic status. *Lamiel* constitutes the
culmination of Stendhal's fictional project in so far as it brings the peculiar conflict
between female freedom and nineteenth-century social and narrative conventions
into the foreground. It does this on the one hand by giving the female character a
centrality never achieved by Mathilde (or indeed Gina), and on the other by giving
her a narrative scope, that of the novel, denied to both Mina de Vanghel and Vanina
Vanini. The next section of this chapter will examine the extent to which each of
the two substantive versions of *Lamiel* places the constantly reasserted freedom of
the heroine at its centre.

Breaking the Chain... Again and Again

Freedom is a recurring theme in Stendhal's works, and has often been a focus of critical studies of the author. As well as Brombert's *Fiction and the Themes of Freedom* and Henri-François Imbert's *Les Métamorphoses de la liberté ou Stendhal devant la Restauration et le Risorgimento*, a number of other critical works published in the 1950s and 1960s examine Stendhal's treatment of freedom, most notably Blin's *Stendhal et les problèmes du roman*, his *Stendhal et les problèmes de la personnalité*, and Starobinski's *L'Œil vivant*. While these works do reference *Lamiel*, they do not pay it the kind of attention that might be expected, given the fact that commentators have always recognized the centrality of the ideal of freedom to the novel and its heroine. This neglect is partly attributable to the fact that Del Litto's revealing edition of the novel was not published until 1971, by which time criticism informed by existentialist ideas about freedom was no longer in favour. As a result, it was feminist critics who first gave serious attention to the theme of freedom in *Lamiel*.

Numerous critics have discussed *Lamiel*'s debt to strong-willed, self-determining eighteenth-century literary heroines, most notably Marivaux's Marianne, Laclos's Mme de Merteuil, and Sade's Juliette. It has been argued, however, notably by Schor and Kara Rabbitt, that the different social and literary context of Stendhal's time worked against the portrayal of an autonomous female subject. Schor's influential study argues that Stendhal's rewritings (or unwritings) of *Lamiel* participate in a logic of Realist representation that militates against the heroine's independent subjecthood, Realist texts being structurally hostile to female energy: 'Unchain the gazelle and let her roam free and the nineteenth-century French novel collapses.'[64] According to this persuasive analysis, *Lamiel*'s character is simply too mobile, too capable of locomotion, to sit comfortably in a Realist narrative. Schor highlights the fact that the description of Sansfin's manipulative education of Lamiel appears for the first time in '*Lamiel II*', and seems designed to confer on the doctor a new structural and psychological dominance over the heroine. According to Schor, then, *Lamiel*'s formidable energy had to be progressively reined in, both thematically and formally, in order to make of her a convincing Realist heroine. Schor's hypothesis is thus pessimistic about the fate of the energetic female in the Realist text.

Many readings of *Lamiel* have, like Schor, highlighted the diminution of the heroine's freedom rather than the manner in which she repeatedly asserts her freedom. Hemmings was the first to point out that the heroine of '*Lamiel II*' can no longer be as fully 'maîtresse d'elle-même' [her own mistress] as her predecessor, once she has become Sansfin's accomplice.[65] Sarah F. Donachie, who echoes many of Hemmings's observations, highlights the greater emotional neediness of the second version of the heroine, as well as her susceptibility to tears, and even states that Lamiel goes from being a 'desiring subject', in '*Lamiel I*', to 'a disposable object of desire' in '*Lamiel II*'.[66] Kara M. Rabbitt claims that while the heroine of '*Lamiel II*' does have some flashes of libertine independence she is ultimately far weaker and less in charge of her own story than her precursor.[67] Longstaffe proposes that the protagonist ultimately becomes Valbaire's slave and is, in Stendhal's *œuvre*, only 'la plus audacieuse et la plus gaie des héroïnes-victimes' [the boldest and gayest of Stendhal's heroine-victims].[68] Crouzet refers to 'le retour du "macho", le domptage de Lamiel, analogue à celui de la "Mégère" shakespearienne, et à celui de Mathilde' [the return of the 'macho', the taming of Lamiel, similar to that of the Shakespearean 'Shrew' and of Mathilde].[69] There is undoubtedly some foundation to such readings: the emotional and intellectual independence of the second version of the heroine does seem more nuanced than that of the first. However, the remainder of this chapter will analyse the plots of '*Lamiel I*' and '*Lamiel II*', as well as the author's written plans for his text, with a view to showing that they reveal not the progressive binding or taming of the heroine's energy but rather her repeated unbinding of the plots that others would weave around her. This demonstration will require minute attention to narrative detail.

Lynn R. Wilkinson has drawn attention, in her article on *Lamiel*, to 'the role of fictions in the construction of the central character'.[70] Certainly, throughout the text(s) of *Lamiel* as we know it, attempts are made by a range of characters to write the heroine's story for her. The Hautemare couple initially adopt her in response to the Abbé Le Clou(d)'s declaration, during his spectacular sermon, that the well-off are duty-bound to give a soul to God. However, the couple (whose circumstances are modest but comfortable) tailor the priest's proposed narrative to the requirements of their own particular plot: they plan to give a soul to God, prevent an unfavoured (because politically liberal) nephew from inheriting their worldly goods, and have someone to look after them in their old age. That the couple want the child to be their creation is further reinforced by Mme Hautemare's response when her husband proposes that they adopt his nephew's child: 'Cet enfant ne sera pas à nous' [That child won't be ours] (*L* 23; see also *L* 189). Upon selecting their child at the Rouen orphanage, the two circulate the story that she is their niece; and henceforth Stendhal's narrative refers to their relationship in these terms. However, the imminent failure of their plot is suggested when, upon the child's arrival at Carville, the villagers correctly deduce that she is a consequence of the Abbé Le Clou(d)'s (literally) hell-raising performance and dub her 'la fille du diable' [the Devil's daughter] (*L* 24, 190). The couple's attempted control of Lamiel's mind is indicated by the allusion to Mme Hautemare's eternal lectures about duty and sinfulness and to M. Hautemare's endless reading lessons. The young girl's freedom of movement is also restricted by her adoptive parents, who restrain her physically as she walks and prohibit her attendance at (and even her witnessing of) the Sunday dance. When the duchess, Mme de Myossens, invites Lamiel to reside with her in her castle, Mme Hautemare negotiates the title of 'lectrice' [reader] for her, lest she be considered a domestic servant; Mme Hautemare's insistence on this point again highlights her desire for authority over Lamiel's plot. In the castle, Lamiel's freedom to elaborate her own plot continues to be circumscribed: she is allowed to walk outside only in the company of one of the duchess's female servants.

However, Lamiel's resistance to externally imposed plots is evident from an early stage in the novel. The first sign of it is her boredom at the age of twelve, which the narrator attributes to 'la présence de l'âme' [presence of spirit] (*L* 26; see also *L* 211). Her abhorred reading classes nevertheless enable her to peruse a medieval adventure story, the *Histoire des quatre fils Aymon* [History of the Four Sons of Aymon], confiscated by M. Hautemare from 'un écolier libertin' [a libertine schoolboy], and to find in it an enjoyment in reading that spurs her on to further readings (*L* 26, 213). When M. Hautemare's domestic collection of books is exhausted, Lamiel steals some editions to exchange at the village grocer's for currants and stories of the eighteenth-century bandits Mandrin and Cartouche. The illicit nature of her subversion of M. Hautemare's plot is underscored by the text; when she eventually tells him about her beloved outlaws, he attempts to correct the ideas she has formed about their admirable qualities. He recognizes Lamiel's 'étrange discours' [extraordinary speech] as alien to the religious narratives that he and his wife have prescribed for their niece (*L* 29; see also *L* 214). In both versions of the text, Lamiel's response to M. Hautemare's horror is to purchase another of the books forbidden to her. In addition, in both instances she begins to write her aunt and uncle into a plot of her own making, imagining for example the unflattering way in which her uncle might have behaved in a couple of the situations handled so admirably by Cartouche and Mandrin.

Once installed in the castle, Lamiel finds a means to subvert the duchess's tight control, leaping through the many rooms of the castle as soon as she knows she is not being watched by the servants. So intense is Lamiel's need for physical exuberance that the enforced gravity of life in the castle, as well as her lengthy daily subjection to the duchess's reading preferences and educational zeal, cause the heroine to fall ill with what Sansfin correctly though privately diagnoses as boredom. Here, as elsewhere in the text, Lamiel's boredom is shown to be a result of her confinement, whether by somebody else's plot or simply by the weather. It is only at this point that the plots of '*Lamiel I*' and '*Lamiel II*' diverge.

'*Lamiel I*'

Focusing for the moment on '*Lamiel I*', the heroine's energy is revitalized by the arrival in Carville of the young, similarly bored Abbé Clément. In one of her conversations with him, she asks him about love and he feels obliged to outline, for her benefit, what he considers to be the universal love plot: love is always dishonouring for women where it does not lead to marriage within forty days; men are respected in direct proportion to the number of young women they dishonour; men always seduce women by speaking about love in a way that leads the latter to want to discover its secret. Her curiosity stimulated by her conversations with the young priest and by her uncle's prohibition against walking in the woods with a young man, Lamiel decides to find out for herself what love is. Shortly after her decision to go walking in the woods with a young man, but before she can enact her plan, Lamiel is sent home from the castle on account of the imminent arrival of the duchess's son, whom she is forbidden by the duchess from seeing. Despite having been sent home with a present of three enormous clothes packages, she wastes no time in donning her cotton cap, clogs, and peasant clothing and heading out to run around the fields. Then, under the influence of the 'profond dégoût' [utter disgust] (*L* 62) produced by her aunt's covetous designs over her fine dresses, Lamiel spends the subsequent months in the fields in order to escape the Hautemare cottage.

When her aunt warns her about men who will want to squeeze her in their arms when they see her alone, and after one drunken young man attempts to do just this, Lamiel's curiosity finally compels her to choose a young man, Jean Berville, to meet in the woods. By her repeated use of the imperative, for the first of very many times in the text of '*Lamiel I*', she expresses that desire for authority over her own life that leads her to take charge of her own defloration.

On the road home after her sexual initiation, Lamiel meets the duchess's son, Fédor (also referred to as Hector or César) de Myossens, with whom she develops a complicity. The duke has qualities — wit, charm, elegance, and knowledge — that appeal to Lamiel, but she cannot love him on account of his readiness to let his behaviour be determined by others or, as the narrator puts it, his lack of 'la force de vouloir' [strength of will/desire] (*L* 71). As befits a character who constantly moulds himself into an object for the gaze of others, Fédor will regard his mistress as a beautiful (if non-compliant) object: 'Mon amour est si ardent qu'il finira par échauffer cette statue si belle' [My love is so ardent that in the end it will warm that beautiful statue] (*L* 81). Despite the duke's Pygmalion fantasy, it is Lamiel who dictates the terms of their relationship, dismissing him imperiously when she judges her first conversation with him to be at an end, and on their second meeting telling him, in her now habitual imperative mode, that he may not speak to her as though she were the duchess's maid. The duke responds by stating that she will play the role of duchess in their relationship, a proposition that pleases Lamiel greatly and of which she takes full advantage throughout their association, exercising a power over him that is as capricious as it is absolute. She forbids him to kiss her except when she ordains it, and demands that he wear black to mourn an alleged cheesemonger relative of hers. Lamiel's high-handed treatment of the young duke points to her will to take absolute control over her own story; she even tells the duke that she would happily treat her uncle in the same way if this were possible.

Lamiel's decision to allow the duke finally to kiss her is prompted by the fact that her aunt has just given her a particularly vigorous lecture about her meetings with the young man. Similarly, her decision later that day to run away with him is a response to her impatience with her aunt and uncle's self-centred complaints about her behaviour: 'C'est pour me moquer d'eux que je me donne à vous' [It's to make fun of them that I'm giving myself to you] (*L* 80). Her definitive rejection of the story prescribed for her by her aunt and uncle is made very clear when their carping causes her to lose any remaining pity at the thought of their lonely futures; she will not look after them in their old age, as they had anticipated. Nevertheless, before the heroine absconds from her home, feeling a sudden pity for her aunt and uncle, she writes a note with details of a face-saving story that they might tell others, thereby conclusively demonstrating that her story is no longer under their rule, but her own.

An ironic awareness of her own self-authorship is evidenced by Lamiel's assurance to César that he has in fact little to do with their decampment; she is the agent and he the accomplice: 'vous m'enlevez fort peu' [you're hardly abducting me at all] (*L* 85). His superfluity to her plot is highlighted again when she decides to proceed to Rouen without continuing to wait for him at the agreed meeting place:

'Je suis bien dupe de l'attendre [...]. Mais qu'ai-je besoin de cette jolie poupée?' [I am a fool indeed to wait for him [...]. But what do I want with that pretty doll?] (*L* 87)

When, armed only with a pair of scissors and a razor tongue, Lamiel is forced to defend herself against the unwelcome advances of her fellow travellers, she learns that her beauty has the power to militate against her status as author of her own story. Later, having become the object of admiration for a group of males in the Rouen hostel, one of them tells her stories of his amorous successes; she gives this self-appointed 'Lovelace' short shrift (*L* 88). The holly-leaf concoction to which the protagonist is introduced that evening by a sympathetic fellow guest safeguards her position as active, self-inventing subject by repelling the admiring gazes and threatening narratives of other people.[71] In a similar repudiation of the position of visual object, she rejects the fashionable clothes that the duke shortly afterwards purchases for her in Rouen and buys instead clothes that make her look like the daughter of a country bourgeois family, on the stated grounds that she does not like being looked at in the street (*L* 94).

Lamiel's role as the duke's puppeteer amuses her and brings her a degree of happiness, but the non-reciprocity it presupposes excludes the possibility of love: 'Lamiel n'éprouva d'autre bonheur que celui de commander' [Lamiel felt only the pleasure of commanding] (*L* 75). The heroine is disappointed in Rouen by the duke's lack of forcefulness; she tells him that she does not want 'un roi fainéant' [a king in name only] but instead wants to see him act of his own volition (*L* 93). If the duke's designs over Lamiel's heart come to naught, however, so do her own hopes for his character. When Lamiel insists that he walk arm in arm with her past his mother on the street, he obeys, but later secretly visits his mother to apologize for his action.

Apart from their few days in Le Havre, occasioned by Lamiel's desire to study the comportment of a famous actress temporarily residing there, the plot imagined by the heroine in Carville unfolds exactly as she had originally planned it. She had told the duke that they would live together in Rouen until he bored her, and despite their nightly trips to the theatre and the literature and geometry lessons that she has him give her, she does indeed decide to leave him when her boredom becomes intolerable. When she orders him to leave her for three days, in the hope of liking him better on his return, he is obliged to obey, just as he had been obliged to consent to accompany her to Le Havre.

Lamiel associates her boredom in Rouen with Fédor's refusal to go running around the fields with her, and his confinement of their walks to the city streets. As soon as he leaves her, she takes to the fields, where a female companion watches in amazement:

> — Courons les champs, ma chère Marthe, lui dit-elle, fuyons cet éternel boulevard de Rouen que le ciel confonde.
> Marthe, la voyant s'égarer à travers champs, suivant de petits sentiers, et quelquefois ne suivant pas de sentiers du tout et s'arrêtant pour jouir de son bonheur lui dit:
> — Il ne vient pas?
> — Qui donc?

— Mais apparemment cet amoureux que vous cherchez?
— Dieu me délivre des amoureux! J'aime mieux ma liberté que tout. (*L* 99)

['Let's go for a run through the fields, my dear Marthe', she said to her, 'let's get away from this unending Rouen boulevard, heaven confound it!'
Marthe, seeing her straying across the fields, following the little pathways and sometimes not following any, and stopping to enjoy her happiness, asked:
'Isn't he coming?'
'Who?'
'That lover you seem to be looking for.'
'Lord save me from lovers! I love my freedom above all else.']

This passage illustrates a key point not only about Lamiel's desire to choose her own path, and her rejection of prescribed paths, but also about the manner in which she elaborates her own route. She proceeds without any defined destination or need of direction, continually improvising the routes she takes, and her happiness arises precisely from her freedom to do this. As is stated very clearly, she prioritizes her freedom over any other goal, including love.[72] It is difficult to imagine any more concise formulation of the existentialist ethic. Indeed, if 'the authentic individual is one who wills her or his own freedom and the freedom of others', it seems appropriate that having decided to leave the duke after her 'essai de liberté' [trial period of freedom] (*L* 102) during his absence, Lamiel should write him a note from Paris to say that she is giving him back his freedom.[73]

The duke attempts to find her and is almost suicidal with distress, all as Lamiel had apparently predicted: 'Toutes les prévisions de Lamiel s'accomplirent' [All Lamiel's predictions came to pass] (*L* 106). Upon her arrival in Paris, she invents a new persona for herself, and fabricates a story designed to win the sympathy and complicity of her hotel manageress, Mme Le Grand. Like Stendhal himself, she finds it difficult to remember the detail of her fictions, so needs to write her story down, in the form of a putative letter to an uncle. Interestingly, from a feminist perspective, the story Lamiel invents to explain her presence in Paris involves her escape from being traded in marriage by her father in the service of his political ambitions; its plot is of the kind found in sentimental novels authored by women during the period of the July Monarchy, and in which a female protagonist is represented as victimized by a male persecutor.[74] Lamiel will in fact soon find herself in danger of becoming ensnared in a plot designed to further a man's social ambitions, though she is very far from being a sentimental heroine.

Two characters, during Lamiel's Parisian phase, try to write her into their plots, but she repeatedly overlays their plans with her own. When Mme Le Grand exhorts her to attend fashionable soirées where she might meet rich young men, she responds by stating her intention to take dance classes and by asking the older woman to accompany her occasionally to the theatre. The plot conceived by Count d'Aubigné/ de Nerwinde is far more threatening to Lamiel's independence. When the drunken count initially conceives 'son projet sur Lamiel' [his plan for Lamiel], he is attracted by an originality that he nevertheless wants to teach her to suppress: 'il y a quelque chose de singulier, d'original chez cette jeune fille. Et moi je veux la former' ['there's something strange and original about that young woman. I want to mould her] (*L* 111). He intends to put this 'jeune gazelle' ['young gazelle'] into a cage to prevent her escaping from him (*L* 117). On receiving a sign of interest from the heroine, he imagines that 'Elle est à moi' ['She's mine'] (*L* 120) and decides that instead of conducting a private affair with her, he will gather some money so that he can show her off in public. The count's narrative pretensions over Lamiel are made explicit by the text: if he is going to make her his mistress, it is at least partly because he longs to have authorship of her story: 'j'aurai à conter son histoire' [I will have to tell her story] (*L* 120). He meditates upon a new name for her, and finally gives her the wildly inappropriate name of Mme de Saint-Serve when, after successfully plotting to acquire money from his sister, he is in a position to flaunt her on his arm at the opera and install her in an apartment. The count's obsession with story-telling, or what the text describes as 'la passion de parler et de raconter' [a passion for talking and telling anecdotes] (*L* 124), is further confirmed by his interest in making of the change in his financial circumstances 'une anecdote piquante et qui me fasse honneur au Cercle' [a witty story that will do me honour at the Club] (*L* 129). Lamiel's absorption into the count's plot is indicated by the fact that she submits to his wishes: he buys her new clothes, tells her what name to call herself, and instructs her to put an end to her relationship with Mme Le Grand. Far from resenting the attempted usurpation of her self-authorship, Lamiel celebrates the central role she now occupies, thanks to the count, within an admiring social circle: 'Elle était ravie du rôle que le comte lui faisait jouer dans le monde et de la hauteur à laquelle il l'avait placée' [She was delighted with the part the count had given her to play in society, and with the height at which he had placed her] (*L* 135). While Lamiel's thoughts and words are not often recounted in the form of direct speech in this part of the story, those around her are impressed by her eloquence to the extent that they compare her, in one draft, to the powerful and independent seventeenth-century courtesan and author, Ninon de Lenclos (*L* 132).

If the count achieves a degree of success in his attempt to write Lamiel into his amorous plot, his power over her is provisional only. He first catches her attention when she learns that he is capable of brutality towards those he considers his social inferiors, because this fact leads her to believe that he is the antithesis of the polite duke. She also realizes that entering into a relationship with the count means that she will be brought to the theatre. At this point in '*Lamiel I*', the heroine is suffering from a boredom bordering on ill health on account of the fact that she can no longer walk or travel by bus without her beauty attracting unwelcome attention, even with the help of her holly paste. Consequently, the prospect of outings with the count is irresistible to her. After a very short time, Lamiel realizes that her admiration for the count's energetic character was misplaced. However, the pleasures of the society into which he introduces her outweigh the tedium of his company. At the end of one week of intimacy with him, Lamiel locks herself in her bedroom. The count is unfazed by the end of their sexual relationship, seeming to believe that all that matters is that her continued presence by his side enhances his social prestige and his 'autorité [...] parmi les hommes de plaisir' [authority [...] among men of pleasure] (*L* 140). The heroine continues to play along with the count's story in public, on the grounds that it allows her to live a physically agreeable life. However, some time after the count has told his friends the truth about his relationship with Lamiel, and after all of these friends have ineffectually played out their own seduction plots around her, she begins an affair with one of these men in order to punish the count. That this 'première infidélité' [first infidelity] (*L* 146) signals Lamiel's reclaiming of authority over her own story is suggested by her sudden return to a speaking and commanding role in the text.

Just after this turning-point, Lamiel absconds from her apartment and encounters the Abbé Clément, whom she persuades to listen to the (carefully edited) story of her life since her departure from the castle. At a subsequent meeting, suggested by Lamiel, she defends her 'mauvaise conduite' [bad conduct] in the following terms: 'Ne suis-je pas maîtresse de moi? À qui est-ce que je fais tort? À quelle promesse est-ce que je manque?' [Am I not my own mistress? To whom am I doing wrong? With whom am I not keeping faith?] (*L* 153) Lamiel's resumption of control over her story is blatant. The young priest's aim, in his conversations with Lamiel, is to persuade her to change her ways, but he signally fails to do this. The narrative of '*Lamiel I*' concludes with her decision to invite a second friend of the count's to play the 'rôle' of her lover, this time for more explicitly authorial purposes: she tells this new man that she wishes to taunt, and provoke the jealousy of, her 'seigneur et maître' [lord and master] and to see the latter's character develop in consequence (*L* 156). Further subversions of the count's narrative authority are outlined in episodes that were sketched by the author but never integrated into the overarching story: in one, Lamiel dresses as a man to offend the count's sense of dignity, and in the other, dressed in a black velvet mask, she places herself among the prostitutes in a bordello visited by the count and his friends; when he begins to talk about her, she unmasks herself and astonishes him (*L* 134, 163).

In a plan that Stendhal sketched out in May 1839, as in one of November of the same year, when he was still working on the first version of the story, the heroine eventually encounters a criminal, falls in love with him, and spoils Sansfin's plan to marry her to the duke. In the November plan, Lamiel does finally consent to Sansfin's marriage plot, after refusing to allow the duke to be robbed by the cronies of her imprisoned lover, Valbaire; however, shortly afterwards, upon seeing the latter chained up, she again frustrates Sansfin by leaving her husband and entering into association with the criminal cronies. Valbaire escapes but is once more arrested before finally killing himself. Lamiel then burns down the Palais de Justice 'pour venger Valbaire' [to avenge Valbaire] (*L* 163). We can never know whether this ending would have been retained by Stendhal, but its survival would seem to be suggested by the fact that in a late plan of March 1841 Lamiel is said to prefer an energetic 'assassin' (now going by the name of the real-life criminal Lacenaire) over the duke (*L* 366). In any case, the ending in which Lamiel dies in a symbolic conflagration of her own making does seem an appropriate conclusion for a heroine so admiring, in both versions of the story, of the careers of Mandrin and Cartouche: 'Leur fin qui arrivait toujours en lieu élevé et en présence de nombreux spectateurs lui semblait noble; le livre ne vantait-il pas leur courage et leur énergie?' [Their end, which always occurred in an elevated place among numerous spectators, seemed to her a noble one; did not the books praise their courage and energy?] (*L* 28; see also

L 214) From the beginning of '*Lamiel I*' to its projected ending, then, the heroine insists on writing her own story.

'*Lamiel II*'

In support of the argument that the second heroine is a meeker creation than the first, Wilkinson cites the opening of '*Lamiel II*', which frames the heroine's story within 'a series of masculine anecdotes'.[75] It is true that the second heroine is more obviously inserted into layers of narrative than was the first — the narrator, who temporarily takes on the persona of a notary's son and one-time guest of the duchess, claims that he will tell the heroine's story, apparently recounted to him by his Carville source or sources over the years — but if she is at the centre of the stories imparted to him, there is no sense that she is contained or disempowered by the swirl of narratives, no sense that she is caught in any textual web:

> La curiosité m'a porté à savoir des nouvelles de Carville, de la marquise maintenant duchesse depuis longtemps, de son fils, des Hautemare. Toutes ces aventures, car il y en a eu, tournent autour de la petite Lamiel, adoptée par les Hautemare, et j'ai pris la fantaisie de les écrire afin de devenir homme de lettres. (*L* 193)

> [Curiosity incited me to find out news of Carville, of the marquise who had long since been made duchess, of her son, and of the Hautemares. All of the events, for there were a few, turn around little Lamiel, adopted by the Hautemares, and I have had the fancy to write them down so that I could become a man of letters.]

The stories that encircle the heroine are presented by the narrator not as immobilizing her but rather as being in motion around her; and the heroine of '*Lamiel II*' will prove just as capable as her predecessor of working her way free of imposed narratives and of devising her own plots. In fact, until the point at which she falls ill with boredom, the heroine of '*Lamiel II*' is virtually indistinguishable from her precursor, and, if anything, is even bolder than she; for example, in the laundry scene, which does not feature at all in '*Lamiel I*', she is instructed to run home by her aunt and, while running instead towards the field where the forbidden Sunday dance takes place, she meets village women with whom she trades insults.

Later in this second version of the narrative, when the heroine has assumed the position of reader for the duchess, it is Sansfin's lessons rather than her conversations with the Abbé Clément that succeed in curing Lamiel of her boredom-induced illness. In '*Lamiel I*', as in '*Lamiel II*', Sansfin is the only character correctly to attribute the heroine's ailment to boredom, but in the second version of the story he deliberately misdiagnoses her with tuberculosis and, after overcoming some resistance from the duchess by exacerbating the young girl's symptoms to prove his point, has her sent home from the castle to serve his own ends. Sansfin then sets about curing Lamiel by reading her accounts of criminal cases from the *Gazette des Tribunaux*. Fed on this diet of sensational news stories, Lamiel's boredom begins to recede.

In 'Lamiel II', Sansfin is presented as an originator of narratives from his first appearance in the newly added opening pages of the second version of the novel, during a parlour game involving stories about past amorous conquests. Later, around the time of the storytelling cure he offers Lamiel, what Hamm calls Sansfin's 'don de l'intrigue' [talent for plotting][76] is further attested by his manipulation of the duchess, whose sense of guilt and indebtedness he reinforces with the imaginative account he gives of the young girl's illness, even going so far as to put accusatory words into the latter's mouth. The doctor then elaborates another narrative that has the effect of persuading all in the village of Carville that the formidable Abbé Du Saillard is jealous of his success in saving Lamiel's life; as intended, this story works to safeguard Sansfin from the priest's fury at his increasing power over the duchess. Fired up by this success, the doctor conceives two further plots: he will seduce Lamiel and he will make himself so indispensable to the duchess that she will marry him, a result which, at worst, would enable him to escape to America as a rich man. Shortly afterwards, Sansfin decides against this particular marriage plot, resolving instead to exploit his powers of persuasion to become a member of parliament, and to enjoy himself in the interim by seducing both Lamiel and the duchess.

The lengthy exposition of Sansfin's redoubtable skills as an originator of narratives serves as a prelude to his attempted conquest of Lamiel. Despite being astonished by the clarity and vigour of her young mind, which makes her unusually difficult to deceive, he does appear to convince her very quickly that he is her only friend in the world and, according to the narrator (though not the subsequent evidence of the text), soon manages to destroy her affection for the Hautemares, in whose home he treats her. He copper-fastens Lamiel's sense of complicity with him, and teaches her discretion, by persuading her to consent to 'un meurtre horrible' [a horrible murder] so as to convince others that she needs continued medical attention and to allow him time to teach her 'le bon sens' [common sense] (L 245), a faculty that he claims she lacks. The murder to which Lamiel is made an accomplice is that of a bird, whose blood she must pour onto a little sponge, held in her mouth. Sansfin plays cleverly here on her obvious appetite for criminal deeds. Throughout the section detailing the doctor's relationship with Lamiel, as in the pages describing the period of her relationship with the count in 'Lamiel I', the heroine speaks only infrequently. A further parallel with the count is suggested by Sansfin's words, which almost exactly repeat the former's formulation: 'Elle sera à moi' [She will be mine] (L 248). But Sansfin's plot is not without its flaws, and it does not achieve its intended conclusion. He imagines wrongly, for example, that the mocking tone he encourages Lamiel to adopt will scare away any handsome men who may come knocking at her door. Nevertheless, if the doctor, like the count in 'Lamiel I', fails ultimately to absorb the heroine into his own plot, his lessons do at least have the merit of teaching her (if such teaching were needed) to suspect other people's motives, including his own.

While administering his lessons in common sense to Lamiel, Sansfin also exploits his growing influence over the duchess to persuade her to increase her popularity (and therefore his own political capital) among the local aristocracy by building a false medieval tower next to the Hautemare cottage and by hosting a great banquet there. Lamiel is reduced to watching the improvised ball that follows this grand meal from the closed windows of a carriage; she has become, in this episode, a mere ancillary to Sansfin's career-driven plot. However, the young girl's resistance to the doctor's various intrigues is demonstrated by the fact that, when she declares that she wants to move into the part of the tower that the duchess has designated for her, she is 'inflexible' against Sansfin's pleas, made on his knees (*L* 256). The reason for Sansfin's opposition to the heroine's plan is not spelled out in the text, but the reason for his concession is: he deduces that her growing vanity has inspired her to rebel against his intellectual superiority over her, and that if he does not grant her wishes now he may not succeed in seducing her in the future. While the Stendhalian narrator does not comment on the accuracy or otherwise of Sansfin's diagnosis, Lamiel's first refusal to play along with his narrative signals both the end of a chapter in Stendhal's text and the beginning of a new phase in her relations with the doctor. As Garnier rightly points out, 'Lamiel ne cessera de déjouer les tentatives de domination de Sansfin (et ceci dans toutes les versions du récit).' [Lamiel will continue to foil Sansfin's efforts to dominate her (and will do so in all of the versions of the story.][77] In the course of the chapter following her refusal to obey Sansfin's wishes, for example, the heroine astonishes him again by returning to the castle rather than moving into the tower as planned. The evolution of Lamiel's relationship with the doctor indicates that, far from submitting to his power, she simply learns what she can from him before asserting her independence, just as she does in the case of the duke in '*Lamiel I*'. According to this reading, Sansfin is a secondary character among others rather than a protagonist in the making.[78]

At the beginning of this next chapter, while Lamiel is still in the cottage, the duchess brings the Abbé Clément to visit her; it is their first meeting in this version of the story. The young priest is both astonished and won over by the young heroine's unexpected 'naïveté charmante' [charming naivety] (*L* 259). Sansfin, upon hearing the two laughing together, immediately sees that his cause is lost. However, if the priest's lessons in history and literature cause Lamiel to reflect on the difference between his version of how the world operates and Sansfin's, she is not at all persuaded by the conventional marriage plot he recommends. Repelled at the thought of marrying a villager, Lamiel decides instead to go to Rouen and earn her living as a book-keeper. This latter plot, entirely of the heroine's making, indicates that she is just as unconvinced by Sansfin's libertine narrative as she is by the Abbé Clément's anodine one: 'Si Lamiel était peu susceptible de sentiment tendre, [...] la méchanceté trop découverte du docteur Sansfin heurtait un peu cette âme encore si jeune' [Though Lamiel was little prone to tender feelings, [...] Doctor Sansfin's too obvious malice jarred a little on her still youthful spirit] (*L* 265). She is hardly recognizable here as the figure whom Jones describes as a 'disciple convaincu du machiavélique Sansfin' [convinced disciple of the Machiavellian Sansfin].[79]

Nevertheless, Sansfin continues to weave his web of stories around Lamiel, firing her curiosity about love by associating the latter with extreme danger and the kind of intrigue that she likes reading about in the stories of *One Thousand and One Nights*. At the same time, the heroine is busy conceiving her own dangerous and secret amorous plots, one being a trip to the woods with a young man and the other being the seduction of the Abbé Clément. Both of these projects would thwart the doctor's own seduction plot in the most humiliating way imaginable for him, attractive young men being those he most envies.

While the heroine's sexual self-initiation is not detailed in '*Lamiel II*' as it is in '*Lamiel I*', its consequences are sketched out twice in Stendhal's very late (March 1842) notes for the novel. In one of these drafts, Lamiel tells the doctor how she had negotiated this rite of passage with a local youth; he is outraged, and even attacks the man in a corridor of the duchess's castle. In a second draft, Lamiel again tells Sansfin how she paid a young man to enlighten her about the meaning of virginity, and again the doctor's reactions are highlighted. His 'fureur et désappointement' [fury and disappointment] (*L* 381) once more lead him to attack the youth, but this time the doctor pays for the latter's silence in order to safeguard his own reputation. Schor maintains that in this very late fragment, 'Stendhal unwrites the most radical episode in the original text — Lamiel's sexual initiation by hire, the ultimate role reversal — by reinscribing Lamiel in the circuit of homosexual exchange from which he had initially so miraculously exempted her.'[80] But the heroine's act has not been unwritten here; the event itself is not detailed as it (arguably) is in '*Lamiel I*', but the initiation is still clearly presented as having taken place, and may still have been included in some form in the projected text. In these late drafts, the heroine's audacity is actually underscored rather than unwritten, because now her act has narrative consequences (even if it still has little if any consequence for Lamiel herself); it is also now presented as a foiling of Sansfin's plot. If the author did hesitate about its inclusion, this may be not because the second Lamiel is meeker or more obedient than the first but rather because the episode risked being misconstrued, in its new textual context, as a submission to the doctor's libertine philosophy rather than as the act of non-compliance presented in these drafts.

Returning now to the actual text of '*Lamiel II*', around the time that the heroine is planning her venture into sexual self-authorship, news of the July Revolution of 1830 reaches Carville and provokes a comically false alarm in the duchess, who summons her son to safety from Paris. The doctor, convinced that his persuasive prestige will enable him to carve out a political role in the new administration, attempts to talk the duchess into allowing her son to return to Paris so that he can accompany the young man and align himself with the winning side; Sansfin's failure to sway the duchess reveals a further shrinkage of his power over the direction of the narrative.

In the final pages of '*Lamiel II*', the duchess repairs to Le Havre and then Portsmouth with her son. Closely mirroring the manner in which she asserts her freedom upon returning from the castle to the family home in '*Lamiel I*', the heroine escapes joyfully into the fields, dressed in peasant clothing. Lamiel is now distanced from Sansfin, who has accompanied the duchess and her son to Le Havre before busying himself for a short time with the furthering of his political career in Paris and the Vendée; the doctor returns to Carville on the pretext of sickness, but he will not reappear in person in the main text of '*Lamiel II*'.

The heroine's sense of exhilaration after her release from the castle is short-lived, however. Subsequent to this escapade, as in '*Lamiel I*', the young girl is confronted by the incontrovertible fact of her aunt's pettiness: Mme Hautemare's manner of acquiring some of Lamiel's fine dresses renders her utterly unlovable in the eyes of the heroine. The latter, by contrast with her precursor, and despite Sansfin's stated success in having put an end to her affection for her adoptive parents, is more upset by the end of her love for her aunt than she is disgusted by the latter's coarseness.[81] Trapped and despairing in the family cottage, unable to install herself in the duchess's abandoned tower for fear of becoming the target of scurrilous neighbourhood gossip, she seeks out the Abbé Clément, but by contrast with his behaviour at end of '*Lamiel I*', he refuses to see her. The heroine's desperation drives her to visit the duchess's right-hand woman in the castle, from the library of which she borrows twenty volumes before remembering a piece of advice from Sansfin: 'juger toujours la situation et s'élever au-dessus de la sensation du moment' [always evaluate the situation and rise above the feeling of the moment] (*L* 311). Lamiel then takes numerous books that the duchess had denied her during her time in the castle; she chooses only those that have not been bound, thereby eluding Mme Anselme's documentation of her borrowings.

As in '*Lamiel I*', at the point where '*Lamiel II*' ends the heroine is once again fully in charge of her own story. She breaks out from the family cottage during the day to read in the woods, and every night she escapes to read *Gil Blas* in the tower. M. Hautemare, who learns that Lamiel has purchased oil from a local shop, is intent on discovering her secret as the narrative tails off, but the final sentence of '*Lamiel II*' leaves him frustrated: 'Ce fut en vain qu'il rôda tout autour de la maison, il ne vit rien d'extraordinaire' [It was in vain that he prowled all around the house, he saw nothing extraordinary] (*L* 315). This then is where '*Lamiel II*' leaves its heroine: revelling in her imagination, beyond the reach of her various self-styled teachers.[82] The story stops just before her uncle is allowed to discover her ruse, and ends in defiantly un-Realistic fashion, with forbidden novels from a past era being consumed in a fantasy medieval tower.

The Impossibility of a Conclusion

The Realist narrative that attempts, according to Schor, to constrain the young heroine reaches no proper conclusion and achieves no unity or completion. As Schor herself says, the text is 'totally inconclusive': 'In the end, Lamiel never does learn to walk in a socially acceptable fashion' and 'succeeds only fleetingly in fettering her walk'.[83] Lamiel's choice of freedom is repeatedly demonstrated by her consistent ability to detach herself from the bonds that would otherwise constrain her. As Beauvoir observes of the novel's heroine, whose story she adapted, intriguingly, for Radio Vichy, 'devant un cœur si résolu, les obstacles matériels ne peuvent manquer de s'aplanir; le seul problème ce sera pour elle de se tailler en un monde médiocre une destinée à sa mesure' [before such a resolute heart, physical obstacles can only be smoothed away; the only problem for her will be to carve out, in a mediocre world, a destiny worthy of her].[84] Instead of being progressively constrained by narratives imposed from without, Lamiel repeatedly breaks free of these narratives and elaborates her own plots.

Among the plots shrugged off by Lamiel is the one dictated by biology: this most curious of characters seems to feel no curiosity at all about her own mysterious origins. As Berthier points out, the heroine's indifference to her anatomical history is continuous with her practice of always inventing her own future(s) rather than allowing her movement to be circumscribed by any prescribed plot.[85] Lamiel's refusal to be defined by her past both anticipates Sartre's definition of freedom and explains why she has so often been associated with nihilism: 'La liberté c'est l'être humain mettant son passé hors de jeu en sécrétant son propre néant' [Freedom is the human being putting his past out of play by secreting his own nothingness]; 'la liberté ne se conçoit que comme néantisation d'un donné' [freedom can only be conceived as the reduction to nothing of a thing that is given].[86] Lamiel relentlessly avoids being defined by her past, thereby evading the seriousness that is, for Sartre, the antithesis of freedom. As Jean-Jacques Labia puts it, 'l'héroïne sait jouer avec la vie' [the heroine knows how to play with her life].[87]

Lamiel is, at every level, a novel about freedom, as is every good work of literature according to Sartre.[88] Freedom is never represented as a given in this novel; it must continually be claimed. It is her instinct for freedom that gives Lamiel her distinctive mobility and that compels her repeatedly to extract herself from situations in which she feels confined. Longstaffe notes that 'Lamiel is the most truly independent of Stendhal's heroines'.[89] In fact, of the primary protagonists of Stendhal's novels, this heroine may be the one who most convincingly epitomizes the existentialist ethos, resisting all efforts by others to instrumentalize her and repeatedly asserting her freedom as a subject.[90] Octave de Malivert, Julien Sorel, and Lucien Leuwen all pursue the realization of their individual projects with great seriousness: Octave feels an overweening sense of duty to others, Julien's project reaches completion when he has adopted the grave persona of the Chevalier de La Vernaye, while Lucien's seriousness nearly earns him social death. Lamiel, by contrast, enthusiastically embraces the lightness of existence: the villagers of Carville may be mistaken when they read modesty into her appearance in peasant clothes, so soon after returning from the castle in a carriage, but her action does highlight the character's lack of vanity, relative to Stendhal's dignity-conscious heroes. Indeed, of the author's male novelistic protagonists, only the impulsive Fabrice del Dongo can rival Lamiel for sheer insouciance; but even the hero of *La Chartreuse de Parme* is too much a superstitious believer in prescribed destiny, too much a puppet of outside forces, whether benign or malign, human or celestial, to equal the irreverent, self-determining Lamiel.[91]

As well as being a novel of freedom, *Lamiel* is about the achievement of joy. Despite Bardèche's claim that Lamiel never achieves that happiness that he considers to be the birthright of the Stendhalian hero, there is much to suggest that she is in fact the happiest of Stendhal's protoganists.[92] She is described as 'parfaitement heureuse' [perfectly happy] during her conversations with the Abbé Clément (*L* 47) as well as during the entire period of Fédor's absence in Rouen (*L* 101). Indeed, she appears to experience her most intense happiness when running around the fields of Rouen during the latter's absence, and on the night she abandons him at the theatre and takes the stagecoach to Paris. There, those in Lamiel's libertine circle cannot understand that she could be so constantly happy while sleeping separately from the count, just as critics tend to assume that, because the heroine does not find love in the course of the narrative proper, she is somehow unhappy or incomplete. But Lamiel does not need to be loved or to love in order to be happy; she only needs her freedom. She explicitly rejects the idea that love is, as it is represented on the stage, 'le plus grand des bonheurs' [the greatest happiness of all] (*L* 100), and tells her companion Marthe, as we have seen, that she loves freedom more than love. Indeed, Lamiel is exceptional among Stendhal's protagonists in that she never experiences love, except in the author's notes for an ending where she is described as 'folle d'amour' [madly in love] (*L* 160) and as 'éperdument amoureuse' [desperately in love] (*L* 161) with Valbaire. However, she is entirely typical to the extent that the choices made by Stendhal's heroes and heroines all ultimately gesture towards a deep scepticism about the capacity of love to guarantee lasting happiness.

For Xavier Bourdenet and Anne Leoni, the heroine's various getaways and adventures repeat on a personal scale the struggle for liberation represented by July 1830, an event that is given a prominent place in '*Lamiel II*'.[93] Ansel also sees Lamiel's personal history as running parallel to that of France in the 1830s; despite holding that the freedom to which she aspires is as self-serving and cynical as the kind endorsed by the July Monarchy, he does acknowledge the uncompromising nature of the heroine's desire for freedom: 'Ce qui est premier chez elle, comme chez Brulard, c'est la revendication d'une liberté entière.' [What is fundamental in her, as in Brulard, is the demand for complete freedom.][94]

There is nothing easy or reassuring about absolute freedom, either for the person who enacts it or for those who witness its enactment. As is appropriate for a character that appears in the text as a direct result of a firework display designed to unsettle a congregation, the heroine's behaviour tends to render other characters uneasy. Her admiration for bandits scandalizes her aunt and uncle, as will, later, her meetings with the young duke. The Abbé Clément describes her to his close friend as 'étonnante' [astonishing], and his unease will become palpable when Lamiel delights in disturbing his composure with her questions about love. The duke falls for the heroine at the moment she first unexpectedly and abruptly takes her leave of him, his amazement changing him into a 'statue' (*L* 72). Her suggestion that they run away together leaves him as paralysed with astonishment as at this first moment. She revels in provoking the duke's unease, for example by telling him that her green cheek is the effect of a recurring skin condition before obliging him to kiss it. Lamiel's statement of her preference for freedom over love leaves a female companion 'pétrifiée d'étonnement' [petrified with astonishment] (*L* 100); the character's behaviour also produces 'étonnement' in Mme Le Grand (*L* 104).

Lamiel disconcerts commentators too. The critic Jules Bois commented in 1889 that 'Lamiel est effrayante d'insouciance, d'insincérité, de cabotinage érotique' [Lamiel is frightening with her carefree attitude, insincerity, and erotic play-acting].[95] Alain refers to her character as 'terrible' on account of her extreme sincerity, and to her 'coquetterie' as 'effrayante' (frightening),[96] while May notes that much criticism of *Lamiel* and its heroine betrays 'un certain malaise de la part des lecteurs les plus perspicaces' [a certain discomfort on the part of the sharpest readers].[97] The historical devaluation of both the novel and its heroine can perhaps be chalked up to the anxiety provoked by the consciousness of freedom with which they present us. The text certainly presents little invitation to the reader to enter into any cosy complicity with its protagonist. By contrast with Stendhal's previous novels, the reader is given relatively little insight into the protagonist's mental processes. The narrator's comments about Lamiel's character lack that paternal, indulgent irony that makes it so apparent that he likes his other protagonists. It is, as a result, the reader who must freely decide how to interpret *Lamiel* and its heroine. This particular reader has chosen to interpret the novel not as an exercise in cynicism, nor as an artistic failure, nor as testament to the triumph of Realism over female desire, but rather as an unrelenting experiment in freedom. According to this reading, there is no 'failure of nerve'[98] in the transition from '*Lamiel I*' to '*Lamiel II*', just an extension of the same fundamental experiment.

The projected ending in which Lamiel dies while vengefully burning down the Palais de Justice has often been interpreted as the heroine's defeat.[99] However, it seems more appropriate, in the context of the reading that has been performed in this chapter, to interpret it as an affirmation, on the heroine's part, of her existential freedom. For Penny Boumelha, the implausible endings of Realist texts often reveal the impossibility of any satisfactory plot resolution for women within that framework. She cites the example of the flood that gives such a catastrophic ending to George Eliot's *The Mill on the Floss*, and which she presents as symbolic of the uncontainable character of female desire:

> The dammed-up energy created by the frustrated ambitions and desires, intellectual and sexual, of the woman is so powerful that it cannot be contained with the forms of mimesis: the repressed and thwarted potential of Maggie conjures into being that destructive, vengeful, triumphant flood.[100]

Lamiel's conflagration is potentially as destructive, vengeful, and triumphant as Maggie's flood; but, in the draft form it takes at least, it seems somehow less serious, less final. In line with the argument put forward in this chapter, in Lamiel's case the implausible resolution may express not so much the impossibility of containing her frustrated energy as the impossibility of containing her energy, and her insistence on joy.

Notes to Chapter 3

1. As the character of Julien Sorel might be understood to demonstrate, the *faculté de vouloir* did not always entail a playful attitude, for Stendhal, who believed for example that English people had the former in abundance, without any of the latter. See *Promenades dans Rome*, p. 146 (27 January 1828), pp. 183–84 (18 April 1828).
2. According to Manzini, Stendhal does not endorse M. Leuwen's ludism. 'Work, Idleness, and Play'.
3. See for example Stendhal, *De l'Amour*, p. 333 (third draft preface); *Orc* I 827.
4. See *OI* II 730–31. See also the contrast established by the author between his own father's 'noir pédantisme' [dark pedantism] and the 'amabilité si gaie et si gentille' [so cheerful and pleasant kindness] of his friend's father (*OI* II 795–96; *Vie de Henri Brulard*).
5. Crouzet, *Le Naturel, la grâce et le réel*, pp. 121, 125; Jefferson, *Reading Realism*, pp. 107, 129. See also Spandri, *L'Art de Komiker'*, pp. 137–53.

6. *Le Deuxième Sexe*, I, 378–79.

7. See for example Adolphe Paupe, *Histoire des œuvres de Stendhal* (Paris: Dujarric, 1903, repr. Geneva: Slatkine Reprints, 1998), pp. 229–39.

8. *Stendhal: A Study of his Novels*, p. 206.

9. *Fiction and the Themes of Freedom*, pp. 177–78.

10. Yves Ansel, *Stendhal littéral: 'Lamiel'* (Grenoble: ELLUG, 2009), p. 208. The other monographs are: Philippe Berthier, *'Lamiel' ou la boîte de Pandore* (Paris: Presses Universitaires de France, 1994) and Thompson, *'Lamiel': Fille du feu*. See also *RHLF*, 109.1 (2009). The conference took place at the University of Aix-en-Provence.

11. For examples of negative reactions to the novel's incompletion, see Prévost, *La Création chez Stendhal*, p. 385; Blin, *Stendhal et les problèmes du roman*, p. 175; Gilbert D. Chaitin, *The Unhappy Few: A Psychological Study of the Novels of Stendhal* (Bloomington: Indiana University Press, 1972), p. 188.

12. While both Anne-Marie Meininger and Jean-Jacques Hamm, in their later editions of the novel, introduce minor variations, they essentially follow Martineau's organization of the text. Stendhal, *Lamiel*, ed. by Anne-Marie Meininger (Paris: Gallimard, 1983) and Stendhal, *Lamiel*, ed. by Jean-Jacques Hamm (Paris: Flammarion, 1993).

13. The terms '*Lamiel I*' and '*Lamiel II*' were first used to distinguish the two main versions of the text in F. W. J. Hemmings, 'Les Deux *Lamiel*: Nouveaux aperçus sur les procédés de composition de Stendhal romancier', *Stendhal Club*, 60 (1973), 287–316.

14. *Mimesis: The Representation of Reality in Western Literature* (Princeton: Princeton University Press, 1946), p. 463. Serge Linkès points out that *Lamiel*, like *Féder*, continues Stendhal's youthful interest in writing comedy for the theatre. 'De *Letellier* à *Lamiel*, la comédie continue', *L'Année stendhalienne*, 1 (2002), 255–80 (p. 265).

15. See for example Bardèche, *Stendhal romancier*, pp. 448–50; Richard, *Littérature et sensation*, p. 114; Jacques Laurent, *Stendhal comme Stendhal, ou le mensonge ambigu* (Paris: Grasset & Fasquelle, 1984), p. 199.

16. Michel Crouzet, '*Lamiel* grotesque', in *Stendhal et le comique*, ed. by Daniel Sangsue (Grenoble: ELLUG, 1999), pp. 267–304 ; Ansel, *Stendhal littéral: 'Lamiel'*, pp. 204, 190. Pearson, in a similar vein, highlights the bizarre tonality of Lamiel with his comment that Stendhal 'set out to write a *Le Rouge et le Noir* for feminists', but instead found himself, particularly in his second version, 'working on a cross between *Lucien Leuwen* and *Beauty and the Beast*'. *Stendhal's Violin*, p. 258.

17. See Ansel, *Stendhal littéral: 'Lamiel'*, pp. 204–05; Gide, 'En relisant *Lamiel*', p. 37. However, Parmentier argues that the refusal to adopt a serious posture is characteristic of the Stendhalian narrator more generally. *Stendhal stratège*, pp. 72–80.

18. *Lamiel*, ed. by Meininger, p. 271. For Meininger, the word 'gouine', now translatable as 'dyke', suggests that the author had come to the realization that Mélanie, the former mistress on whom he had partly modelled Lamiel, had been lesbian; according to Meininger, this retrospective discovery gave rise to his detachment from the character (pp. 29–30). However, Garnier notes that the *Dictionnaire historique de la langue française* indicates that 'gouine' only acquired the connotation of homosexuality in 1867; at the time of writing *Lamiel*, it would simply have meant, according to Littré, 'coureuse, femme de mauvaise vie' [a manhunter, a loose woman]. *La Femme comme construction*, section 4.3.4. This point is echoed in Ansel, *Stendhal littéral: 'Lamiel'*, p. 35.

19. Garnier's careful examination of the manuscript from which the note is drawn throws serious doubt on the hypothesis of an allusion to Lamiel; in addition, like Henri Martineau, Garnier reads the word 'sérieux' [serious] as 'suivi' [coherent]. *La Femme comme construction*, section 4.3.4.

20. *Stendhal et les problèmes du roman*, p. 175.

21. *Stendhal romancier*, p. 450; see also pp. 442–43.

22. *La Création chez Stendhal*, p. 378.

23. *Le Deuxième Sexe*, p. 388; *Le Naturel chez Stendhal*, p. 351.

24. *L'Ironie dans les romans de Stendhal*, p. 174.

25. *The Unhappy Few*, p. 173.

26. *Stendhal et le roman*, p. 65.

27. 'Débauches en ébauche: La Vie marginale de Lamiel', in *Esquisses/ Ebauches: Projects and Pre-Texts in Nineteenth-Century French Culture*, ed. by Sonya Stephens (Oxford: Lang, 2007), pp. 81–89

(p. 84). For West Sooby, the seeds of Lamiel's marginalization are present in the earliest details of her plot. For an example of a study that privileges Sansfin over Lamiel, see for example Michel Crouzet, 'Les Français du King φιλιππε', in *Le Dernier Stendhal*, pp. 365–433.

28. See Serge Linkès, 'Le manuscrit de *Lamiel*: la fin d'une énigme?' in *Le Dernier Stendhal 1837–1842*, ed. by Michel Arrous (Paris: Eurédit, 2000), pp. 463–77; Serge Linkès, 'Éditer le manuscrit inachevé: Vraies et fausses vertus du numérique', in *Recherches & Travaux*, 72 (2008), 185–99. Linkès' demonstration suggests that the division into two successive versions is misleading. Our own analysis will nevertheless retain the conventional distinction with a view to showing how little the two traditionally recognized versions differ from one another in their treatment of the heroine's freedom. Linkès has also demonstrated that a close study of the manuscripts reveals that Stendhal dictated a first version of the novel in May 1839 rather than October 1839, as previously believed. His new edition of *Lamiel* is due to appear in the third Pléiade volume of Stendhal's *Œuvres romanesques complètes*.

29. Garnier makes this point, and also offers an excellent overview of critical interpretations of the allegedly diminished role of the heroine. *La Femme comme construction*, section 3.2.

30. *Stendhal littéral: 'Lamiel'*, p. 139.

31. '*Lamiel*, conte dépolitisé?', *RHLF*, 109.1 (2009), 35–50 (p. 44).

32. West Sooby notes that the author's projected stories relating to Sansfin are often contradictory and impossible to make sense of. 'Débauches en ébauche', p. 87.

33. See Hemmings, 'Les Deux *Lamiel*', pp. 289–90.

34. Ansel refutes what he calls the 'idée reçue' [received idea] of a Lamiel who rebels against her circumstances and seizes her freedom, an idea propagated by feminist analyses inspired by Beauvoir — Bolster, May, and Naomi Schor are named in a later footnote. He goes on to say that the heroine is in fact no 'briseuse de chaînes' [breaker of chains] because she is effectively dependent on men for her upkeep, and therefore a prostitute. *Stendhal littéral: 'Lamiel'*, pp. 177, 180. Leaving aside the question of whether the heroine of '*Lamiel I*' can be described as a prostitute, and indeed the equally complex question of the prostitute's necessary non-feminism, to define feminism as the achievement of financial freedom from men seems excessively reductive.

35. As May puts it, the heroine is not a revolutionary, but rather 'l'incarnation féminine du rebelle et de l'anarchiste; toute forme d'autorité sociale et politique lui est également suspecte' [the female incarnation of the rebel and the anarchist; all forms of social and political authority are equally suspect to her]. 'Le Féminisme de Stendhal', p. 202. John West Sooby, similarly, maintains that Lamiel is 'a figure of revolt' rather than of revolution. 'Revolution and Revolt in Stendhal's *Lamiel*', *Nineteenth-Century French Studies*, 22.1–2 (1993–94), 90–99 (p. 94).

36. According to a note of 13 April 1839, the woman was sighted as she turned down the rue Saint-Denis (*L* 3). The steamer encounter is attributed by Meininger to a trip made by the author around Normandy in late 1838. Stendhal, *Lamiel*, ed. Meininger, p. 230. Del Litto likens the effect of the glimpse of the young woman on the street to the astonishment produced, in *Mémoires d'un touriste*, by the sighting of a fellow passenger on a boat trip along the Loire in June 1837 (*L* v–vi). The young Breton woman described in this latter episode shares many similarities with the later Lamiel: the narrator is struck by the novelty of her appearance and by the naturalness and ironic awareness demonstrated by her conversation. Stendhal, *Voyages en France*, pp. 246–47. An authorial note on the manuscript of *Le Rose et le Vert* (*Orc* II 1437, n. 4) claims an affinity between Mina and the woman with the green hat.

37. On this point, see for example Jacques Dubois, 'Une sociologie amoureuse', *RHLF*, 109.1 (2009), 5–20 (p. 10); Didier Philippot, '*Lamiel* ou le paradoxe romanesque', in *Le Dernier Stendhal*, pp. 167–206 (pp. 185–87); Pierre-Louis Rey, '"Un peu trop grande et trop maigre"', *RHLF*, 109.1 (2009), 51–60 (especially pp. 52, 55).

38. Bardèche complains of *Lamiel* that 'Ce roman n'est qu'une préface' [This novel is only a preface], being concerned only with the description of a heroine-to-be, a pre-heroine, rather than with a heroine proper. *Stendhal romancier*, p. 440.

39. On the priority of character over plot in Stendhal, see for example Bardèche, *Stendhal romancier*, p. 421. Many critics have remarked, nevertheless, on what Jefferson calls the 'lack of characterological clarity' of many of Stendhal's creations. *Reading Realism*, p. 182.

40. On the centrality of the theme of energy to *Lamiel*, see Thompson, *'Lamiel': Fille du feu*.
41. *Stendhal romancier*, p. 431.
42. *En lisant en écrivant* ([Paris]: Corti, 1980; repr. 1981), pp. 42, 58.
43. *Reading for the Plot*, p. 76.
44. See for example Blin, *Stendhal romancier*, p. 436.
45. Stendhal, *Lamiel*, ed. by Hamm, pp. 17–18. Thompson, similarly, describes the text as 'essentiellement ludique et joyeux' [essentially playful and joyous]. *'Lamiel': Fille du feu*, p. 63, while Rita Zaffarami Berlinghini links its extraordinary freedom to the author's revisiting of his adolescence with the writing of *Vie de Henry Brulard*. 'Lamiel ou l'émancipation de la femme', in *Le Dernier Stendhal*, pp. 267–77 (pp. 267–70).
46. *Stendhal littéral: 'Lamiel'*, p. 18.
47. *Stendhal littéral: 'Lamiel'*, pp. 192–93.
48. ' "Ce qu'elle aimait par-dessus tout, c'était une conversation intéressante." Bavardage et commérage dans *Lamiel*.' *L'Année Stendhal*, 2 (1998), 95–111. Naomi Schor, by contrast, claims that *'Lamiel II'* represents an attempt by Stendhal to 'Balzacize' his writing. *Breaking the Chain: Women, Theory, and French Realist Fiction* (New York: Columbia University Press, 1985), p. 145. For Schor, this 'Balzacization' is undertaken because *'Lamiel I'* is 'an *unwritable text*' (as distinct from Barthes's writable text), insofar as it is 'a text which cannot but be unwritten, a text which contains within it the principles of its own nonclosure, its own undoing' (pp. 141, 142).
49. Dennis Porter, for whom Lamiel is 'the freest and most unpredictable character in all of Stendhal's fiction', maintains that the text adopts a fairytale register in order to permit the representation of a female protagonist who departs from the literary stereotypes of sexual exploiter or exploited victim. 'Lamiel: The Wild Child and the Ugly Men', *Novel*, 12.1 (1978), 21–32 (p. 25).
50. 'En relisant *Lamiel*', p. 24.
51. For Bordas, the centrality of conversation to *Lamiel* militates against any immobilization of textual structures. ' "Ce qu'elle aimait par-dessus tout" '. On the significance of the laundry for female sociability, see Alain Corbin, *Time, Desire and Horror: Towards a History of the Senses*, trans. by Jean Birrell (Cambridge: Polity Press, 1995), pp. 24–25. I have already written about the *Lamiel* laundry scene from the perspective of female sociability in Maria Scott, 'Le Thème de l'amitié féminine chez un "tendre ami des femmes" ', *L'Année stendhalienne*, 8 (2009), 101–15.
52. That this scene has something obsessional about it for Stendhal is suggested by the fact that Julien, Lucien, and Fabrice are also thrown by their horses into the mud; that it is intended to be comical, in line with Hobbes' theory of laughter, is suggested by two passages in Stendhal, *Racine et Shakespeare*, p. 284 ('Le Rire'), p. 324 ('Causes du rire').
53. On the rebellious qualities of nineteenth-century French washerwomen, see Corbin, *Time, Desire and Horror*, p. 24.
54. *Stendhal comme Stendhal*, p. 199.
55. 'Le Dépucelage de Lamiel', in *Amicitia Scriptor: Littérature, Histoire des Idées, Philosophie: Mélanges offerts à Robert Mauzi*, ed. by Annie Becq et al. (Paris: Champion, 1998), pp. 293–313 (p. 310).
56. 'Le Dépucelage de Lamiel', p. 304. Philippot too emphasizes Lamiel's lack of physical desire in this scene. *'Lamiel'*, pp. 171–75. Interestingly, the female critic Pauline Wahl Willis refers to the absence of 'tendresse' [tenderness] in the Berville passage rather than to the absence of desire. 'Lamiel de Stendhal à feu et à sang', in *The Play of Terror in Nineteenth-Century France*, ed. by John T. Booker and Allan H. Pasco (London: Associated University Presses, 1997), pp. 122–29 (p. 126).
57. *The Rise of the French Novel* (London: Hamish Hamilton, 1979), p. 165.
58. See for example Ansel, *Stendhal littéral: 'Lamiel'*, pp. 93, 98, 198.
59. 'Le Dépucelage de Lamiel', p. 299.
60. 'Lamiel: The Wild Child and the Ugly Men', p. 26. For similar points, see also Garnier, *La Femme comme construction*, section 4.2.3 and Rey, ' "Un peu trop grande et trop maigre" ', p. 52.
61. See Tracy, *De l'amour*, p. 52.
62. See Marie de Gandt, 'Lamiel-Psyché, la figure de l'esprit', *L'Année stendhalienne*, 8 (2009), 79–100 (p. 82). Keith A. Reader argues, albeit for different reasons, that the subversive power of female sexuality is central to *Lamiel*. 'Le Discours du pouvoir dans *Lamiel*', in *Stendhal: l'Écrivain, la société et le pouvoir* (Grenoble: Presses Universitaires de Grenoble, 1984), pp. 265–76.

63. Rosalind Coward, *Female Desire* (London: Paladin, 1984; repr. 1987), p. 141.

64. *Breaking the Chain*, p. 142. Schor's hypothesis now seems less well-founded in the light of Linkès's recent genetic analysis of the manuscript.

65. 'Les Deux *Lamiel*', p. 315.

66. 'Unwriting the "Amazone": Gender Trouble in Stendhal's *Lamiel*', in *Love and Sexuality: New Approaches in French Studies*, ed. by Sarah F. Donachie and Kim Harrison (Oxford: Lang, 2005), pp. 17–32 (p. 29).

67. 'L'Enfant libertine: Pouvoir discursif et volonté narrative dans *Lamiel* de Stendhal', *Nineteenth-Century French Studies*, 31.1–2 (2002–03), 66–83 (pp. 74–75).

68. 'Le Coup de pistolet', pp. 23, 27. See also Moya Longstaffe, 'Freedom, Feminism, and Further Reflections on Simone de Beauvoir, Stendhal, and Claudel' in *Claudel Studies*, 22.1–2 (1995), 109–22.

69. 'Le Dépucelage de Lamiel', p. 302. See also Bolster, *Stendhal, Balzac et le féminisme romantique*, p. 171.

70. 'Gender and Class in Stendhal's *Lamiel*', *Romanic Review*, 80.1 (1989), 57–74 (p. 66).

71. For Berthier, by this act Lamiel 's'affirme sujet' [asserts her subjecthood]. *'Lamiel' ou la boîte de Pandore*, p. 86. Rey makes a similar point. '"Un peu trop grande et trop maigre"', p. 59.

72. Lamiel also declares her lack of interest in love to the hotel manageress (*L* 108). Many commentators have nevertheless emphasized Lamiel's qualities as a lover. See for example Alain, *Stendhal*, pp. 59–63 and Philippot, *'Lamiel'*. Philippot explicitly refutes the 'feminist' interpretation of *Lamiel* as a story about freedom rather than love (p. 178).

73. Linda A. Bell, *Sartre's Ethics of Authenticity* (Tuscaloosa: University of Alabama Press, 1989), p. 4. While Bell is referring here to Sartre's idea, the ethics of reciprocity is far more central to Simone de Beauvoir's thinking than to Sartre's. Caitriona MacKenzie paraphrases Beauvoir's ethics as follows: 'We affirm ourselves as subjects only by accepting the freedom and independence of the other.' 'A Certain Lack of Symmetry: Beauvoir on Autonomous Agency and Women's Embodiment', in *Simone de Beauvoir's 'The Second Sex': New Interdisciplinary Essays*, ed. by Ruth Evans (Manchester: Manchester University Press, 1998), pp. 122–58 (p. 132). For Sartre, the figure of the sadist attempts to appropriate the other's freedom. See *L'Être et le néant*, pp. 473–74. In 'Lamiel II', Sansfin attempts to exercise control over Lamiel precisely in the gesture of teaching her how to be free of received ideas. On this point, see Berthier, *'Lamiel' ou la boîte de Pandore*, p. 51. On the influence of Sade on *Lamiel*, see Alain Goldschläger, 'Stendhal, mauvais disciple de Sade', *L'Année stendhalienne*, 4 (2005), 193–203.

74. See Cohen, *The Sentimental Education of the Novel*.

75. 'Gender and Class', p. 62.

76. Stendhal, *Lamiel*, ed. by Hamm, p. 16.

77. *La Femme comme construction*, section 3.2.3. Thompson and Ansel too point out that Lamiel frees herself very easily of Sansfin's attempts to control her. Thompson, *'Lamiel': Fille du feu*, p. 90; Ansel, *Stendhal littéral: 'Lamiel'*, pp. 108, 124. See also the author's 'Plan' of January 1840: 'Lamiel est grandie et sachant résister à un homme tel que Sansfin' [Lamiel is older and able to stand up to a man like Sansfin] (*L* 38).

78. Drawing on her own transcriptions of the *Lamiel* manuscripts by way of example, Garnier demonstrates that if the revisions that Stendhal made to his original version of the text were designed to give more importance than before to secondary characters such as Sansfin and the duchess, this is in line with the author's usual practice, for example in *Lucien Leuwen*, and does not contradict his original plans for *Lamiel*. *La Femme comme construction*, section 3.2.2.

79. *L'Ironie dans les romans de Stendhal*, p. 180.

80. *Breaking the Chain*, p. 143.

81. Lamiel's distress in this episode, and her desire to 'se réserver au moins la faculté d'aimer son oncle' [at least keep her ability to love her uncle] (*L* 307), appear to contradict Hilary Hutchinson's claim that Sansfin's education makes of her 'un être incapable d'aimer' [a being incapable of love]. 'Lamiel et l'immoralisme gidien', *Stendhal Club*, 25.100 (1983), 501–10 (p. 506).

82. For Pauline Wahl, the novel is driven by the author's interest in the teaching relationship, or 'pygmalionism'. She argues that Stendhal explores the 'possibility of liberty for the pupil in *Lamiel*

I and the possibility of control for the teacher in *Lamiel II*'. 'Stendhal's *Lamiel*: Observations on Pygmalionism', in *Pre-text, Text, Context. Essays on Nineteenth-Century Literature*, ed. by R. Mitchell (Columbus: Ohio State University Press, 1980), pp. 113–19 (p. 117).

83. *Breaking the Chain*, pp. 139–40.

84. *Le Deuxième Sexe*, I, 388.

85. '*Lamiel' ou la boîte de Pandore*, p. 12.

86. *L'Être et le néant*, pp. 65, 560–61. For Sartre, 'le néant' [nothingness], is the very condition of human freedom; it is the activity of our consciousness, permitting us to detach ourselves from the immanence and plenitude of being.

87. 'Un "conte d'hiver": *Lamiel*', in *Stendhal-Balzac: Réalisme et cinéma*, pp. 213–18 (p. 214).

88. 'C'est bien le but final de l'art: récupérer ce monde-ci en le donnant à voir tel qu'il est, mais comme s'il avait sa source dans la liberté humaine.' [This is the the final aim of art: recover this world by giving it to be seen as it is, but as if it had its source in human freedom.] Jean-Paul Sartre, *Qu'est-ce que la littérature?* (Paris: Gallimard, 1948; repr. with preface 2008), p. 64. See also the argument he makes for an intimate link between the reading of literature and the exercise of freedom in S. de Beauvoir and others, *Que peut la littérature?*, pp. 107–27.

89. *Metamorphoses of Passion*, p. 243. Affirmations of Lamiel's radical freedom are made in Berthier, '*Lamiel' ou la boîte de Pandore*; Gandt, 'Lamiel-Psyché'; Anne Leoni, 'Le Vert de houx', *RHLF*, 109.1 (2009), 61–70; Maryline Lukacher, 'Lamiel, lectrice de Stendhal', *L'Année stendhalienne*, 4 (2005), 179–92; May, 'Le Féminisme de Stendhal'; Thompson, '*Lamiel': Fille du feu*; Zaffarami Berlinghini, '*Lamiel* ou l'émancipation de la femme'. Nevertheless, Crouzet remarks that Lamiel is wrongly said to be 'une heroïne très affranchie' [a very liberated heroine]. 'Les Français du King φιλιππε', p. 411

90. Ingrid Galster, in her article on Beauvoir's radio adaptation, refers to Lamiel as 'cette créature existentialiste avant la lettre' [this proto-existentialist creature]. '*Lamiel* à Radio Vichy. Une adaptation de Simone de Beauvoir', *L'Année stendhalienne*, 5 (2006), 131–51 (p. 145). Leoni too attributes an existentialist outlook to the heroine. 'Le Vert de houx', p. 70.

91. On Fabrice's essential passivity, see for example Ansel, *Stendhal littéral: 'Lamiel'*, p. 126; Émile Faguet, *Politiques et moralistes du dix-neuvième siècle*, 3 vols, 8th edn (Paris: Société française d'imprimerie et de librairie, [nd]), III, 56; Allan H. Pasco, 'The Unheroic Mode: Stendhal's *La Chartreuse de Parme*', *Philological Quarterly*, 70.3 (1991), 361–78 (p. 367).

92. For Bardèche, the novel lacks 'l'image du bonheur' [the image of happiness], even if it seems clear to him that the heroine would have achieved happiness had her story been continued. *Stendhal romancier*, pp. 439–40.

93. Xavier Bourdenet, 'Lamiel ou l'histoire en miroir à propos de 1830', *RHLF*, 109.1 (2009), 21–33; Leoni, 'Le Vert de houx'.

94. *Stendhal littéral: 'Lamiel'*, p. 170.

95. Quoted in Paupe, *Histoire des œuvres de Stendhal*, p. 232.

96. *Stendhal*, pp. 59, 60.

97. 'Le Féminisme de Stendhal', pp. 201–02.

98. Wilkinson, 'Gender and Class', p. 70.

99. Berthier is unusual in the optimistic reading he gives to this ending, which he presents as the heroine's final act of self-determination. '*Lamiel' ou la boîte de Pandore*, p. 90.

100. 'Realism and the Ends of Feminism', in *Grafts: Feminist Cultural Criticism*, ed. by Susan Sheridan (London: Verso, 1988), pp. 77–91 (p. 87).

CONCLUSION

When Prosper Mérimée protested to his friend Stendhal that the latter had created an implausible character in the figure of Mathilde de La Mole, the author pointed, in his defence, to the existence of his own former lover Alberthe de Rubempré and of Mary de Neuville, an aristocratic mutual acquaintance whose elopement with a social inferior had been a source of great scandal among those of her class.[1] Mérimée responded by reiterating that Mathilde is still 'impossible en apparence' [seemingly impossible], and thus in contravention of the precepts laid down in Boileau's *Art poétique* (where it is stated that even the truth can lack verisimilitude). He also observed that any literary modification of the 'problème' [problem] of Alberthe would necessarily make an impossibility of the extraordinary fact.[2]

Various commentators, in the wake of Mérimée, have pointed to the strain that Mathilde's character places on our understanding of *Le Rouge et le Noir* as a Realist novel.[3] Interestingly, the novel's famous defence of itself, surely its most frequently cited passage, hinges on the figure of Mathilde and the alleged impossibility of her character. It is ostensibly as a means of parrying anticipated charges of indecency in his portrait of her passion for Julien that the narrator compares the novel to a mirror walking along a road. Commentators have been unanimous in discerning covert praise for Mathilde in this famous passage.[4] Some have also noted the apparent contradiction between the novel-as-mirror defence and the claim that the heroine's character is a figment of the author's imagination: the passage simultaneously claims that Mathilde is an entirely invented, impossible character, and that she needs to be represented because the novel is a mirror that must reflect both ugly reality (mud) and beautiful ideals (blue sky). The apparent inconsistency might of course be resolved if we understand that the author tacitly identifies Mathilde with the ideal rather than with the mud of the roads. After all, Alberthe de Rubempré was known by Stendhal and others in her inner circle as Mme Azur. The text refers several times to the blueness of Mathilde's eyes, and the narrator even once describes them as 'd'un bleu céleste' [heavenly blue] (*Orc* I 607). It is possible that the novel's depiction of the young heroine is not as intentionally parodic as has usually been assumed; what is certain, however, is that it is the reader who must decide on the nature of what he or she finds reflected in the mirror.

This project began with a belief, developed as an undergraduate student, that Mathilde de La Mole was a more fascinating character than Julien Sorel. As a doctoral student, I came to believe that Stendhal had constructed *Le Rouge et le Noir* on the model of Hans Holbein's famous *vanitas* painting, *The Ambassadors* (1533), with Mathilde as the semi-invisible death's-head at its centre, poking fun at the orthodoxies of her society, and at us. Just as Mathilde is unseen by Altamira and Julien Sorel as they pour scorn on the vanity of the ballgoers around them, even when she places her head quite literally between them, many readers choose not to see her, or to see her only as marginal and superfluous. Mathilde became, for me, emblematic of the position of the female within the French Realist text, as theorized by Shoshana Felman: 'The woman (is) predestined to be, precisely, *the realistic invisible*, that which realism as such is inherently unable to see.'[5]

But all of Stendhal's young and fearless heroines have something of Holbein's anamorphic skull about them.[6] They do not fit easily into their represented social contexts or their conventional narrative frameworks. They repeatedly surprise and scandalize other characters, who are often led to categorize them as mad, or at the very least as *mauvaises têtes*. However, to earn the reputation of '*mauvaise tête*' [*a wrong-headed person*], described by the narrator of *Le Rouge et le Noir* as 'le plus grand anathème en province' [the greatest anathema in the provinces] (*Orc* I 771), is perhaps not as dangerous a prospect, in Stendhalian terms, as to align oneself with those 'gens sages et modérés' [sensible and sober people] evoked in the first chapter of that novel, who 'exercent le plus ennuyeux *despotisme*' [exercise the most tiresome *tyranny*] over public opinion in small towns, and who confer the epithet on any inhabitant of Franche-Comté who dares to build walls in the Italian style (*Orc* I 354).[7] The disrespect shown by Stendhal's heroines towards social conventions problematizes our understanding of him as a Realist author. One of the hallmarks of the literary style which is said to have begun with Stendhal and Balzac, and which subsequently came to dominate the nineteenth century, is its pessimism in relation to the possibility of individual freedom; and Stendhal's young heroines do achieve a significant degree of freedom, even if one subscribes to the hypothesis that the endings they meet are punitive. Other characteristics of literary Realism, such as the explicability of characters' behaviour, the logical unfolding of events, and the avoidance of literary exaggeration, also come under considerable strain in the texts that feature these heroines. Their contravention not only of social rules but also of the (nascent) rules of Realism goes a long way towards explaining why Stendhal's young heroines have, historically, scandalized many of their readers.

This book began by considering the freedom of readers to interpret texts in the way suggested to them by their particular situations. Fetterley wrote in the 1970s about the need for critics to become resisting readers, alert to the misogyny enshrined in canonical literary texts. Naomi Segal develops this argument by proposing that female readers occupy a peculiarly privileged position, in that their active exclusion by such texts can lead them 'to read in a deconstructive way', seeking out 'unconscious meaning'.[8] However, Stendhal's fiction places the feminist reader in an unusual position, because it gives extraordinarily free rein to strong and fearless heroines. One tradition of feminist response, beginning with the work of Clara Malraux and Simone de Beauvoir, has consequently emphasized the unusual levels of agency demonstrated by his heroines, or at least their occupation of the subject position. A second strategy has been to identify 'the traces of masculine assumptions'[9] in his depictions of women. Accordingly, many feminist critics have pointed to the eventual price paid by his heroines for their assertion of their freedom; others have highlighted their immobilization and marginalization by an apparently inexorable textual logic, or their idealized qualities, or their conformity to literary stereotypes; others again have drawn attention to Stendhal's denigration of a literary style associated in his time with female authors, and his consequent contribution to the marginalization of women within nineteenth-century French literary history.

The argument presented in this book situates itself at the optimistic end of the spectrum of feminist criticism; but it does not depend upon any supposition of feminism on the part of the author. It has tried to demonstrate that Stendhal's texts lend themselves very easily to a sympathetic reading of heroines that have often been seen as unsympathetic or unworthy of the love of heroes and readers alike. It has, in addition, argued that Stendhal's independent young heroines can be understood to enact a mode of freedom that is recognizably grounded in the science of Ideology, by which the author was heavily influenced, while also anticipating the thinking of French existentialism. All four of the heroines discussed in this book assert a freedom that will later find echoes in the work of Sartre and Beauvoir: all elaborate their own destinies and adopt a playful, unserious approach to life, even where the personal and moral stakes are high.

Blin reminds us that Balzac amusingly read *La Chartreuse de Parme* as Mosca's story.[10] But similar readerly projections are in evidence everywhere in Stendhal criticism, as the first chapter of this book attempted to show (without in any way claiming exemption from the general rule). In one sense, then, there is no possibility of reading Stendhal, or any other author for that matter, with what Adrienne Rich called 'fresh eyes';[11] we will always find our own preoccupations emblazoned across any text on which we choose to cast those eyes. Stendhal knew this, and even designed his fictions accordingly. In the preface to *Armance*, for example, he explains how he satirized both industrialists and aristocrats in the work: just as turtle doves see the Tuileries gardens differently from those who walk in the gardens, the reader will understand the satire according to his or her position in society. Similarly, in his projected article on *Le Rouge et le Noir*, Stendhal writes of how he attempted, by his inclusion of two heroines, to appeal to two distinct female audiences, representatives of 'deux *exigences opposées*' [two *opposing demands*], the chambermaids and provincial women in pursuit of a sentimental experience and the more sceptical Parisian ladies, interested primarily in accurate reflections of society (*Orc* I 825). If we cannot read with neutral eyes, then, we can however make a case for the legitimacy of what we find in a text.

It is important to recognize the extent to which our individual situations colour our readings. But we do not distort texts when we bring our lives to bear on them. We simply give them the only kind of life that texts can ever have.

Notes to the Conclusion

1. On the sequence of the exchange, some of which has been lost but can be deduced from the surviving evidence, see Robert Vigneron, 'Stendhal et Sanscrit', *Modern Philology*, 33.4 (1936), 383–402 (p. 400). Stendhal could also have pointed to the existence of Giulia Rinieri, another acknowledged inspiration for the character of Mathilde. It was after having read *Vanina Vanini*

in the *Revue de Paris* of December 1829 that Giulia introduced herself to the author and embarked on an affair with him, leading to an unsuccessful marriage proposal in November 1830. On Stendhal's affair with Alberthe, and Alberthe's interesting love life, see Alan Raitt, 'An unpublished letter by Mérimée', *Modern Language Review*, 65.2 (1970), 282–89.

2. *HB*, p. 53.

3. See for example Claudine Vercollier, 'Un personnage problématique: Mathilde de la Mole', *University of Toronto Quarterly*, 68.2 (1999), 642–54. Lawrence R. Schehr presents Mathilde as a figure of the unrepresentable, or 'an interruption', in the novel. *Rendering French Realism* (Stanford: Stanford University Press, 1997), p. 48.

4. *Orc* I 670–71. Prendergast, for example, associates the references in this passage to her madness with her resistance to social and literary stereotyping. *The Order of Mimesis*, pp. 139–40. See also Felman, *La 'Folie'*, p. 42.

5. Shoshana Felman, 'Women and Madness: the Critical Phallacy', in *Balzac,* ed. by Michael Tilby (London: Longman, 1995) pp. 266–83 (first publ. in *Diacritics*, 5.4 (1975), 2–10), p. 275. For an elaboration of the preceding hypothesis, see Maria Scott, 'Stendhal, Mathilde et le regard oblique', in *L'Œil écrit*, ed. by Johnnie Gratton and Derval Conroy (Geneva: Slatkine, 2005), pp. 221–36. The main problem with the 'anamorphic' hypothesis is that it relies upon the hackneyed idea that, as Pearson puts it, 'Stendhal is the goal of interpretation' and that 'a secret message' must be decoded in order to gain access to the newly 'unambiguous author'. *Stendhal's Violin*, pp. 115, 116.

6. Kosei Kurisu points out that the relationship between Stendhal's early heroines and their societies is characterized by 'étrangeté' [strangeness]. 'Armance, Mina de Vanghel, Mathilde de La Mole: Le Thème de la singularité chez les héroïnes stendhaliennes', *Stendhal Club*, 74 (1976–77), 123–32.

7. In the *Roman de Métilde* (1819), Stendhal refers to the 'mauvaise tête' of his own alter ego, who loses the love of Métilde on account of the 'folies' [mad acts] and 'imprudences' prompted by his 'passion folle' [mad passion]. Stendhal, *Œuvres complètes*, IV, 379. He also acknowledges his own 'réputation de mauvaise tête' [reputation as wrong-headed] among his acquaintances (*OI* II 483).

8. *The Unintended Reader* (Cambridge: Cambridge University Press, 1986), p. xiii.

9. Longstaffe, *Metamorphoses of Passion*, p. 306.

10. *Stendhal et les problèmes du roman*, p. 162.

11. 'When We Dead Awaken: Writing as Re-Vision', *College English*, 34.1 (Oct 1972), 18–30 (p. 18).

BIBLIOGRAPHY

Works by Stendhal

Chroniques pour l'Angleterre: Contributions à la presse britannique, ed. by Renée Dénier and Keith G. McWatters, 8 vols (Grenoble: ELLUG, 1980–95)

Correspondance générale, ed. by Victor Del Litto and others, 6 vols (Paris: Champion, 1997–99)

De l'Amour, ed. by Henri Martineau (Paris: Garnier Frères, 1959)

Lamiel, trans. by T. W. Earp (Norfolk, CN: New Directions, 1952)

Lamiel, ed. by Jean-Jacques Hamm (Paris: Flammarion, 1993)

Lamiel, ed. by Anne-Marie Meininger (Paris: Gallimard, 1983)

Le Rose et le Vert, Mina de Vanghel, Tamira Wanghen, ed. by Jean-Jacques Labia (Paris: Flammarion, 1998)

Œuvres complètes, ed. by Victor Del Litto and Ernest Abravanel, 50 vols (Geneva: Cercle du Bibliophile, 1967–1974)

Œuvres intimes, ed. by Victor Del Litto, 2 vols (Paris: Gallimard, Bibliothèque de la Pléiade, 1981–82)

Œuvres romanesques complètes, ed. by Yves Ansel, Philippe Berthier, and Xavier Bourdenet, 3 vols (Paris: Gallimard, Bibliothèque de la Pléiade, 2005–)

'The Pink and the Green': Followed by 'Mina de Vanghel', trans. by Richard Howard (New York: New Directions, 1988)

Promenades dans Rome, ed. by Victor Del Litto (Grenoble: Millon, 1993)

Racine et Shakespeare (1818–1825) et autres textes de théorie romantique, ed. by Michel Crouzet (Paris: Champion, 2006)

The Red and the Black: A Chronicle of the Nineteenth Century, ed. and trans. by Catherine Slater (Oxford: Oxford University Press, 2009)

Romans et nouvelles, ed. by Henri Martineau, 2 vols (Paris: Gallimard, Bibliothèque de la Pléiade, 1952)

Rome, Naples et Florence, ed. by Pierre Brunel (Paris: Gallimard, 1987)

Vanina Vanini, trans. by David Coward, in *The Oxford Book of French Short Stories*, ed. by Elizabeth Fallaize (Oxford: Oxford University Press, 2010), pp. 7–29

Vanina Vanini et autres nouvelles, dossier and notes by Xavier Bourdenet (Paris: Gallimard, 2010)

Voyages en France, ed. by Victor del Litto (Paris: Gallimard, Bibliothèque de la Pléiade, 1992)

Other works

ALAIN, *Stendhal* (Paris: Rieder, 1935)

ALGAZI, LISA G., *Maternal Subjectivity in the Works of Stendhal* (Lewiston, NY: Mellen, 2001)

—— 'Stendhal féministe?', *L'Année stendhalienne*, 4 (2005), 29–40

ANDRIEU, JACQUELINE, 'De Mina de Vanghel à Lamiel ou Héroïsme, amour et vraisemblance', *Stendhal Club*, 76 (1976–77), 321–31

ANSEL, YVES, '*Lamiel*, conte dépolitisé?', *RHLF*, 109.1 (2009), 35–50

——'Sartre' in *Dictionnaire de Stendhal*, ed. by Yves Ansel, Philippe Berthier, and Michael Nerlich (Paris: Champion, 2003), pp. 653–54

——'Stendhal et la femme "en deux volumes"', *L'Année stendhalienne*, 8 (2009) 139–68

——*Stendhal littéral: 'Lamiel'* (Grenoble: ELLUG, 2009)

——*Stendhal littéral: 'Le Rouge et le Noir'* (Paris: Kimé, 2001),

ATTUEL, JOSIANE, *Le Style de Stendhal: Efficacité et romanesque* (Bologna: Pàtron, 1980)

AUERBACH, ERICH, *Mimesis: The Representation of Reality in Western Literature* (Princeton,: Princeton University Press, 1946)

AUTHIER, CATHERINE and LUCY GARNIER, 'Giuditta Pasta, le travestissement et la "féminité" chez Stendhal', *L'Année stendhalienne*, 8 (2009), 117–38

BALZAC, HONORÉ DE, *Mémoires de deux jeunes mariées*, (Paris: Gallimard, 2002)

BARBÉRIS, PIERRE, 'Qu'est-ce qu'un personnage littéraire au féminin? A propos de Louise de Rênal', *HB. Revue Internationale d'études stendhaliennes*, 4 (2000), 47–73

BARDÈCHE, MAURICE, *Stendhal romancier* (Paris: La Table ronde, 1947)

BARTHES, ROLAND, *S/Z* (Paris: Seuil, 1970)

BAUDELAIRE, CHARLES, *Œuvres complètes*, ed. by Claude Pichois, 2 vols (Paris: Gallimard, Bibliothèque de la Pléiade, 1975–76)

BEAUVOIR, SIMONE DE, *Le Deuxième Sexe*, 2 vols (Paris: Gallimard, 1949; repr. 1976)

——*L'Existentialisme et la sagesse des nations* (Geneva: Nagel, 1986)

——'Littérature et métaphysique', *Les Temps modernes*, 1.7 (1946), 1153–63

——et al., *Que peut la littérature?* ([Paris]: Union générale d'éditions, 1965), pp. 73–92

BELL, LINDA A., *Sartre's Ethics of Authenticity* (Tuscaloosa: University of Alabama Press, 1989)

BELL, SHEILA, *Stendhal: 'Vie de Henry Brulard'* (London: Grant and Cutler, 2006)

BERSANI, LEO, *A Future for Astyanax: Character and Desire in Literature* (Boston: Little, Brown, 1976)

BERTELÀ, MADDALENA, *Stendhal et l'Autre: L'Homme et l'œuvre à travers l'idée de féminité* (Florence: Olschki, 1985)

BERTHIER, PHILIPPE, *'Lamiel' ou la boîte de Pandore* (Paris: Presses Universitaires de France, 1994)

——'Stendhal Club', *Revue des sciences humaines*, (1991), 139–59

——'Stendhal entre Julia et Simone', *L'Année stendhalienne*, 8 (2009), 187–95.

——*Stendhal et la Sainte famille* (Geneva: Droz, 1984)

BLIN, GEORGES, *Stendhal et les problèmes de la personnalité* (Paris: Corti, 2001 [1958])

——*Stendhal et les problèmes du roman* (Paris: Corti, 1954)

BLÜHER, KARL ALFRED, 'L'Amour tragique dans les premières nouvelles de Stendhal', *Stendhal Club*, 96 (1982), 374–87

BOLL-JOHANSEN, HANS, *Stendhal et le roman: Essai sur la structure du roman stendhalien* (Aran: Éditions du grand chêne, 1979)

BOLSTER, RICHARD, *Stendhal, Balzac et le féminisme romantique* (Paris: Minard, 1970)

——'Stendhal, Mme de Duras et la tradition sentimentale', *Studi Francesi*, 107.36 (1992), 301–06.

BORDAS, ÉRIC, ' "Ce qu'elle aimait par-dessus tout, c'était une conversation intéressante": Bavardage et commérage dans *Lamiel*', *L'Année Stendhal*, 2 (1998), 95–111

BOUMELHA, PENNY, 'Realism and the Ends of Feminism', in *Grafts: Feminist Cultural Criticism*, ed. by Susan Sheridan (London: Verso, 1988), pp. 77–91

BOURDENET, XAVIER, 'Lamiel ou l'histoire en miroir à propos de 1830', *RHLF*, 109.1 (2009), 21–33

——'Mme Grandet, ou comment l'amour vient aux femmes', *L'Année stendhalienne*, 8 (2009), 169–86

BROMBERT, VICTOR, *Fiction and the Themes of Freedom* (New York: Random House, 1968)

BROOKS, PETER, *The Novel of Worldliness: Crébillon, Marivaux, Laclos, Stendhal* (Princeton: Princeton University Press, 1969)

——Reading for the Plot: Design and Intention in Narrative (New York: Knopf, 1984)

BRUYAS, JEAN-PAUL, La Psychologie de l'adolescence dans l'œuvre romanesque de Stendhal (Aix-en-Provence: La Pensée Universitaire, 1967)

BUTLER, JUDITH, Gender Trouble: Feminism and the Subversion of Identity (London: Routledge, 1990)

CAILLOIS, ROGER, Les Jeux et les hommes: Le Masque et le vertige, revised and augmented edn ([Paris]: Gallimard, 1967)

CHAITIN, GILBERT D., The Unhappy Few: A Psychological Study of the Novels of Stendhal (Bloomington: Indiana University Press, 1972)

CHILCOAT, MICHELLE, 'Idéologie et romantisme: Habitude et réflexion', L'Année stendhalienne, 4 (2005), 41–66

COHEN, MARGARET, 'In Lieu of a Chapter on Some French Women Novelists', in Spectacles of Realism: Body, Gender, Genre, ed. by Margaret Cohen and Christopher Prendergast (Minneapolis: University of Minnesota Press, 1995), pp. 90–119

——The Sentimental Education of the Novel (Princeton: Princeton University Press, 1999)

CONSTANS, ELLEN, 'Au nom du bonheur: Le Féminisme de Stendhal', Europe, 652–53 (1983), 62–74

——'Les Problèmes de la condition féminine dans l'œuvre de Stendhal', 2 vols (Lille: Service de reproduction des thèses de l'université Lille III, 1978)

COQUILLAT, MICHÈLE, La Poétique du mâle (Paris: Gallimard, 1982)

CORBIN, ALAIN, Time, Desire and Horror: Towards a History of the Senses, trans. by Jean Birrell (Cambridge: Polity Press, 1995)

CORRÉDOR, MARIE-ROSE, 'Aux sources du discours clinique: La Correspondance avec Félix Faure et François Bigillion (mai 1805 à février 1806)', in Lire la correspondance de Stendhal, ed. by Martine Reid and Elaine Williamson (Paris: Champion, 2007), pp. 57–63

COUDERT, MARIE-LOUISE, 'Mathilde mal aimée', Europe, 519–21 (1972), 136–41

COWARD, ROSALIND, Female Desire (London: Paladin, 1984; repr. 1987)

CROUZET, MICHEL, 'Le Dépucelage de Lamiel', in Amicitia Scriptor: Littérature, Histoire des Idées, Philosophie: Mélanges offerts à Robert Mauzi, ed. by Annie Becq et al. (Paris: Champion, 1998), pp. 293–313

——'Les Français du King φιλιππε', in Le Dernier Stendhal 1837–1842, ed. by Michel Arrous (Paris: Eurédit, 2000), pp. 365–433.

——Le Héros fourbe chez Stendhal ou Hypocrisie, politique, séduction, amour dans le beylisme (Paris: SEDES, 1987)

——'Lamiel grotesque', in Stendhal et le comique, ed. by Daniel Sangsue (Grenoble: ELLUG, 1999), pp. 267–304

——Nature et Société chez Stendhal: La Révolte romantique (Villeneuve d'Ascq: Presses Universitaires de Lille, 1985)

——Le Naturel, la grâce et le réel dans la poétique de Stendhal: Essai sur la genèse du romantisme, Tome II (Paris: Flammarion, 1986)

——'Le Rouge et le Noir': Essai sur le romanesque stendhalien (Paris: Presses Universitaires de France, 1995)

——'Stendhal et le récit tragique', in Stendhal Europeo: Atti del congresso internazionale Milano, 19–21 Maggio 1992 (Fasano: Schena, 1996), pp. 107–62

——et al., ed. Stendhal: Mémoire de la critique (Paris: Presses de l'Université de Paris-Sorbonne, 1996), pp. 219–37

DEGUISE, PIERRE, 'Stendhal et Sartre. Du naturel à l'authentique', French Review, 42.4 (1969), 540–47

DEL LITTO, VICTOR, 'Stendhal romancier réaliste?', in Stendhal-Balzac: Réalisme et cinéma: Actes du XIᵉ congrès international stendhalien, Auxerre, 1976, ed. by Victor Del Litto (Grenoble: Presses Universitaires de Grenoble, 1978), pp. 7–12

———*La Vie intellectuelle de Stendhal: Genèse et évolution de ses idées* (1802–1821) (Grenoble: Presses Universitaires de France, 1959)

DÉMAR, CLAIRE, *Ma loi d'avenir: 1833: Ouvrage posthume; suivi d'un Appel d'une femme au peuple sur l'affranchissement de la femme* (Paris: Au bureau de la Tribune des femmes, 1834)

DESALMAND, PAUL, *Sartre, Stendhal et la morale: ou la Revanche de Stendhal* (Paris: Pocket, 2005)

DESTUTT DE TRACY, ANTOINE LOUIS CLAUDE, *De l'amour* (Paris: Les Belles Lettres, 1926)

———*Élémens d'idéologie*, 4 vols (Paris: Courcier, 1817–18)

DONACHIE, SARAH F., 'Unwriting the "Amazone": Gender Trouble in Stendhal's *Lamiel*', in *Love and Sexuality: New Approaches in French Studies*, ed. by Sarah F. Donachie and Kim Harrison (Oxford: Lang, 2005), pp. 17–32

DUBOIS, JACQUES, 'Une sociologie amoureuse', *RHLF*, 109.1 (2009), 5–20

FAGUET, ÉMILE, *Politiques et moralistes du dix-neuvième siècle*, 3 vols, 8th edn (Paris: Société française d'imprimerie et de librairie, [nd])

FALLAIZE, ELIZABETH, 'Simone de Beauvoir and the Demystification of Women', in *A History of Feminist Literary Criticism*, ed. by Gill Plain and Susan Sellers (Cambridge: Cambridge University Press, 2007), pp. 85–99

FÉLIX-FAURE, JACQUES, 'La Douloureuse Destinée de Victorine Bigillion', *Stendhal Club*, 1 (1958), 9–14

FELMAN, SHOSHANA, *La 'Folie' dans l'œuvre romanesque de Stendhal* (Paris: Corti, 1971)

———'Women and Madness: The Critical Phallacy', in *Balzac*, ed. by Michael Tilby (London: Longman, 1995) pp. 266–83 (first publ. in *Diacritics*, 5.4 (1975), 2–10)

FETTERLEY, JUDITH, *The Resisting Reader: A Feminist Approach to Feminist Fiction* (Bloomington: Indiana University Press, 1978)

FINCH, ALISON, *Women's Writing in Nineteenth-Century France* (Cambridge: Cambridge University Press, 2000)

FLOWER MACCANNELL, JULIET, 'Stendhal's Woman', *Semiotica*, 48.1–2 (1984), 143–68

FROGER, NATHALIE, 'Femme publique, femme privée: La Dialectique impossible de l'héroïne stendhalienne', *Stendhal Club*, 133 (1991), 39–51

GALSTER, INGRID, '*Lamiel* à Radio Vichy. Une adaptation de Simone de Beauvoir', *L'Année stendhalienne*, 5 (2006), 131–51

GANDT, MARIE DE, 'Lamiel-Psyché, la figure de l'esprit', *L'Année stendhalienne*, 8 (2009), 79–100

GARNIER, LUCY, 'La Femme comme construction dans la fiction stendhalienne', unpublished doctoral thesis, University of Oxford, 2007

———'"La Femme par M. de Stal": *Lucien Leuwen* et la sexualité féminine chez Stendhal', *L'Année stendhalienne*, 9 (2010), 93–119

———'"On ne naît pas femme, on le devient": Les Lettres à Pauline et la condition féminine', in *Lire la correspondance de Stendhal*, ed. by Martine Reid (Paris: Champion, 2007), pp. 11–25

———'Stendhal's *Mina de Vanghel* and the question of feminism', *Nineteeth-Century French Studies*, 34.3–4 (2006), 252–61

GÉFIN, LASZLO K., 'Auerbach's Stendhal: Realism, Figurality, and Refiguration', *Poetics Today*, 20.1 (1999), 27–40

GENETTE, GÉRARD, *Figures II* (Paris: Seuil, 1969)

GIDE, ANDRÉ, 'En relisant *Lamiel*', in Stendhal, *Lamiel*, ed. by Jean-Jacques Hamm (Paris: Flammarion, 1993), pp. 21–37

GIRARD, RENÉ, *Mensonge romantique et vérité romanesque* (Paris: Grasset, 1961)

GOETZ, WILLIAM R., 'Nietzsche and *Le Rouge et le noir*', *Comparative Literature Studies*, 18.4 (1981), 443–58

GOLDSCHLÄGER, ALAIN, 'Stendhal, mauvais disciple de Sade', *L'Année stendhalienne*, 4 (2005), 193–203

GORMLEY, LANE, '"Mon roman est fini": Fabricateurs de romans et fiction intratextuelle dans *Le Rouge et le Noir*', *Stendhal Club*, 21 (1979), 129–38

GRACQ, JULIEN, *En lisant en écrivant* ([Paris]: Corti, 1980; repr. 1981)

GUÉRIN, MICHEL, *La Politique de Stendhal: Les Brigands et le bottier* (Paris: Presses Universitaires de France, 1982)

HAGE, ANNE, 'Crime et châtiment dans *Le Rouge et le Noir*', *L'Année stendhalienne*, 2 (2003), 179–209

HEMMINGS, F. W. J., 'Les Deux *Lamiel*: Nouveaux aperçus sur les procédés de composition de Stendhal romancier', *Stendhal Club*, 60 (1973), 287–316

—— *Stendhal: A Study of his Novels* (Oxford: Clarendon Press, 1964)

HIGONNET, MARGARET, 'Frames of Female Suicide', *Studies in the Novel*, 32.2 (2000), 228–41

HOOG, ARMAND, 'Le "rôle" de Julien', *Stendhal Club*, 78 (1978), 131–42

HUTCHINSON, HILARY, 'Lamiel et l'immoralisme gidien', *Stendhal Club*, 25.100 (1983), 501–10

IMBERT, HENRI-FRANÇOIS, *Les Métamorphoses de la liberté ou Stendhal devant la Restauration et le Risorgimento* (Paris: Corti, 1967)

JACCARD, ANNIE-CLAIRE, 'Julien Sorel: La Mort et le temps du bonheur', *Europe*, 519–21 (1972), 113–27

JATON, ANNE-MARIE, 'De *l'amour* et *Lucien Leuwen*: Une poétique de l'obstacle', in *Le Plus Méconnu des romans de Stendhal: 'Lucien Leuwen'*, ed. by Société des études romantiques (Paris: SEDES-CDU réunis, 1983), 89–98

JEFFERSON, ANN, *Reading Realism in Stendhal* (Cambridge: Cambridge University Press, 1988)

—— 'Varieties of Female Agency in Stendhal', in *From Goethe to Gide: Feminism, Aesthetics and the French and German Literary Canon 1770–1936*, ed. by Mary Orr and Lesley Sharpe (Exeter: University of Exeter Press, 2005), 65–79

JONES, GRAHAME C., *L'Ironie dans les romans de Stendhal* (Lausanne: Éditions du Grand Chêne, 1966)

—— 'Les Murs et l'emprisonnement dans *Le Rouge et le Noir*', *Stendhal Club*, 25.100 (1983), 449–63

KRISTEVA, JULIA, 'Stendhal et la politique du regard: L'Amour d'un égotiste', in *Histoires d'amour* (Paris: Denoël, 1983), pp. 319–40

KURISU, KOSEI, 'Armance, Mina de Vanghel, Mathilde de La Mole: Le Thème de la singularité chez les héroïnes stendhaliennes', *Stendhal Club*, 74 (1976–77), 123–32

LABIA, JEAN-JACQUES, 'Un "conte d'hiver": *Lamiel*', in *Stendhal-Balzac: Réalisme et cinéma*, pp. 213–18

LAFORGUE, PIERRE, *1830. Romantisme et histoire* (Saint-Pierre-du-Mont: Eurédit, 2001)

LAURENS, GILBERT, 'Le Mythe d'Hérodiade chez Stendhal, III', *Stendhal Club*, 106 (1985), 131–47

LAURENT, JACQUES, *Stendhal comme Stendhal ou le mensonge ambigu* (Paris: Grasset & Fasquelle, 1984)

LEONI, ANNE, 'Le Vert de houx', *RHLF*, 109.1 (2009), 61–70

LINKÈS, SERGE, 'De *Letellier* à *Lamiel*, la comédie continue', *L'Année stendhalienne*, 1 (2002), 255–80

—— 'Éditer le manuscrit inachevé: Vraies et fausses vertus du numérique', in *Recherches & Travaux*, 72 (2008), 185–99

—— 'Le Manuscrit de *Lamiel*: La Fin d'une énigme?' in *Le Dernier Stendhal 1837–1842*, ed. by Michel Arrous (Paris: Eurédit, 2000), pp. 463–77

LONGSTAFFE, MOYA, 'Le Coup de pistolet, le concert et l'audace féminine: La Fin de la chasse au bonheur', *L'Année Stendhal*, 4 (2000), 5–27

—— 'Le Dilemme de l'honneur féminin dans l'univers masculin du duel: Le Crime de la duchesse Sanseverina', *Stendhal Club*, 75 (1976–77), 305–19

—— 'Freedom, Feminism, and Further Reflections on Simone de Beauvoir, Stendhal, and Claudel', *Claudel Studies*, 22.1–2 (1995), 109–22

—— *Metamorphoses of Passion and the Heroic in French Literature — Corneille, Stendhal, Claudel* (Lewiston, NY: Mellen, 1999)

LUKACHER, MARYLINE, 'Lamiel, lectrice de Stendhal', *L'Année stendhalienne*, 4 (2005), 179–92

MACKENZIE, CAITRIONA, 'A Certain Lack of Symmetry: Beauvoir on Autonomous Agency and Women's Embodiment', in *Simone de Beauvoir's 'The Second Sex': New Interdisciplinary Essays*, ed. by Ruth Evans (Manchester: Manchester University Press, 1998), pp. 122–58

MALRAUX, CLARA, 'Les Grandes Sœurs de Mathilde de la Mole', *Confluences*, 30 (1944), 262–64

MANZINI, FRANCESCO, 'Stendhal, Imagination and Inconsequentiality: the Dirt of Politics and the Politics of Dirt in the *Vie de Henry Brulard*, *Lucien Leuwen* and *La Chartreuse de Parme*', *Dix-Neuf* (forthcoming)

—— *Stendhal's Parallel Lives* (Oxford: Lang, 2004)

—— 'Work, Idleness, and Play in Stendhal's *Lucien Leuwen*', *Dix-Neuf*, 16.1 (2012), 28–37

MARIETTE, CATHERINE, 'De l'Amour: Essai d'idéologie ou "fragments d'un discours amoureux"', in *Persuasions d'amour: Nouvelles lectures de 'De l'Amour' de Stendhal*, ed. Daniel Sangsue (Geneva: Droz, 1999), pp. 79–88

MARILL-ALBÉRÈS, FRANCINE, *Le Naturel chez Stendhal* (Paris: Nizet, 1956)

MAY, GITA, 'Le Féminisme de Stendhal et *Lamiel*', *Stendhal Club*, 20 (1977–78), 191–204

MÉRIMÉE, PROSPER, *HB suivi de XIX lettres à Stendhal* (Geneva: Slatkine Reprints, 1998)

MILLER, NANCY K., *The Heroine's Text: Readings in the French and English Novel, 1722–1782* (New York: Columbia University Press, 1980)

MITCHELL, JOHN, *Stendhal: 'Le Rouge et le Noir'* (London: Arnold, 1973)

MORETTI, FRANCO, *The Way of the World: The 'Bildungsroman' in European Culture* (London: Verso, 1987)

MOSSMAN, CAROL A., *The Narrative Matrix: Stendhal's 'Le Rouge et le Noir'* (Lexington, KY: French Forum, 1984)

NERLICH, MICHAEL, 'Renaissance', in *Dictionnaire de Stendhal*, pp. 591–92

PARMENTIER, MARIE, '*Le Rouge et le Noir*, un "roman pour femmes de chambre"?', *L'Année stendhalienne*, 4 (2005), 205–30

PASCO, ALLAN H., 'The Unheroic Mode: Stendhal's *La Chartreuse de Parme*', *Philological Quarterly*, 70.3 (1991), 361–78

PAUPE, ADOLPHE, *Histoire des œuvres de Stendhal* (Paris: Dujarric, 1903, repr. Geneva: Slatkine Reprints, 1998)

PAVET-JÖRG, PIERRETTE, 'Le Temps des héroïnes stendhaliennes', in *Le Dernier Stendhal*, pp. 207–31

PEARSON, ROGER, *Stendhal's Violin: A Novelist and his Reader* (Oxford: Clarendon Press, 1988)

PEYTARD, JEAN, *Voix et traces narratives chez Stendhal* (Paris: Les Éditeurs français réunis, 1980)

PHILIPPOT, DIDIER, 'Lamiel ou le paradoxe romanesque', in *Le Dernier Stendhal*, pp. 167–206

PIZZORUSSO, ARNALDO, '*Mina de Vanghel* ou l'antipode de la raison', *Travaux de linguistique et de littérature*, 13.2 (1975), 631–40

PORTER, DENNIS, '*Lamiel*: The Wild Child and the Ugly Men', *Novel*, 12.1 (1978), 21–32

PRENDERGAST, CHRISTOPHER, *Balzac: Fiction and Melodrama* (London: Arnold, 1978)

—— *The Order of Mimesis: Balzac, Stendhal, Nerval, Flaubert* (Cambridge: Cambridge University Press, 1986)

PRÉVOST, JEAN, *La Création chez Stendhal: Essai sur le métier d'écrire et la psychologie de l'écrivain* (Paris: Mercure de France, 1951)

—— *Essai sur les sources de 'Lamiel'. Les Amazones de Stendhal. Le Procès de Lacenaire* (Lyons: Imprimeries réunies, 1942)

RABBITT, KARA M., 'L'Enfant libertine: Pouvoir discursif et volonté narrative dans *Lamiel de Stendhal*', *Nineteenth-Century French Studies*, 31.1–2 (2002–03), 66–83

RABINE, LESLIE W., *Reading the Romantic Heroine: Text, History, Ideology* (Ann Arbor: University of Michigan Press, 1985)

RAITT, ALAN, 'An unpublished letter by Mérimée', *Modern Language Review*, 65.2 (1970), 282–89

READER, KEITH A., 'Le Discours du pouvoir dans *Lamiel*', in *Stendhal: l'Écrivain, la société et le pouvoir* (Grenoble: Presses Universitaires de Grenoble, 1984), pp. 265–76

REID, MARTINE, 'Sur le personnage féminin et Mme de Rênal. Réponse à Pierre Barbéris', *L'Année stendhalienne*, 8 (2009), 197–212

REY, PIERRE-LOUIS, '"Un peu trop grande et trop maigre"', *RHLF*, 109.1 (2009), 51–60

RICH, ADRIENNE, 'When We Dead Awaken: Writing as Re-Vision', *College English*, 34.1 (Oct 1972), 18–30

RICHARD, JEAN-PIERRE, *Littérature et sensation* (Paris: Seuil, 1954)

RODGERS, CATHERINE, 'Étude féministe de cinq auteurs: Cinquante ans de recul', in *Cinquantenaire du 'Deuxième Sexe'*, ed. by Christine Delphy and Sylvie Chaperon (Paris: Syllepse, 2002), pp. 139–42

ROGERS, NANCY, 'The Wasting Away of Romantic Heroines', *Nineteenth-Century French Studies*, 11.3–4 (1983), 246–56

ROUSSEAU, JEAN-JACQUES, *Émile ou de l'éducation* (Paris: Flammarion, 1966)

SARTRE, JEAN-PAUL, *L'Être et le néant: Essai d'ontologie phénoménologique* (Paris: Gallimard, 1943)

—— *Qu'est-ce que la littérature?* (Paris: Gallimard, 1948; repr. with preface 2008)

SCHEHR, LAWRENCE R., *Rendering French Realism* (Stanford: Stanford University Press, 1997)

SCHOR, NAOMI, *Breaking the Chain: Women, Theory, and French Realist Fiction* (New York: Columbia University Press, 1985)

SCOTT, MARIA, 'Comédie et liberté chez Stendhal: Une étude de ses actrices', *L'Année stendhalienne*, 11 (2012), 217–31

—— 'Les Femmes et la faculté de vouloir dans *Les Promenades dans Rome*' in *'Façons de voir': Enquêtes sur les 'Promenades dans Rome'*, ed. by Xavier Bourdenet and François Vanoosthuyse (Grenoble: ELLUG, 2011), pp. 247–64

—— 'Performing Desire: Stendhal's Theatrical Heroines', *French Studies*, 62 (2008), 259–70

—— 'Le Réalisme et la peur du désir? Le cas de *Lucien Leuwen*', *L'Année stendhalienne*, 9 (2010), 35–57

—— 'Simone de Beauvoir on Stendhal: in Good Faith or in Bad?', *Irish Journal of French Studies*, 8 (2008), 55–71

—— 'Stendhal, Mathilde et le regard oblique', in *L'Œil écrit*, ed. by Johnnie Gratton and Derval Conroy (Geneva: Slatkine, 2005), pp. 221–36

—— 'Stendhal's Heroines: Escaping History through History', *Nineteenth-Century French Studies*, 37.3–4 (2009), 260–72

—— 'Stendhal's Muddy Realism', *Dix-Neuf*. 16.1 (2012), 15–27

—— 'Stendhal's Rebellious Mothers and the Fight Against Death-by-Maternity', in *Birth and Death in Nineteenth-Century French Culture*, ed. by Nigel Harkness and others (Amsterdam: Rodopi, 2007), pp. 139–51

—— 'Le Thème de l'amitié féminine chez un "tendre ami des femmes"', *L'Année stendhalienne*, 8 (2009), 101–15

SEGAL, NAOMI, *The Unintended Reader* (Cambridge: Cambridge University Press, 1986)

SPANDRI, FRANCESCO, *L'Art de Komiker': Comédie, théâtralité et jeu chez Stendhal* (Paris: Champion, 2003)

STAROBINSKI, JEAN, *L'Œil vivant* (Paris: Gallimard, 1961)

TALBOT, ÉMILE, ed., *La Critique stendhalienne de Balzac à Zola* (York, SC: French Literature Publications Company, 1979)

THOMPSON, CHRISTOPHER W., 'Conflict, Gender and Transcendence in *Le Rouge et le Noir*', *Nineteenth-Century French Studies*, 22.1–2 (1993–94), 77–89

—— '*Lamiel*': *Fille du feu: Essai sur Stendhal et l'énergie* (Paris: L'Harmattan, 1997)

——'*Vanina Vanini* ou la répétition tragique', *L'Année Stendhal*, 4 (2000), 29–36

TURNELL, MARTIN, *The Rise of the French Novel* (London: Hamish Hamilton, 1979)

VALÉRY, PAUL, *Variété II* (Paris: Gallimard, 1930)

VERCOLLIER, CLAUDINE, 'Un personnage problématique: Mathilde de la Mole', *University of Toronto Quarterly*, 68.2 (1999), 642–54

VIGNERON, ROBERT, 'Stendhal et Sanscrit', *Modern Philology*, 33.4 (1936), 383–402

WAIS, KURT, 'Stendhal zwischen Novelle und Roman: Mina de Vanghel und ihre Schwestern', *Stendhal Club*, 96 (1982), 435–49

WALLER, MARGARET, *The Male Malady: Fictions of Impotence in the French Romantic Novel* (New Brunswick, NJ: Rutgers University Press, 1993)

WEIAND, CHRISTOF, 'Stendhal ou le romanesque du vrai', in *Simone de Beauvoir: 'Le Deuxième Sexe'. Le Livre fondateur du féminisme moderne en situation*, ed. by Ingrid Galster (Paris: Champion, 2004), pp. 241–55

WEST SOOBY, JOHN, '*Armance*: Le Choix d'un destin', *Stendhal Club*, 25. 100 (1983), 490–500

——'Débauches en ébauche: La Vie marginale de *Lamiel*', in *Esquisses/ Ebauches: Projects and Pre-Texts in Nineteenth-Century French Culture*, ed. by Sonya Stephens (Oxford: Lang, 2007), pp. 81–89

——'Revolution and Revolt in Stendhal's *Lamiel*', *Nineteenth-Century French Studies*, 22.1–2 (1993–94), 90–99

——'La Société et le jeu dans *Le Rouge et le Noir*', in *Stendhal: l'Écrivain, la société et le pouvoir* (Grenoble: Presses Universitaires de Grenoble, 1984), pp. 99–114

WILKINSON, LYNN R. 'Gender and Class in Stendhal's *Lamiel*', *Romanic Review*, 80.1 (1989), 57–74

WILLIS, PAULINE WAHL, '*Lamiel* de Stendhal à feu et à sang', in *The Play of Terror in Nineteenth-Century France*, ed. by John T. Booker and Allan H. Pasco (London: Associated University Presses, 1997), pp. 122–29

—— (as PAULINE WAHL), 'Stendhal's *Lamiel*: Observations on Pygmalionism', in *Pre-text/ Text/Context. Essays on Nineteenth-Century Literature*, ed. by Robert L. Mitchell (Columbus: Ohio State University Press, 1980), pp. 113–19

ZAFFARAMI BERLINGHINI, RITA, '*Lamiel* ou l'émancipation de la femme', in *Le Dernier Stendhal*, pp. 267–77

INDEX

Printed in Great Britain
by Amazon

40052706R00084